THE ELEMENTS OF
DISASTER PSYCHOLOGY

THE ELEMENTS OF DISASTER PSYCHOLOGY

Managing Psychosocial Trauma

An Integrated Approach to Force Protection and Acute Care

By

JAMES L. GREENSTONE, ED.D., J.D., DABECI

CHARLES C THOMAS • PUBLISHER, LTD.
Springfield • Illinois • U.S.A.

Published and Distributed Throughout the World by

CHARLES C THOMAS • PUBLISHER, LTD.
2600 South First Street
Springfield, Illinois 62704

© 2008 by CHARLES C THOMAS • PUBLISHER, LTD.

ISBN 978-0-398-07784-6 (hard)
ISBN 978-0-398-07785-3 (pbk.)

Library of Congress Catalog Card Number: 2007032833

With THOMAS BOOKS *careful attention is given to all details of manufacturing
and design. It is the Publisher's desire to present books that are satisfactory as to their
physical qualities and artistic possibilities and appropriate for their particular use.*
THOMAS BOOKS *will be true to those laws of quality that assure a good name
and good will.*

Printed in the United States of America
LAH-R-3

Library of Congress Cataloging-in-Publication Data

Greenstone, James L.
  The Elements of disaster psychology : managing psychosocial trauma : an
integrated approach to force protection and acute care / by James L. Green-
stone.
     p. ; cm.
  Includes bibliographical references and index.
  ISBN 978-0-398-07784-6 (hard) -- ISBN 978-0-398-07785-3 (pbk.)
  1. Crisis intervention (Mental health services) 2. Emergency management--
Psychological aspects. 3. Disasters--Psychological aspects. 4. Disaster victims-
-Rehabilitation. I. Title.
  [DNLM: 1. Crisis Intervention--organization & administration. 2. Disaster
Planning--methods. 3. Disasters. 4. Emergency Services, Psychiatric--organi-
zation & administration. 5. Health Personnel--psychology. WM 401 G815ea
2007]
  RC480.6.G7193 2007
  616.89'14--dc22
                                                           2007032833

This book is dedicated to those who put their boots on the ground when their intervention is desperately needed and requested. They go into harm's way to provide for the psychological well-being of those who cannot provide for themselves.

This book is written in a straightforward, no nonsense, user-friendly, field guide format. It is designed for the types of crisis interveners who will use it. It is also written with the hope that such disasters into which they must go will be few and far between.

And finally, this work is dedicated to Doctor Sharon Cohen Leviton. She is a skilled intervener from whom I have learned much about this discipline.

Also, to Doctor Edward Stephen Rosenbluh, my life-long mentor in Crisis Intervention.

George Santayana in 1905, "Progress, far from consist-ing in change, depends on retentiveness. . . . Those who cannot remember the past are condemned to fulfill it."

FOREWORD

It was with significant insight, that Doctor Greenstone has chosen the title, *The Elements of Disaster Psychology*. He has succeeded in constructing a unique text that will help restore health to those whose lives have been impacted by disasters. To the reader, he has succeeded in providing these elements.

Elements! They are the fundamental building blocks of all things. Water or H_2O is the result of a proper combination of elements without which life could not be sustained on our planet. Critical physiological elements are vital to maintaining physical health. Imbalance or deficiency of such elements leads to disease or injury susceptibility. Identifying the essential elements for psychological health and repair is equally important. The area of disaster psychology has been awaiting a concise printing of such "elements" relevant to managing psychological trauma from disasters. Doctor Greenstone has delivered.

This is not just a text. It is a tool! A tool is a purposely designed, useful instrument. Such is a valid description of *The Elements of Disaster Psychology*. Not to be left on the shelf, this text is to be carried with those providers rendering psychological assistance to people who have sustained the impact of a disaster.

Called to deliver such psychological assistance, figuratively, the reader is to "bring," recalling the principles learned in this book to the care delivery site, as well as quite literally, to bring the text as a self-contained guide for just-in-time review at the care delivery site during a disaster response as well.

Readers who are familiar with the many publications of Doctor Greenstone, know that he has a unique style. It is a style that fosters learning and delivers application to likely-to-be encountered clinical scenarios. Why is he able to effectively write in such a manner? It is because he has done and continues to do that about what he writes.

Through his dedicated and lengthy career, he has applied, modified and where appropriate even rejected the theories that abound, demonstrating through clinical encounters what works and has useable value to the readers.

Doctor Greenstone writes in a most meaningful way. His writing concisely penetrates the reader's previous assumptions. He challenges the reader to replace these assumptions with bite-sized bullets of knowledge. Through his years of validated field experience he then takes these bullet points of knowledge and assimilates them into ready-to-use tools and skills. Armed with scientific clinical knowledge and field-proven skill applications, the reader's confidence is strengthened. The reader is now encouraged to engage.

Engagement in the context of a disaster is the willingness to show up and to perform your duties when the need is present. Jim has succeeded in constructing these elements in a manner that will encourage clinical providers who read this text to have a stronger desire to perform their duties willfully as they will be better prepared for the likely encounters.

Go ahead! Get started! And when you are finished reading, put this text in your response grip for ready access to these essential elements of disaster psychology.

RAYMOND E. SWIENTON, MD, FACEP

Doctor Swienton is one of the founders and editors of the American Medical Association (AMA) National Disaster Life Support (NDLS) programs. He is an editor of the popular textbook entitled *Medical Response to Terrorism: Preparedness and Clinical Practice.* He is an Associate Professor of Emergency Medicine and serves as the Co-Director of the Section of Emergency Medical Services (EMS), Homeland Security and Disaster Medicine at the University of Texas Southwestern Medical Center at Dallas.

PREFACE

It is not possible to write a book that covers adequately all areas of disaster work. This author decided to limit the scope of this work to two important areas. These include the immediate psychological care of those affected by the disaster, and the less well-considered area of force protection. Force protection focuses on the psychological preparation and care for disaster responders so that they will improve their job in assisting others. It may even appear that what is good for the victims is also appropriate care and preparation for the responders. This author subscribes to this philosophy. The format is direct and unadorned, and will be thoroughly explained later. As the book was being designed and written, additional areas of concern were added that address special issues expressed by both first and second responders. It seemed important to add as much of the real world as possible and to short-cut the theory surrounding this type of response. Other publications and trainings have and will cover this effectively. A substantial bibliography and suggested reading are also provided herein to help in this particular quest either pre or post-incident. The point of this approach is to help you accomplish what you have signed on to do and to do it in the most expeditious and effective manner possible. My long-time colleague and mentor Doctor Edward S. Rosenbluh once said that, "In order to be helpful, we must be effective." This book is dedicated to that premise. What is here will help you to be effective when handling the psychosocial problems of victims and of responders as they present. In addition, it may help prevent crises from occurring in the first place. Responders must learn how to take care of themselves first if they are to be truly effective responding to the needs of others.

The elements are the basics of any discipline. Knowledge of them is critical to achieving success. *The Elements of Disaster Psychology: Man-*

aging Psychosocial Trauma focuses on those basics that are needed by crisis and disaster responders in the field. This book is an integrated approach to force protection and acute care. The presentation is ordered in such a way as to provide quick and easy access to the information needed from the initial deployment, to the final debriefing. Tables of contents were developed that respond to specific needs. The main table of contents is prescriptive in nature so that it can be used as a self-contained guide to disaster response. Other tables help guide users to specific types of crises or to procedures and techniques. These tables guide the user to the chapters of the book that are related. These chapters contain more useful checklists and procedural notes that are related to the crisis management process. The entire work is designed to be user-friendly and to provide those in the field with what they need when they need it. This is done without the theory that often accompanies. Those who want theoretical depth are guided to other sources that can provide such information. This is an uncomplicated book that reflects what is known in this field, and then funnels it to the intervener.

Although there are few extensive works in the field of disaster response, *The Elements of Disaster Psychology* can serve as a companion text in the field, or stand by itself in the disaster intervener's gear bag. It is what is needed to get the job done, and nothing more. The lists, procedures, suggestions, and guidelines are field-tested and directly related to field situations. Because no two situations are the same, allowance is made for such differences and additional suggestions are offered for making the necessary adjustments.

Disaster Psychology and Crisis Management have been reduced to their basic elements so that they can be applied as broadly as possible, and are presented in a format that is useful both for the experienced professional and for the novice. I know of no other text that approaches the subject so directly. Much time has been spent eliminating confusion about procedures and about how to deal with crises. This book reinforces the theoretical framework that postulates Crisis Intervention as a viable discipline in its own right. In fact, a scientific study by the New York Academy of Medicine in 2005 demonstrated the efficacy of this discipline. New Yorkers who received emergency crisis intervention in the workplace following the World Trade Center disaster suffered from fewer mental health problems for up to two years after the disaster occurred. This work was published in the *International*

Journal of Emergency Mental Health and was conducted by Richard Adams, Ph.D., and Charles Figley, Ph.D.

Because this is a practical guide, most theory has been purposely omitted. It is suggested that *The Elements of Disaster Psychology: Managing Psychosocial Trauma* be used as a supplement in related emergency management, crisis intervention and disaster psychology classes. This work is also appropriate for first and second responder training, and for Medical Reserve Corps, both uniformed and nonuniformed. The experienced disaster intervener can use this book independently in the field, in training and in the office.

This book is designed to aid in practical, day-to-day, on-the-scene disaster response and crisis intervention by all interveners. In addition to listing the areas covered in the chapters, the table of contents is a *step-by-step* guide to the intervention and disaster response process. It should be used by disaster responders to guide an intervention in an orderly fashion. For the experienced responder, the table of contents is a helpful reminder of the steps to be taken during any disaster situation. Novices may need to read the entire book carefully before they can use the table of contents effectively. They should understand that the full value of this book depends on their gaining theoretical depth and practical training. Interveners can also look up material according to the activity they want to perform or by the responder's role (e.g., First Responder, Secondary Responder, Medical Reserve Corps member, etc.). These listings are located at the back of this book for added convenience when under field conditions.

Because this is an elements book, please remember as you peruse it that:

1. It is not intended to cover everything for every situation.
2. This work is intended to get you started regardless of where you begin.
3. This is not a finished work. Much more could be added and as we learn more, some could possibly be eliminated or changed. Perhaps some of you reading this book of elements will add to it and eventually finish it. Perhaps there will come a time when such work is no longer necessary.
4. For the most part, theory and research have not been included. The bibliography is intended to guide you in this direction should you so desire.

5. This is intended as a user-friendly guidebook for those directly involved in the field as well as for the novice.

J.L.G.

ACKNOWLEDGMENTS

Doctor Sharon C. Leviton who is always there for me and for the discipline with her knowledge and skills in disaster crisis management. I thank her for her expert contributions to this book.

Suzanne Raif, my editorial assistant, without whom I would not have accomplished the completion of this book.

Doctor Judy Versola-Russo for her encouragement and suggestions about how to title this book to make it most useful.

Weldon Walles for his encouragement and ideas given over many years of work together.

David Isch, Director of Ethics, Department of Ethics, Harris Methodist Fort Worth Hospital for his help in understanding some of the ethical issues related to disaster response and decision-making.

Doctor W. Rodney Fowler, Crisis Intervention Pioneer. You will find his wisdom emanating from the words in this book.

Karen Ray, Doctoral Student, Capella University, Harold Abel School of Psychology for her invaluable assistance in developing the Greenstone Disaster Mental Health Triage System and for her suggestions to make this work stronger.

Lieutenant Roger Dixon, Fort Worth Police Department for his friendship, encouragement and insights into disaster security.

Chaplain Mitchale Felder, Fort Worth Police Department for his enduring friendship and encouragement as I moved through the process of creating this work.

Doctor Ray Swienton, M.D., for preparing the Foreword to this work and for his encouragement. Doctor Swienton is one of the founders and editors of the *American Medical Association* (AMA) *National Disaster Life Support* (NDLS) programs. He is an editor of the popular textbook entitled *Medical Response to Terrorism: Preparedness and Clinical Practice.* He is an Associate Professor of Emergency Medicine and serves as the Co-Director of the Section of Emergency Medical Services (EMS), Homeland Security and Disaster Medicine at the *University of Texas Southwestern Medical Center at Dallas.*

Detective Jeffery Dunn for his input, friendship and encouragement.

The Texas State Guard Medical Brigade (MRC) and Commanding General, BG Marshall H. Scantlin for providing the structure in which to learn.

Doctor Edward S. Rosenbluh, Crisis Intervention pioneer and teacher. The real deal. My colleague and mentor in this field for over forty years.

CONTENTS

THE ELEMENTS OF
DISASTER PSYCHOLOGY

"Marines Call It That 2,000-Yard Stare." Painting by Tom Lea. Courtesy of the U. S. Army Art Collection, U. S. Army Center of Military History.

Chapter 1

UNDERSTAND THE GENERAL PRINCIPLES OF PREPARING TO RESPOND: THE PSYCHOSOCIAL ASPECTS OF DISASTERS AND DISASTER INTERVENTION

Crisis intervention during man-made or natural disasters is similar to such intervention done in other venues. It differs in that whatever intervention is done, must be done for more victims over a longer period of time than, and with the overlay of other problems and concerns for both the victims and for the interveners. Whereas an intervention into the life of a suicidal victim on any given day may have an end point for the intervener, disaster interventions may need to move from one person to the next over extended periods of time with or without relief. The intervention techniques may be the same in both the short-term and longer-term need for assistance. The differences may be measured in the resilience and stamina of the intervener as well as the specific training to be able to respond in these situations. Not everyone can, or should be expected to, do this type of work. However, if you are involved, these are some of the issues about which you should be aware, and some of the important steps to take:

1. Prepare, prepare, prepare.
2. Obtain the specific types of training that will allow you to function in your respective area.
3. Expect to be part of a team.
4. Be a part of a team.
5. Know your chain of command.
6. Understand the Incident Command System and how to access

it.

7. Understand and develop triage skills.
8. Know the meaning of triage under disaster conditions and that it may be different than nondisaster conditions.
9. Know physical first aid as well as emotional first aid.
10. If you are not called to intervene, don't show up unannounced.
11. Work in teams of at least two interveners.
12. Practice, practice, practice.
13. Maintain your certifications as required.
14. Prepare by learning about the effects of disaster on those experiencing it.
15. Expect disasters to be unpleasant.
16. Train as though your life and the lives of others depended on it. Someday, it will.
17. Remember that there is really no panacea for stress reactions in times of disaster or terror events.
18. Recognize the interplay between distress responses, behavioral changes and psychiatric stress during a disaster or terror event.
19. Recognize that risk factors will increase psychological problems based on degree of exposure, the level of exhaustion, physical harm that has occurred and the presence of a preexisting mental disorder.
20. The scene of a disaster may present as an awful, scary, and terifying place to all including crisis interveners. Prepare for this. Most of us do not operate in such circumstances on a daily basis. Exercises can go only so far. Be ready for that which you really do not expect or that in which you do not want to be.
21. Understand what Weapons of Mass Destruction are.
22. Know that CBRNE stands for Chemical release, Biological release, Radiological event, Nuclear detonation, and Explosive devices or incidents. You will hear these terms.
23. The greatest challenges for a civilian caught in a catastrophic situation are often
    a. No personal protection equipment.
    b. Fear and anxiety.
    c. Cultural issues that may hinder aid. Eg. Taking off one's clothing to be decontaminated.
    d. Keeping families together. Don't forget this.
24. Risk perception may be affected by:

     a. The fact that the threat may be invisible.

     b. The fact that the threat may be odorless.

     c. The exposure and uncertainties. Long-term effects. Cancer?

     d. Multiple unexplained symptoms. Level of exposure. No exposure? Headaches, nausea and fatigue are examples.

     e. Unfamiliarity with disaster situations which depart greatly from nondisaster scenarios.

     f. Grotesqueness.

     g. Moral outrage.

25. Mass panic is unusual. Historically, it is not a common reaction to disaster.

26. Panic may be the result of a serious perceived threat combined with limited or no avenues of escape for the victims.

27. Perceived threats do not have to be real to affect the victim. Reality is always in the eye of the beholder. If the victim or sufferer thinks that it is real, it is real to that person. Never try to talk someone out of their perceptions. It cannot be done and it demonstrates your lack of understanding.

28. Become familiar with the National Incident Management System. Knowledge will assist you in understanding the responses made to disasters at various levels.

29. Remember, and never forget when involved in disaster response.

     a. Eat when you can.

     b. Sleep when you can.

     c. Go to the bathroom when you can. Now, go back and read this again. You will be glad you did.

30. Refer to Table 1.1. *Matrix of Suggested Disaster Crisis Responder Activities at all Levels of Responder Involvement.* Columns should be read down rather than across for ease of understanding.

Table 1.1. Matrix of Suggested Disaster Crisis Responder Activities
at all Levels of Responder Involvement.

INFO TO READ	PREPARATION	MITIGATION - PREVENTION	RESPONSE	RECOVERY- CONSEQUENCES MANAGEMENT	RESPONDER SURVIVAL	SKILLS
Elements of Crisis Intervention	Mind-set adjustment	Train on the emotional hazards of disaster response	Respond when deployed	Intervener Survival	Utilize a buddy system to take care of each other.	Maintain Crisis Inter-vention skills
Elements of Disaster Psychology	Disaster Crisis Intervention Training	Teach disaster response to teams.	Psycho-social triage.	Team tactical debriefing.	Complete CPR Training	Psycho-social triage
State volunteer protection laws	Incident Command System training	Train non-psychological responders re disaster response	Physical Fitness	Psychological debriefing	Blood-Borne Pathogens Training	Disaster response skills
HR 4698 Disaster Relief Volunteer Protection Act of 2006	Team training and plans development.	Practice training and refine plans	Establish emergency commo	Restock supplies and equipment	Certifications to Teach, and Teach F.A., CPR, BBP	Maintain Health Care Licenses
Public Health Laws	Train on psychosocial disaster triage system	Standard of care vs. Sufficiency of care	Function in assigned roles.	Evaluate response and corrective actions	Practice intervener survival skills.	Personal survival skills
Medical Reserve Corps response to liability issues	Wellness training for all responders	Stress inoculations	Disaster Crisis Intervention	Provide referral sources for victims of the disaster and follow-up	Take time to attend to your own psychological needs.	Suicide recognition and interven-tion training
Emergency Manage-ment Assistance Compact	24 hour call-out bag	Physical Fitness	Establish triage areas	Provide post disaster referral sources for responders and follow-up	Eat, Sleep, Water, Routine and Rigorous physical activity	Communica-tion skills
Legal Guidelines in Crisis Intervention	Personal Survival Gear	Health Hazards	Establish working relationship with Medical personnel	Assist with community crisis recovery	Environmental threat assessment	Legal aspects of disaster intervention
Good Samaritan Law	Complete First Aid Courses	Danger issues of disaster crisis response	Set up staffed area for MUPS individuals		Medical Threat Assessments	
Incident Command System	National Disaster Life Support Courses		Attend to child victims			BDLS ADLS
Volunteer Protection Act	Three-day Call-Out Bag (72 hour)		Keep families together and attend to them		Critical Incident Stress Issues	
Websites	First Aid Equipment		Use appropriate disaster forms			

Key:

MUPS = Medically Unexplained Physical Symptoms; Often mistakenly call the "Worried Well."
BDLS = Basic Disaster Life Support.
ADLS = Advanced Disaster Life Support
CPR = Cardiopulmonary Resuscitation
BBP = Blood Borne Pathogens
FA = First Aid
Commo = Communications
Preparation = What to do to get ready.

Mitigation = What to do to be proactive and prevent problems during response.
Response = What to do when the balloon goes up.
Recovery = What to do post – response.
Info to read = Related resources of which to be aware.
Responder survival= Issues of intervener survi-val.
Skills = Skills to develop and to maintain.

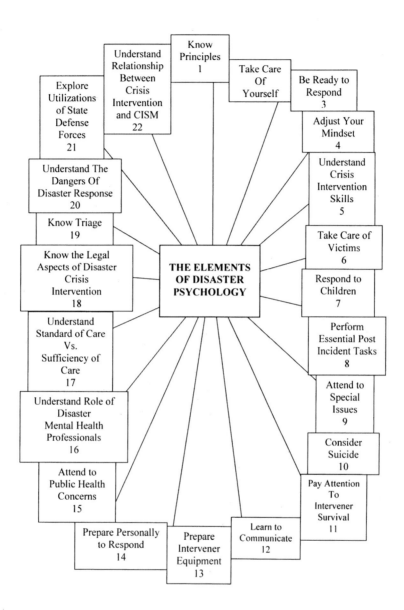

Figure 1.1. The Elements of Disaster Psychology.

Chapter 2

TAKE CARE OF YOURSELF: YOUR FIRST RESPONSIBILITY

If you do not take care of yourself, you can hardly be expected to take care of others. You must come first if you have a serious intent to be effective when dealing with others. Many times disaster personnel experience feelings of guilt if they take time for themselves, take a time-out in order to eat, if they have food when others do not, and on and on. The paradox is that you have a responsibility to care for yourself if you have any hope of being effectively helpful to disaster victims. If you fall out, those who need you may be lost. Take this particular mandate of "take care of yourself" as vital, and the point from which all else emanates. Taking care of one's self including both physical care and psychological care is essential. Do not get hurt either way. In many ways, this entire book is about taking care of yourselves. The principles that are applied to helping others are many times the same principles that must be applied to our own well-being. Acute care crisis intervention for victims is the basis of psychological force protection for responders. Take care of yourself. Take care of your co-responders. Take care of victims. In that order. To do otherwise, degrades your capabilities and responsibilities to help others in need.

1. Plan to take care of yourself and to provide for your own needs.
2. Assemble personal gear that will allow you to subsist over extended time periods.
3. Put together a "go bag" with your professional resource information and tools of the trade that you might need to use with victims of a disaster.

4. Be able to function on your own.
5. Prepare yourself to detect and to respond to hazards, physical and psychological.
6. Be alert to hidden threats.
7. Know when you need to take a "time-out."
8. Keep a watchful eye on your co-workers.
9. Attend to co-workers and teammates quickly.
10. Know what to stay away from; this is as important as knowing what to get involved in.
11. Approach all scenes and victims with great care and caution.
12. Attend to your own safety before attending to others in crisis.
13. Know that if you get hurt, or if you go into crisis, you will be able to help no one.
14. Eat when you are hungry.
15. Be sure that you have foodstuffs for yourself when you need it.
16. Use your equipment sparingly. You may need to assist many.
17. Use the victim's equipment and supplies to assist them if possible and practical.
18. Be prepared to ask for assistance if you need it.
19. Know from where your back-up is coming.
20. Wear appropriate personal protective equipment.
21. Learn to trust your equipment.
22. Understand the dangerous elements in which you may be working. See the chapter on Dangerousness.
23. Understand the effects of vicarious trauma and compassion fatigue. All interveners are vulnerable.
24. Learn steps to take to manage your own stress.
25. Know the signs of stress in yourself. Watch for them.
26. Understand the limitations of your own body and mind under disaster conditions.
27. Be prepared to defend yourself both physically and psychologically.
28. Take care of your own personal hygiene when time allows.
29. Always sleep, eat and defecate when time allows. Do not put off these specific functions.
30. Crisis Interveners are not supermen or superwomen. Don't pretend you are.
31. Let your family and loved ones know where you are and that you are okay.

32. Accept that responders can have the same symptoms of psychological responses as others. This includes veteran responders.
33. Try to always work with a "buddy." Working alone may not be safe or secure.
34. You cannot be all things to all people. Know what you can do and do that. If you give all of yourself to every victim, you will have nothing left to give.
35. Rely on your support systems just as you advise others to rely on theirs.
36. See Figure 2.1 below.

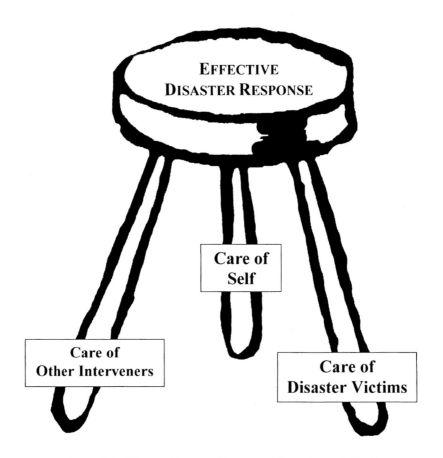

Figure 2.1. Effective Disaster Response Three-Legged Stool.
The stool cannot stand without all three legs in place and active.

Chapter 3

BE READY TO RESPOND TO THE CALL-OUT AND DEPLOYMENT

This one is not as easy as it may sound. Readiness must occur on several levels to be effective. Here we will deal with personal readiness and those lists that will help you to prepare. Also, psychological readiness and physical readiness will be emphasized. It is one thing to pack your bags. It is another to have the most helpful mindset and to be in reasonable physical condition. As you have already learned, taking care of yourself is paramount. Part of this care is your equipment, your mental readiness, and your physical shape. All of these work together. Long hours on your feet, reliance on what you can provide, and a readiness for what you will encounter all play a part in being ready to respond. As many times as you have heard this, taking care of you must occur before you can ever expect to take care of others. From a psychological standpoint, individuals may not prepare well because to do so brings the reality of disaster work into focus. If one prepares, the possibility exists that they may have to act on that preparedness. Denial may be marginally helpful in other situations. It is not helpful here. If you are determined to respond when called, then acknowledgment and acceptance of the possibilities must be your reality. No one wants a disaster with all that it implies. People get hurt. Some will surely die. All will need assistance. There will never be enough to go around. What we do must be effective and responsive. We may have only one chance. This effectiveness is dependent on our preparation and readiness to be called and to respond at any time with everything we need.

1. Get ready now.
2. Take readiness seriously.
3. Prepare your own family so that they can take care of themselves.
4. Prepare your family for the eventuality of your deployment.
5. Pack your bags. See Appendix 1, Form 21.
6. Keep your bags packed. Change out seasonal clothing as necessary. Replace out-of-date items and consumables as needed.
7. Begin to prepare yourself for the psychological eventualities on a disaster response. Talk to those with more experience. Become aware of your own worries and concerns. Awareness may be more important than worrying about having these concerns.
8. Refer to the other areas of this book that deal with the psychological eventualities of disaster work and recommended intervention procedures. Procedures suggested for intervention into the crises of disaster victims must be applied to us and to those with whom we work. Force protection and disaster intervention have similar tenants. Take care of self; Take care of other responders; Take care of disaster sufferers.
9. Prepare yourself physically. If you require medications, plan for this during a deployment. Be sure that you have what you need. Do not depend that these things will be available from other responders or from the local economy.
10. If you need to get in better shape than you are currently, do not put this off. Each will develop a program specific to needs.
11. Personal, family, psychological and physical readiness are critical to overall success in a deployment.
12. Consider developing a short-term pack and a long-term pack. The short-term pack should be designed to get you through approximately 24 hours of deployment. The long-term pack should provide for your needs for approximately 72 hours.
13. Keep your gear at arm's length. Keep it packed and know where it is at all times.
14. Respond to a deployment as previously directed or currently ordered.
15. Responding without being directed to deploy is generally not acceptable.
16. When deployed, respond in a timely manner.
17. Observe time requirements for responding.

18. Advise your leadership of any time restrictions you may have.
19. If you say you will be there, be there.
20. Update your family about your situation when possible. They should already know that contact with you and by you may be limited. Keep them informed.
21. Find out if someone on your team who remained behind will take responsibility for informing families of the current status of the deployment. This can help allay many fears and concerns of family members.
22. Be sure that your employer knows ahead of time that you might be called to respond.
23. Investigate and understand employment protections that you might have if deployed.
24. The better informed your employer, the less likelihood of problems later.
25. Do nothing to jeopardize your employment. Be aware of the possibilities.
26. Be clear to your team leadership about your ability and availability to be called-up.
27. Be sure to have your medical records updated and copies available as needed.
28. U.S. Department of Health, Education and Welfare, Public Health Service, Form PHS – 731 (Rev. 9-77), International Certificates of Vaccination is a valuable form to have with you.
29. Keep Form PHS – 731 up-to-date. Other forms may also be available and work as well.
30. Be sure that you have all necessary vaccinations and immunizations related to your assignment or possible hazards that might be encountered.
31. If you are unable to respond to an alert or call-up, let your team leadership know as soon as possible.
32. When you have packed your gear, practice carrying same. Often, you will have no help in moving your personal gear and there may be no electricity to power elevators and the like. Pack so that you can carry what you bring.
33. Remember that your personal gear is for your use and survival during a call-up or deployment.
34. This author has been on deployments where more time was spent attending to the medical and psychological problems of

disaster workers than providing direct services to disaster victims. While force protections is vital to the success of any deployment, pre-existing medical or psychological conditions should be ameliorated prior to deployment. Sick or ailing personnel responding to a call-up may be of no help to anyone, least of all themselves.

35. Get ready. Be ready. Stay ready.

Chapter 4

ARRIVE AT THE DISASTER SITE OR STAGING AREA PREPARED TO INTERVENE: ADJUST YOUR MINDSET

Everyone wants to help. Disasters bring out this aspect of human nature in most of us. However, wanting to help, being ready and able to help, and being ready to provide effective help are very different matters. Just showing up is not always helpful. Showing up even though you have not been requested can cause more problems than are solved by this action. Many disaster teams require that members be activated by the team prior to actual deployment. This is a good idea. It is also a good idea for all responders to be familiar with the National Incident Management System and its related procedures.

Once you have been activated, what you do next is important to your ultimate helpfulness:

1. Be sure you know to where you should report. Be sure.
2. Take time to get the address and directions to the staging area.
3. Ask about the safest route to the reporting area.
4. Get the name, callback number and radio call sign of the person activating you.
5. Listen carefully to the instructions provided to you prior to deployment.
6. To what type of situation are you being deployed? Find out.
7. Take appropriate equipment with you that you have previously prepared.
8. Take last minute items as needed. These might include fresh food or fruit, medications, special comfort items, seasonal

clothing, fresh water and the like.

9. Dress for the environment into which you are going to the extent that you can, i.e., uniform, boots, sweater, jacket, etc. depending on weather and situation.

10. Begin adjusting your mindset to the reality of the disaster and what you are about to see and experience. Early-on, put on your "game face." Mentally shift from your regular environment to the disaster environment.

11. Regarding mindset adjustments, see Chapters 17, 18 and 20 specifically. Know with what you are getting involved and begin the adjustment process early. This will pay off for you as you respond.

12. When you arrive at the staging area or reporting site, immediately report to the area or site supervisor.

13. Determine what equipment or gear you will need immediately and where to secure the remainder of your belongings.

14. If there is anything that would prohibit you from certain activities, let your supervisor know prior to assignment.

15. Inquire regarding threat assessments that have been performed and the results.

16. Are there psychological threats as well as physical threats present?

17. Determine early-on if you will need personal protective equipment other than just your personal clothing or uniform. Acquire what you need before proceeding further.

18. If personal protective equipment (PPE) is needed, utilize it during your interventions and time in the area. PPE works only if you use it. Once you have been contaminated it may be too late.

19. Be sure the personal protective equipment fits you and that you know how to use it. Get help if you need it.

20. Once deployed, you may be required to assist a disaster victim at anytime. Be ready from the time you are called to intervene as needed. Do not be surprised by such requests. You may have little or no down-time from the moment you are deployed or arrive on scene. Be ready to go.

UNDERSTAND THE NATIONAL INCIDENT MANAGEMENT SYSTEM (NIMS)

1. A comprehensive approach to disaster incident management.
2. A national approach.
3. Applicable to all jurisdictions and levels.
4. Applicable across disciplines.
5. Previous disasters have shown the need for a system that provides a coordinated response, standardization and interoperability.
6. NIMS is flexible. It allows all responding organizations to work together.
7. Its standardization improves interoperability and the overall response.
8. The National Incident Management System includes:
   a. The Incident Command System.
   b. Multi-agency Coordination Systems.
   c. Public Information Systems.
9. NIMS preparedness includes:
   a. Planning, training and exercises.
   b. Personnel qualifications and certification.
   c. Equipment acquisition and certification.
   d. Publication management.
   e. Mutual aid and Emergency Management Assistance Compacts.
10. Resource management includes standardized:
    a. Descriptions
    b. Inventories
    c. Mobilization
    d. Dispatch
    e. Tracking
    f. Recovery
11. NIMS identifies requirements for communications, information management and information sharing.
12. Awareness and knowledge of the National Incident Management System is a must for all disaster responders.
13. The Incident Command System is a critical functional part of the NIMS and knowledge of how to function within it is critical. Courses specific to ICS are available online and in class-

rooms. Know this system and be prepared to function under its guidelines.

Chapter 5

UNDERSTAND CRISIS INTERVENTION SKILLS, PROCEDURES AND MODELS, AND HOW TO APPLY THEM

Basic to the understanding of disaster psychology and its application is knowing what works in these situations and what does not work. Generally, the mode of intervention is not treatment or psychotherapy. This may or may not be needed later. And the need for treatment later may well be related to the initial methods and techniques used that are helpful and effective in these situations. Many years ago, an early pioneer in this field, Dr. Edward Rosenbluh, said, "In order to remain helpful, we must remain effective." What is most often needed in the early stages of a disaster is crisis management. Not crisis treatment or crisis resolution, but crisis management. This involves such things as, but are not limited to, structure, answers, honesty, direction and guidance. The model of intervention may vary according to style and training, but the goal is the same (see Chapter 22).

1. Understand and respond to the timeliness of a crisis.
2. Remember that crises are self-limiting.
3. Remember that crises are time-limited.
4. Understand that most reactions to a crisis or disaster situation are normal, to be expected and usual under the circumstances.
5. Know the threats presented by your particular situation.
6. Adjust to the reality that you cannot attend to or preserve every victim.
7. Be prepared to attend to and to preserve each victim.
8. Learn to accept that some victims will die or will be dead when

     you get there.

9. Encourage self-reliance among victims.
10. Follow the model for crisis intervention of Immediacy, Control, Assessment, Disposition, Referral, and Follow-up.
11. Remember that different people may respond differently to the ostensibly same situation.
12. Accept your duty to normalize.
13. Educate others so that panic will not ensue.
14. Exude confidence even though you may be scared or uncertain.
15. Although you will be involved with victims, acknowledge problem ownership.
16. Avoid overidentification with victims.
17. Recognize symptoms of psychological stress such as anger, self-blame, isolation, withdrawal, blaming, fear, feeling stunned, variations in mood, feelings of helplessness, the tendency to deny, memory problems, family discord, sadness and grief.
18. Recognize the physiological symptoms such as limited or no appetite, chest pains, body aches, headaches, gastrointestinal problems, hyperactivity, drug and/or alcohol abuse or misuse, trouble getting to sleep or trouble staying asleep, troubled dreams and nightmares, low energy levels and fatigue even after rest or sleep.
19. Provide stress inoculations for interveners. Previous experience in successfully handling stressful situations often acts as an inoculation in that it prepares the intervener when they encounter the next stressful situation.
20. Emphasize the team approach.
21. Force fluids for interveners.
22. Use fluids as indicated for victims.
23. Understand that personal attacks aimed at you are seldom really personal attacks aimed at you.
24. Remember that responses of victims may be mediated or exaggerated by their cognitive functioning, physical health, personal relationships, duration and intensity of normal life disruption, personal meaning attached to the disaster or related events, the usual psychological well-being of the victim pre-crisis, and by elapsed time since the disaster occurred.
25. Always perform an immediate assessment of victims or suffer-

ers when encountered.

26. Enlist the assistance of those able to be of help.
27. Support those who need supporting.
28. Listen, listen, listen.
29. Help victims to reconnect with usual and normal support systems.
30. Expect that victims may need help accessing support systems.
31. Do not be too quick to offer advice to sufferers.
32. Provide the needed psychological structure for a victim.
33. Provide the needed physical structure for a victim.
34. Return control of the victim's life to the victim at the instant that they are able to exercise this control.
35. Do not be too quick to say that you understand what the victim is experiencing.
36. Remember that your credibility as an intervener is constantly-being evaluated by the victim.
37. Victims want to talk to somebody; they will not talk to just anybody.
38. Do not tell victims to stop feeling what they are feeling.
39. Do not tell victims that they should not feel the way that they feel.
40. Do not become a "pollyanna" intervener. You are not helping anyone except perhaps yourself.
41. Do not tell a victim not to cry.
42. Please do not invoke the deity as the cause of the disaster or crisis event.
43. Do not challenge the perceptions of the victims. Crisis is always in the eye of the beholder.
44. Never say that you don't think things are really as bad as the sufferer reflects that they are.
45. Be careful that your responses to victims do not elicit negative responses or reactions to your intervention. Credibility is at issue here.
46. Be respectful of a victim and their desires.
47. Be true to your style of intervention. You cannot do it effectively my way; I cannot do it effectively your way.
48. Triage those with abnormal responses from those with "normal responses."
49. Treat within the scope of your competency and resources.

50. Identify those at high risk for immediate referral and treatment.
51. Normalize responses.
52. Empathize with victims.
53. Reduce psychological arousal.
54. Access support for the most distressed victims.
55. Screen for depression and suicide.
56. Ask if the victim has felt depressed; have they lost interest in things that they would normally have interest in; have they had thoughts that their life was not worth living; and have they had recent thoughts about killing themselves.
57. Assess suicidal possibilities by focusing on the lethality of the means and the specificity of the plan.
58. Assess for stress disorders by assessing startle responses, emotional numbing, emotional arousal or emotional avoidance and the persistence of the symptoms.
59. Assess for possibilities of alcohol or substance abuse by asking if they have felt that they should cut down; have others annoyed them by telling them to cut down on drinking; have they felt guilty about their own drinking; and do they routinely need a drink to start the day in order to overcome a hangover.
60. Those involved may present with many symptoms.
61. Symptoms presented may not be expected and yet will appear.
62. Watch your sufferers for signs of agents to include nausea, muscle aches, respiratory problems, unusual fatigue, and dizziness.
63. Expect many questions about certainty of exposure or degree of exposure
64. Try to respond to questions about long-term effects of agents in a realistic manner based on what you actually know rather than based on unsubstantiated or rumor information.
65. Expect twice the number of psychological casualties as you have physical casualties.
66. Expect up to one-fourth of victims to remain calm.
67. Expect confusion, bewilderment and the inability to care for self in up to three-quarters of victims.
68. Expect confusion, anxiety, emotional flailing, trial-and-error problem-solving behavior, and even a rare panic in up to one-quarter of victims.

Immediacy. Action must be taken now.

Control. The disaster intervener must provide structure and support for the subject and for the situation.

Assessment. Often missed even by experienced interveners. You must know what it is that presents in front of you before you can make an effective decision about what to do.

Disposition. Once you know what you have, then you can do what is needed to resolve or to manage the incident: Intervene in a crisis.

Referral. Sometimes help is needed beyond the initial intervention. If you have done the previous steps effectively, the possibility of a successful referral increases.

Follow-Up. This is probably the hardest step to follow. Time and other duties often prevent us from finding out what actually happened to the disaster victim. One great benefit of the follow-up is that it may provide significant information about the effectiveness of the intervention and provide material that can be duplicated in training.

Figure 5.1. The Greenstone Crisis Intervention Model.

Chapter 6

TAKE CARE OF VICTIMS AND REFER AS NEEDED

Once the initial intervention and crisis management is initiated, consideration of what a victim needs to progress should be anticipated and planned. Each will need to be handled individually rather than lumped together with others. What we must do in the midst of large groups of victims and the surrounding chaos is to individualize what we do to the degree that we can. Although our approach may be different than it might be in nondisaster time, it is important to be sensitive and specific to the degree that we can. Treat each in the way you would like a disaster intervener to treat a member of your family under the same circumstances. Do not ignore the reality of the surrounding situation, while at the same time attempting to provide the best psychological care possible. Realize that you may be limited as to what you can do.

1. Consider the needed movement from "Standard of Care" to "Sufficiency of Care" for those you may need to assist. See Chapter 17 for more information.
2. Do not dismiss the "Worried Well."
3. Provide for the needs of those who have multiple unexplained physical symptoms. (MUPS)
4. Prepare for outbreaks of medically unexplained symptoms of the symptomatic unexposed. (OMUS)
5. Understand that the OMUS or MUPS are real and require real crisis intervention.
6. Keep OMUS or MUPS individuals together and attend to their

needs.

7. Reduce harmful overstimulation by either removing the sufferer from the crisis situation or by removing the crisis situation from the sufferer.

8. Help victims to "get past" the incident rather than dwelling on trying to "get over" what has happened. They can get past it, they cannot get over it.

9. Remember that effective intervention now may reduce the need for long-term treatment later.

10. Recognize the need for "critical incident stress debriefings" and when they are inappropriate.

11. Know that rigorous physical activity, within one's own limitations, is a great stress damper.

12. Appreciate the fact that some of those involved in a disaster will seem quite okay at first. They may deteriorate later. They may not deteriorate at all in your presence.

13. Do not assume that victims cannot function effectively at certain times.

14. Understand that those who may seem to function well immediately, may not be able to keep it up over extended time periods.

15. Cry if you need to.

16. Cry with the victim if they need you to do so.

17. As appropriate, get involved with the victims in their recovery activities.

18. Participating in recovery activities alongside victims helps to reduce their fears and suspiciousness about who you are and your willingness to help.

19. Normal responses can include apprehension, worry, edginess and problems with concentration.

20. Additional normal responses include attempts to flee the scene and more altruistic behaviors.

21. Provide effective risk communication.

22. Provide education as needed.

23. Facilitate reunions with family and friends.

24. If insomnia is observed, treat symptomatically.

25. Protect survivors from further harm.

26. Keep families together.

Chapter 7

RESPOND TO CHILDREN WHO ARE VICTIMS OF THE DISASTER

KNOW THE REACTIONS OF AND RESPONSES TO CHILDREN IN DISASTER

Learn what to expect from children in disaster situations. Do not assume anything, and be prepared to deal effectively with whatever presents. Usually, children are quite resilient in the same stressful situations wherein adults may have great difficulty. Of course, the reverse may also be true. Respond to children's questions and do not assume that they want more than they ask for. Try not to impose your own sense of the disaster on a child. Be as honest as you can to give them a sense of control and empowerment in a situation that may have been quite disruptive to their usual life.

1. Children's reactions to disasters and terror events will vary with age.
2. Note that children under five years of age may experience nightmares, separation anxiety and fears and even regressive-behaviors.
3. Note that the reactions of children between 6 and 11 years of age may include unusual disruptive behaviors, withdrawal, decrease in school performance and grades and difficulty concentrating.
4. Be aware that the symptoms of adolescents may mirror those of adults.
5. For children, routine is important. Disasters interrupt routine.

Try to reestablish as soon as possible and practical.

6. There may be much uncertainty among all who are involved on both sides of the helping equation.
7. Most will be unfamiliar with what is happening or with what is being released.
8. Mass panic among those affected could occur but is generally a rare occurrence. Many times, clear crisis communications can stem the tide of this type of event. A sense of loss-of-control over one's life and surroundings may produce panic. Often in disaster situations, even victims can perform in useful and reasonable ways.
9. Most behavior by victims of a disaster is normal given the circumstances. How are you supposed to feel? How are you supposed to act? This goes for children too.

UNDERSTAND THE GUIDELINES TO ASSIST PARENTS TO HELP THEIR CHILDREN

1. The objective for victims of a disaster is not to get over what has happened. The goal must be to get past these occurrences in order to survive. There is no way to turn off feelings. However, feelings do not prevent appropriate and healthy behavior unless we choose to let them.
2. We must be ready psychologically for what comes.
3. Remember, that what you are feeling now is a normal reaction to what has happened.
4. If we are going to be ready to handle more, we must find, I repeat, must find a way to get past this and go on with our individual and collective lives.
5. We must return to a normalcy and a routine as soon as possible.
6. Turn the TV off and live your life. Just as it is not always good to talk repeatedly about a traumatic event, although many are led to believe it is, TV is the electronic equivalent of talking about it, and seeing it, over and over again. Every time you re-see the events, it dredges up all of the feelings and emotions that we have been experiencing from the beginning. And, it does not make any of it any better. Turn off the television. Limit

your viewing time and the viewing time of your children. If something really bad or important happens, you know that the media will keep repeating it over and over again. Checking the news in the morning for a short time, and in the evening for a short time will probably get all of the information that you need and want. In the time that you have left over, do what you would normally do.

7. Get back into your basic routines such as eating, drinking fluids, sleeping and exercising.

8. Be sure that your family eats regularly, even if you don't feel like it.

9. Get plenty of fluids, preferably water, even if you are not thirsty.

10. Try to get back on your regular sleep schedule. If you are having trouble sleeping, at least rest on a regular basis. Contact your medical doctor if this continues. You may need to get something to help you to get drowsy and to fall off to sleep.

11. Exercise. Rigorous physical activity, within your ability and according to your doctor's orders, is one of the best stress dampers about which we know. And it is all within your control.

12. If you need to travel: Expect delays. Find out what you can take with you and what you cannot. Remain alert to possible problems, and be prepared to react for your own safety. Do not leave luggage unattended. Report any luggage that is unattended. Avoid large congregations of people. Know how to exit your surroundings.

13. Adjust daily activities as needed. Find your new normal, and get on with things as they are rather than wishing that things were as in the past. They will never again be that way, and we all must find a way, for our self, to get on with life. We determine if we do this, not the disaster.

14. We must find for ourselves a way to extract normalcy out of the chaos and to move on. The alternative is not a good one. Go to work. Do your job. Help others. Be productive. Encourage all family members to do the same.

15. Get the facts on possible threats such as anthrax, tularemia, influenza, botulinum, smallpox, chemical, nuclear and explosive threats, etc. Do not accept rumors and misinformation from anyone including the media. Panic is not the answer. Find out

what you need to know from reliable sources. Use common sense to figure out what is really possible and what is not, once you have the information.

16. Make personal and family plans concerning actions that you will take in case you encounter a threat.
17. Increase your awareness of your surroundings.
18. Report to the authorities anything that seems actually threatening or inappropriate. Don't touch it. Keep others away. Teach your children the same thing. Paranoia is not useful. Awareness is.
19. Seek help early if you need assistance dealing with your own stress. Crisis prevention is as important as crisis intervention.
20. Talk as a family; plan as a family.
21. Find time for fun and relaxation.
22. Find something each day to laugh about.
23. Volunteer to assist others. This is a good way to "get outside" your own problems.
24. Hug those close to you. Do it often.
25. Be patient with yourself and with each other.
26. Seek spiritual guidance often and as it may be needed.
27. Avoid the tendency to stereotype other people.
28. Anger is to be expected. A lot is going on around us. However, lashing-out verbally or physically seldom brings relief. It may create more personal grief.

REVIEW THE THIRTY STEPS TO HANDLING DISASTERS FOR CHILDREN AND FAMILIES

1. Listen to your kids. Often, they will have a broad array of feelings and concerns.
2. Let feelings be. Do not discount them.
3. Understand your child's words. Be sure that they can understand yours. Do not be euphemistic.
4. When you grieve, allow your children to see some of it and to take part in their own grieving.
5. Remember that managing your grief is your job and not the job of your children.
6. Reassure again and again. Feeling safe is critical for kids.

7. Honesty is important and you cannot know all about everything. Kids can accept that, you must also.
8. Reassure that they will be taken care of and that as parents you are doing everything possible to remain safe and to be there for your child.
9. Straight talk works best. Age-appropriate "straight" talk works even better.
10. Let your child see how you handle your life during these times. They will learn from this.
11. Provide structure, limits, support and guidance.
12. Converse with your child about what he or she needs from you. These needs may include a hug, time to talk, time to play or time to be with you. Adapt to the age and maturity of the child.
13. Establish a sense of purpose for your family.
14. Focus on your life and try to remain positive.
15. Do not abandon personal or family projects.
16. Routine is essential for all members of the family trying to recover from a disaster.
17. Exercise control over your life to the degree possible. Respond to other areas of life as control returns.
18. Keep expectations realistic for all.
19. Do not assign roles to children that are not age-appropriate. You are inviting problems.
20. Do what is necessary to remain healthy.
21. Stay active with friends and other families.
22. Hear your child's feelings and understand the behavior that might result. Set limits and provide stability, structure and continuity.
23. Pay attention both to the verbal and to nonverbal behavior of your kids.
24. Use laughter as a stress manager and reducer.
25. Exercise regularly. Rest sufficiently. Relax often.
26. Maintain the continuity of the familiar around you.
27. Listen, hear and respond. Do not lecture.
28. Seek ways to maximize recovery for everyone in the family.
29. Participate in support groups either separately or with your children.
30. Seek professional help early.

KNOW THE SPECIFIC GUIDELINES ABOUT WHAT PARENTS CAN DO TO HELP THEIR CHILDREN COPE WITH FEELINGS

1. Physical support is as crucial as emotional support. Hold your child.
2. Find time to let your child see your feelings and stress to them that feelings are okay at any age. Avoid the gore.
3. Provide age-appropriate and accurate information to questions raised by your kids.
4. Remember, you might need to repeat information and reassurances many times. Do not assume that all is understood immediately.
5. Allow your child to rely on his or her security blanket or toy, as needed.
6. Watch what your child does while playing alone and with others. Children may express feelings of fear or of anger while playing with toys and with friends.

Chapter 8

PERFORM ESSENTIAL POST-INCIDENT TASKS

It is not over until it's over. Post-incident tasks and procedures may be as important as any other part of a disaster intervention. Taking care of yourself, your team and others with whom you work is critical to mental well-being and to the preparation for next time.

What is below are suggestions to be supplemented by current needs. Not everything is appropriate for everybody. For example, not all exposed to a disaster will need to be psychologically debriefed, nor will they require therapy. What is needed should be evaluated on an individual basis with plans and interventions developed accordingly.

1. Post-incident debriefings should never be an afterthought. Debriefings may take many forms, and the form used should depend on the person and his or her specific needs.
2. Not everyone exposed to stress or stressful situations need to be psychologically debriefed.
3. A careful evaluation should be made to determine who needs what.
4. Stressful situations can be examined in a group setting.
5. Stressful situations can be examined individually.
6. Some stressful experiences do not need to be examined at all.
7. Do not make the assumption that all affected by disaster and resulting crisis need the same thing to assist them.
8. This author's experience tells him that those who have experienced significant stress in their life as a result of a disaster or other personal tragedy will find a way to handle these times

even if we do nothing.

9. Our job is not to impose ourselves. Our job is to provide the assistance actually needed.

10. The goal of our work with severely stressed individuals should be to help them get past the incident and to get on with their life. Our goal is not to help them get over what they are feeling. To do otherwise is like trying to teach a pig to sing. Soon you will see the impossibility of the task and you will annoy the pig. Just don't do it.

11. Be clear about your goals and intentions. Victims will pick them up even if you do not say a word. If the tables were turned, so would you.

12. Psychological debriefings are not the same as tactical or administrative debriefings. They should not be mixed together.

13. If involved in a psychological debriefing, insist that tactical or administrative issues are not allowed in this venue.

14. Post-disaster attention to yourself, to other team members and to victims of the high stress must be individualized. Some may benefit from group work. Others from individual outreach. Some may benefit from knowing that support is available if they ever need it.

15. Timing of any intervention is crucial to its effectiveness. Some things may be needed immediately. Some may be needed on-scene. Some may need to be delayed until an appropriate time that takes into account other things that are going on. Trying to debrief someone who is actively working or in the middle of a family tragedy may be inappropriate. Early work in the area of disaster intervention indicated that working alongside a disaster victim, as an initial approach, may yield huge benefits later. These may come in the form of trust and validation of what you are offering, or will offer, to the victim. Don't forget this.

16. Effective response to those who have experienced post-trauma stress should be the least amount necessary to provide an effective intervention. Sometimes less really is more. Overdoing it may serve to create more problems. If you are unsure about how much to do, consult with another intervener or a crisis intervener supervisor. A very wise man once told this author, "When in doubt of what to do, stand still." Standing still is not inactivity. It is a time to gather that which is needed to make the

correct and most beneficial move. Just doing things is not usually helpful.

17. When doing a formal debriefing in a group, use a standard format. Do not be uneasy about some deviation from the format. However, structure may prove to be important.

18. There are many successful models that can be used for group debriefings. The same is true for individual debriefings.

19. When doing an individual debriefing, a standard format can be used also.

20. Individual debriefings or crisis interventions may be adapted as appropriate to the individual being debriefed.

21. Make team psychological debriefings a regular event that is to be seen as part of the overall disaster response.

22. Encourage all disaster responders to take part of post-incident debriefings.

23. Those who do not participate should be contacted individually.

24. The importance of healthy responders cannot be overstated. Post-incident care can work to make this happen.

25. Post-incident issues and problems can help the responder to understand their own vulnerability. In crisis intervention, knowing what to stay away from is just as important as knowing in what to be involved. Interveners must learn to evaluate this in themselves.

26. Being vulnerable, having uncomfortable feelings, not wanting to "do that again," resistance to responding, guilt and the like should not be seen as anything other than the strength of knowing oneself.

27. Those responding uncomfortably to responding to a disaster scenario should be assisted in accepting what they feel, and then adjusting performance expectations accordingly. No responder can be all things to all people all of the time. This reality is sometimes hard for some to accept. Acceptance is the key; not agreement (see Chapter 17).

28. If you are responding alone, ask to be debriefed post-incident. Let leadership know of your need. Many times, responders are reluctant to ask for assistance in this area. Actually, it demonstrates that post-incident care is related directly to the incident care that you and others are able to provide.

29. Attendance at either individual or group debriefings should be

mandatory. Participation should not be mandatory. Those not attending should be contacted individually. Punishment is not an issue. Strengthening interveners is the real issue. Maybe, "Mandatory with discretion" expresses this best.

30. Pay attention to your co-responders. Early support may avoid later problems. We are all in this together and need to be interested in how each of us are doing.

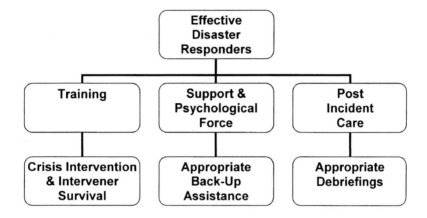

Figure 8.1. Requirements for Effective Disaster Responders.

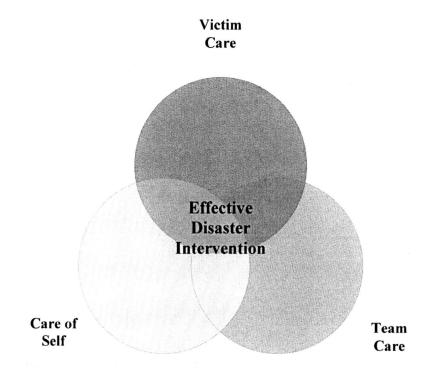

Figure 8.2. Components of Effective Disaster Crisis Intervention.

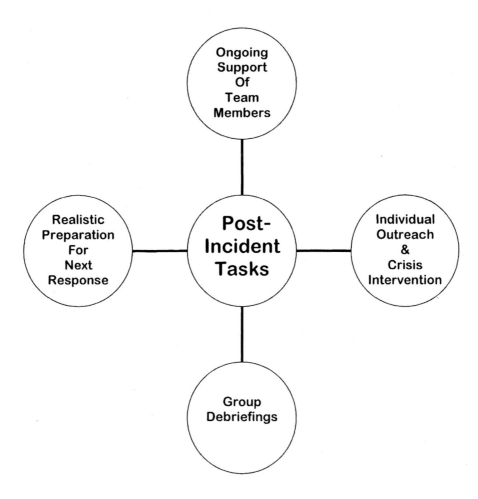

Figure 8.3. Post-Incident Tasks and Psychological Force Protection.

Chapter 9

ATTEND TO SPECIAL ISSUES AND CONCERNS

DEVELOP UNCOMMON SENSE

Pay close attention here. These guidelines may contradict common sense in some instances. What you must develop is "uncommon sense," or that ability to respond based on your training rather than your emotions. Often victims of any disaster will respond emotionally. And, while we may appropriately empathize and share their feelings, we must respond effectively at all times.

RESPECT THE CRIME SCENE

1. Remember that a disaster site is also a crime scene. Do not disturb anything unless absolutely necessary to save life.
2. Note where moved items were before movement and report this to authorities as required.
3. Remember that dead bodies are also part of the crime scene.
4. Resist the temptation to cover corpses unless instructed to do so.
5. Be careful about refusing to let survivors see those who have died. Would you want to see your loved one under these circumstances?

Note: Some of the information regarding the use of translators in this chapter has been adapted from James L. Greenstone, *The elements of police hostage and crisis negotiations: Critical incidents and how to respond to them.* (Binghamton, NY: The Haworth Press, Inc., 2005). Reproduced by permission.

6. Treat those who have died and survivors with respect.
7. Inquire of authorities concerning what is allowed and what is not allowed within a crime scene.

AVOID EUPHEMISMS

When informing others about a death, avoid euphemistic phrases. Short simple, and to the point statements seem to work very well.

USE TRANSLATORS EFFECTIVELY

The method of using a translator during a disaster or crisis with a non-English-speaking crisis victim is often compromised by lack of proper training for interveners and by misunderstandings about effective procedure. Translators are of value only if they, or their agency, can be trusted, and if their contribution to the intervention fosters the ability of the crisis intervener/responder/caregiver to give care to the victim. One common mistake is allowing the translator to conduct the intervention or the treatment. Regardless of the language spoken, and translated, the disaster responder/crisis intervener must conduct the actual intervention with the victim. This is true even if the translator happens to be a trained intervener or other caregiver.

1. Translators must be chosen carefully prior to an actual incident. If this person can participate in training scenarios, so much the better.
2. Whenever possible, translators should be recruited from reputable agencies that provide such services.
3. In the alternative to an agency, a specific person with the required skills should be sought, evaluated and trained by the intervention team.
4. The translator acts as only a "word machine" for the crisis intervener.
5. The translator does not conduct the ongoing crisis management with the subject.
6. Translators must be able to say to the sufferer exactly what the intervener says in the same way as the intervener says it.
7. Similarly, he or she must be able to say to the intervener exact-

ly what the victim or sufferer says and in the same way that he or she says it.

8. Translators should not paraphrase what either the intervener and victim says.

9. Information about the victim's tone, inflection, cultural meanings and the like will be given directly to the intervener if such nuances may not successfully cross cultural boundaries. The translator should be instructed to do this by the intervener.

10. Translators should not add personal interpretations about what the victim or intervener are saying unless specifically asked for by the intervener.

11. The translator should be fluent specifically in English and in the language of the non-English-speaking victim.

12. The translator should have no conflicts of interest that would prevent them from relating information accurately or from working with the intervener in the management of the crisis. This must be explored before the translator is used.

13. When using the translator, the crisis intervener should speak in short phrases in order to allow for accurate translation. This is called "chunking," and takes practice.

14. The translator should translate in short and exact phrases.

15. The translator is not part of the intervention unless specifically needed.

16. Remember: The translator only translates. Nothing more.

UNDERSTAND RESPONDER SECURITY

It seems to this author that the importance of security issues and security planning is relegated by most in much the same way as are psychosocial issues. If one asks, most reply that security and psychosocial concerns are important, but it seems to end there. When we practice, we do not practice realistically in either area. Even though we are taught by those who seem to know that for every traumatic injury, there will be three to five psychological injuries, do we practice with 50 psychological victims when we train to care for ten trauma victims? Hardly! When we train, do we deal with the security issues as we might in-fact find them the day the balloon goes up? Another, "Hardly!"

And, what about the ethical aspects of security? How far is a community or a community law enforcement officer willing or allowed to go to prevent the overrunning and contamination of a crowded emergency room? An emergency room filled to the brim with other disaster victims?

Further, it is this author's experience and observation that, not only have we not dealt with these issues, but also that we really do not know how to deal with them. Many believe that somehow it will just be taken care of. Police personnel are often present at disaster training scenarios. We assume therefore that should a real disaster occur they will have no more pressing assignments than to staff our security details.

What about security personnel? How are they really trained and to do what? What about the "boots-on-the-ground" disaster workers? If a person goes into crisis, or if someone responds in anger, or fails to respond calmly, what then? It has been observed that the first thing that usually happens is a call for the police who are on the scene to handle the situation. Little or no attempts are made by the disaster responders to intervene. Most are not trained and do not know what to do. And, we do not provide the training because we assume that this is really not part of our job. In this author's opinion, "Wrong answer again."

The following may be useful as we begin to approach this area in a measured, accurate and definitive way. Not to do so will get us hurt. And, if we get hurt, or cannot continue to provide for other victims, where does that leave our entire disaster response?

1. Start with the premise that team security, scene security and individual security are parts of your responsibilities as an intervener.
2. Plan for the possibility that the security you provide will be the only security you may have.
3. Early on, appoint a physical force protection officer to be responsible for the security of your team.
4. Appoint a psychological force protection officer to help insure the psychological well-being of your team members.
5. Do not assume the presence of professional police or security personnel.
6. Assure that all disaster team members are trained in Crisis In-

tervention and have the opportunity to practice these skills during training exercises.

7. Consider the ethics of security issues that might be faced during times of disaster. How far are you willing to go to insure the protection and security of your team members or of other victims? Hospital ethicists and disaster ethicists can be a great help here. Many have never faced these types of questions.

8. Remember that ethics are often the result of reasoned deliberation rather than personal opinion. Be willing to engage in the process.

9. Under what conditions is force authorized and to be utilized? Deadly force? Equal force?

10. Provide basic security training for all team members.

11. Discuss the ethical ramifications attendant to security issues.

12. Be sure that all training simulations include security issues. Train to play.

13. Consider team responses in the absence of police personnel; without security personnel.

14. Accept the reality that you may have to deal with angry, resistant, emotionally disturbed and just plain difficult people under great stress. These are usual in disasters.

15. Develop basic self-defense techniques. Learn to take care of yourself so that you can effectively take care of others.

16. Know how to interact helpfully with trained security personnel should they be present.

17. Know something about the laws regarding use of force, continuum of force and responding to force against you or others you serve.

18. Understand basic issues regarding weapons, loading, unloading, disabling, recognizing, signs of presence, and the like.

19. Recognize the seriousness of this area of your responsibilities during a disaster. If you already have, validate your thinking. If you have not, plan accordingly.

20. Remember that a crisis intervener who is in a crisis because of a preventable security breach is of little use to disaster victims.

21. Awareness, preparation and training are key to successful intervention in crisis situations just as they are to successful security response.

22. Learn to play the "What if" game as you develop security acu-

men. Anticipate, anticipate, anticipate.

23. Know what is required to insure that your situation or scene is secure.

24. Perform a threat assessment for every scene into which you enter.

25. Consider the available assets to be used to secure the area in which you and your team are operating.

26. Under what conditions would you consider abandoning your area of operations?

27. Train all personnel and all security personnel about how to deal with persons in crisis with or without the availability of police.

28. Security personnel, regardless of background, should be trained in the following:
    a. Security procedures
    b. Enforcement procedures
    c. Civilian "use of force"
    d. "Citizen's" arrest laws and procedures
    e. Self-defense
    f. Emotional crisis intervention
    g. Physical crisis intervention

29. The area of security is often an area of assumptions rather than of careful analysis, planning and training.

30. The only acceptable assumption is that law enforcement will not be there. If they are, great. If not, you must be ready.

31. Be sure that if law enforcement or security personnel are present, they know the correct actions to take given the specific disaster scene. Work together. Both have this responsibility.

Chapter 10

CONSIDER THE ISSUES OF SUICIDE

USE THE TEN STEPS TO DEALING WITH THE POTENTIAL SUICIDE

The potential for suicide can be a major concern during and after the advent of a disaster. Depending on the emotional depths to which victims are forced because of the losses experienced, considerations of suicide may be present. It is important that disaster interveners be aware of the possibilities and take appropriate and skillful action. Look for such expressions both in adults and in children.

1. If you suspect suicide, take action now! Don't wait until it's too late.
2. If you can talk openly about suicide, maybe it will be easier for the sufferer to speak of it. Using the word, "suicide" will not make the person suicidal. Tell the sufferer, "I don't want you to die."
3. Never say, "You don't really want to do that." They really do want to do it.
4. Never ask, "Why do you want to do that?" They probably do not know "why," and the question will increase their defensiveness. Ask present-oriented questions if you need information such as, "What happened?"; "How do you feel?"; "What's going on?"

Note: A special acknowledgment is made to Doctor Sharon Leviton, Crisis Intervention Specialist, for her material that aided in the development of this specific section. Some of the material in this chapter has been adapted from James L. Greenstone, *The elements of police hostage and crisis negotiations: Critical incidents and how to respond to them* (Binghamton, NY: The Haworth Press, Inc., 2005). Revisions reproduced by permission.

5. Remember that a suicidal person will have trouble focusing on the future and that, "Things will get better." Keep your focus on the present and what can be done to assist them now.
6. Never challenge the sufferer to, "Go ahead and do it." You may be giving him or her permission to do the act that you will regret for the rest of your life.
7. Be careful of whom you call to talk with the victim. They may be part of the problem. e.g., family members, minister, doctor. Evaluate potential to be helpful to others.
8. Remember: Suicide has nothing to do with death. Suicide has to do with conflict in a person's life between the sufferer and at least one other person or institution, either present or absent in their life at the moment. Death may be only the unfortunate by-product of the suicidal gesture.
9. If you believe that the person is suicidal, do not leave them alone. Stay with them.
10. Rule of Thumb: Check out the "specificity of the suicidal plan," and the "lethality of the suicidal means." The more specific the plan and the more lethal the means, the greater the risk of suicide. Ask the sufferer what he or she intends to do and how. See and learn how to use the Lethality Scale in this chapter.

UNDERSTAND ADOLESCENT SUICIDE

Even without the occurrence of a disaster or other major traumatic event, the teenage years are a period of turmoil for just about everyone experiencing them. Many changes are taking place both emotionally and physically and new social roles are being learned. Sometimes solutions to problems are not readily available to the teen and the result can be loneliness. The more that interveners understand about the unique nature of teen suicidal actors, the better prepared they will be to intervene effectively. Combine this information with what we know about the impact and stressors of a disaster, and we begin to understand the magnitude of this potential problem.

Speculation about how our life will turn out is not an unusual thing for any of us to do. With teens, it can be particularly difficult to understand everything that is going on around them. Family problems, divorce, embarrassment and even poor grades in school can exacerbate a sense of great concern about one's life and the reasons to continue or to end it. Teens may have some difficulty recognizing the bigger picture that just as things change, so do feelings and inner turmoil. It may become too much to handle for the young mind and depression can result. Such depression increases the risk of suicidal behavior. A disaster may include the total risk. There may be a need for support during these times and such support might come from a parent, a good friend or a mental health professional. However, recognition of the problem by those closest to the teen is the first step in the process toward better mental help at these times. Denial will not make the problem go away. Undoubtedly, it will make the problem worse as the loneliness and the feelings of not being understood increase. To the contrary, with effective help, most can recover from the depression fairly quickly.

What To Look For

As you intervene, stay alert to what you may observe. Mood swings are normal. A lot of swings in mood often accompany teen years. Everyone feels sad at times. Feeling sad is not our focus here. A depressed mood that continues for two weeks or more could be a significant sign that deserves our attention. Listen to what your teens say. Watch what teens do. Help could be needed if you hear: "I am sleeping much later than I used to." Or, "I'm not sleeping well and I wake up early in the morning." "I am beginning to take a lot of naps," could be cause for some concern. Changes in appetite and unplanned weight gains or losses are additional clues. Remember that you do not have to be a highly-trained mental health professional to pay attention to the signs of suicide in teenagers during disaster operations, or to take appropriate action when needed.

Listen For

- "I am very restless."
- "I don't want to see anyone; not even friends and family."
- "I can't seem to concentrate anymore."
- "I've lost interest in everything."
- "I feel guilty," or "I feel hopeless and helpless."
- "I seem to be withdrawing more and more."
- "My mood keeps changing."

• "Life is just not worth living anymore."

More Clues

1. It seems to be that young people who have attempted suicide in the past are at greater risk.
2. Talking about suicide does not obviate the need for concern and intervention. Those who talk about suicide may actually do it. It is a myth to think otherwise.
3. Feelings of loneliness, hopelessness and rejection are significant.
4. Alcohol use and abuse may be a part of suicidal behavior. Some teens who abuse alcohol or drugs are more likely to consider, attempt or succeed at suicide than are non-abusers.
5. Those planning to kill themselves may give away personal possessions, discard things that are usually meaningful to them, or begin cleaning their own room.
6. The teen may suddenly become cheerful, or even appear upbeat, after a bout with depression. The sudden change may foretell that they have made the decision to end their own life. Do not put off getting help in these circumstances.
7. Remember that one of the most dangerous times occur when severe loss of any kind has been experienced or personal humiliation has been felt. Disaster events can exacerbate this.

Some Findings

1. Those who talk of helplessness and hopelessness may be at great risk.
2. Talking about suicide will not prevent it from happening as some believe.
3. Depression and the ultimate risk of suicide may have biological as well as psychological causes.
4. A family history of suicide may be a significant risk factor in predicting suicidal behavior in teens.
5. The suicide rate for teens is about the same as the national average. Although not as high as the media would have us believe, suicide among teenagers is a serious health problem.
6. Males seem to commit suicide more than females. Females attempt suicide more often, however. This may be a changing

phenomenon in our society as traditional roles change.

Intervention Guidelines

1. The American Psychiatric Association and The American Psychological Association provide much insight into teen suicide and suicide intervention.
2. Many times persons who are depressed, or depressed and suicidal, will find it hard to talk to anyone about what they feel.
3. Feelings of worthlessness and hopelessness may contribute to this unwillingness to reach out to others.
4. Those with suicidal ideations may even deny their own emotions or think that talking to someone will only burden the listener.
5. Remember, a person who is suicidal may truly believe that no one cares anyway.
6. Some may feel that others will make fun of them.
7. Although much of the reluctance to reach out and to express themselves may be justified by previous encounters, such can make the problems worse.
8. Most of those who may contemplate suicide will leave some clues.
9. In many cases, the teen who is suicidal has spoken with, or at least tried to speak with, someone about what they are experiencing.
10. If the teen alludes to the subject of suicide or brings it up directly, take it seriously and take some time to talk about it.
11. The difference that this small act of talking and listening can make could be inestimable.
12. Reassure the troubled teen that he or she has those around them that are ready and willing to help.
13. Do not be afraid to listen to the teen in crisis and to try to understand their dilemma of wanting to live on the one hand and die on the other. It is part of their experience.
14. Sometimes it is hard to let someone else know that there is a need to talk about something as serious as our emotions.
15. Avoid the tendency, when talking with a person who is suicidal, to preach or to lecture to them about why they should not kill themselves.

16. It will not be helpful to point out to the teen all of the reasons that they should stay alive or the things for which they have to live.
17. Listen and reassure. I repeat for emphasis, listen and reassure!
18. Depression and suicidal tendencies can be treated successfully. Tell them that also, but only after you have listened a lot and reassured as needed.
19. We know that depressive disorders respond well to psychotherapy and to medication.
20. Antidepressants can act within two to three weeks and are often used in addition to psychotherapy.

ATTEND TO DISASTER GRIEF

Disaster, and the ensuing stress, may create crisis in a person's life. Crisis usually involves loss. In fact, loss may be the common denominator of crises. If the loss is significant, substantial grief results. If the loss is minor, sufferers may be able to manage the loss through their usual coping mechanisms. With great loss, the grief may require the intervention of a trained crisis responder.

Interveners must recognize at least three elements that affect the grief of the sufferer. These are:

1. The intensity of the emotions resulting from the loss.
2. The perceived effects of the loss in the long term to the life of the sufferer.
3. The personal value attached to the experienced loss.

It is important that responders remember that crisis is always in the eye of the beholder. The above listed elements are also determined by the eye of the beholder. Perception is the reality of the crisis victim. It is with the recognition of these basic points that the crisis responder remains effective.

1. Encourage sufferers to express their emotions. Allow this without judgment on your part.
2. Let the victim take the time needed and necessary to express feelings before attempting to address options or alternatives.
3. Assure sufferers that their emotions are normal and accepted as such.

4. Assure them that they can live through even the loneliest and very painful experience.
5. As an intervener, reach out to the disaster victim in ways that you consider appropriate and effective given the immediate circumstances.
6. Reach out physically only with permission.
7. During the grief process, those suffering may experience:
    a. Dizziness, off balance and/or lack of coordination.
    b. Erratic appetite.
    c. Disturbed sleep patterns and/or feeling drugged without having taken medications.
    d. Feeling not "in sync" with their own body.
    e. Irritability, anger and/or rage.
    f. A disconnect with family and with friends.
    g. Feelings of "falling apart" and/or disorientation.
    h. Sadness.
    i. Lack of personal control and/or hopelessness.
    j. Confusion and/or inability to make decisions.
    k. Feelings that nothing has meaning or that nothing matters anymore.
    l. Feeling frozen in time.
    m. That too much effort is involved in doing even the most basic behaviors.
    n. Embarrassment about personal feelings.
    o. Guilt.
    p. An overwhelming sense of panic.
    q. The sense that nothing will ever be right again.
    r. A feeling of spinning around.
    s. Resentment that the loss has occurred.
    t. Relief that the ordeal leading to the loss is over and then experiencing guilt for feeling this way.
    u. Emptiness and/or numbness.
    v. Being pushed down or buried.
    w. Being very small.
    x. Turmoil.
    y. Ambivalence.
    z. Euphoria at one moment; depression the next.
8. Disaster interveners should encourage victims to do the following as a part of self-intervention:

a. Feel their own feelings and allow them to be whatever they are at the moment.

b. Avoid major changes in their life that would disenfranchise them further.

c. Avoid making any major decisions for the time being.

d. Remain with that which is familiar as a form of psychological security.

e. Set realistic expectations concerning all major areas of their life.

f. Seek out those others who are helpful and comforting.

g. Avoid the well-intentioned who are not helpful. Being well-intentioned does not always translate into helpful behavior.

h. Identify those areas of life over which some control is still recognized and maintained and exercise that control as soon as possible. This may help return that sense of control to those other areas of life seen as less controlled because of the crisis and loss.

i. Maintain a daily routine. The pre-crisis routine would probably work best.

j. Care for self through exercise, vitamin supplements, realistic work and rest schedules. Do not put this off.

k. Let the process of recovery take as long as it takes. Imposing limits is seldom helpful or therapeutic.

l. Allow for discovery and utilization of personal strengths.

9. Interveners can help sufferers to do the following:

a. Concentrate on the present instead of the distant future. Live for today and view each day as a victory.

b. Enjoy family members and relationships; Allow talk about thoughts and feelings.

c. Finish project previously started or begin a new project or hobby.

d. Remember that each person copes in ways specific to them. Sufferers should listen to their own needs.

e. Accept personal responsibility for one's own life and state of mind. Set realistic goals.

f. Reach out to others and let them know the victim's wants and needs as appropriate.

g. Encourage open and honest communication and set the tone for others with whom they may associate.

h. Work with family, friends and co-workers to help build and maintain a sense of control, purpose and hope.

i. Remember that there will be good times as well as bad times. Focus on the good and never lose hope.

j. Share thoughts and feelings only as the victim desires. Understand that sometimes talking with others eases emotional weight. Sometimes talking to others can provide insight and new directions.

k. Talk about their experiences only when they so desire to do so. Do not be forced by others, no matter how well meang.

l. Remember that professional help is available and should be considered early if the need arises.

m. Recognize that self-help groups can aid in the healing process.

n. Remember that expressing feelings with others can be a great release.

o. Live each day as fully as possible.

p. Knowing that a decision to make the most out of life can be of substantial help to them.

q. Choose small goals and constructive ways to use them.

r. Ask, "What is important to me right now?" and "What do I cherish?"

s. Think of the needs of other families, their own family, friends and others who are important to the sufferer.

t. Keep a daily journal of feelings, thoughts and experiences.

u. Direct personal energy into living each day as it comes and making each day count by what is put into it.

v. Keep close at hand those things that have historically given them pleasure and surround themselves with familiar things.

w. Keep up with local and national news in a realistic manner so as not to overload on either.

x. Ask others to go out or to just drop by for a visit.

y. Understand that wanting to be alone is okay.

z. Maintain self-respect even though it may sometimes seem difficult.

KNOW HOW TO USE THE LETHALITY SCALE

Figure 10.1
LETHALITY SCALE

	0 Points	1 Point	2 Points	3 Points	4 Points	Total
Age, Male	0-12 yrs.		13-44 yrs.	45-64 yrs.	65 and up	
Age, Female	0-12 yrs.	13-44 yrs.	45 and up			
Personal Resources Available	Good	Fair		Poor		
Current Stress	Low		Medium		High	
Marital Status	Married with Children	Married without Children		Widowed or Single	Divorced	
Current Psychological Functioning	Stable		Unstable			
Other problems or symptoms	Absent		Present			
Communication Channels	Open		Blocked			
Physical Condition	Good	Fair			Poor	
Suicide by close Family Member	No		Yes			
Depressed or Agitated Now	No				Yes	
Prior Suicidal Behavior	No		Yes			
Reactions by Significant Others to the Needs of the Person	Helpful			Not Helpful		
Current Financial Stress	Absent		Present			
Suicidal Plan of the Person	Has none	Plan with few details	Person has selected means for suicide		Person has highly specific plan for suicide	
Occupation of Person	Non-helping profession or	MD, dentist, attorney, or helping professional	Psych, police officer or unemployed			

Figure 10.1–*Continued*

	occupation					
Residence	Rural	Suburban	Urban			
Living Arrangements	Lives with others				Live Alone	
Time of Year		Spring				
Day of Week		Sunday or Monday or Wednesday				
Recent Occurrence of Arguments with Spouse or Significant Other	No	Yes				
Recently, Person's Significant Other was:		The focus of a disappointment	Lost to person in some significant way			
					Total Points	

Name of person being evaluated:
Date and Time Scale completed:
Name of Intervener completing this scale:

Comments and Action Notes:

Criteria

Minimal Risk (0-15 points)   _____
Low Risk (16-30 points)   _____
Medium Risk (31-46 points) _____
High Risk (47-60 points)   _____

Directions for Use: Circle response in appropriate row and column. Place points from top of column in the far right column. Sum all scores under total points and match with total criteria. Scale can be administered multiple times on same person as more information becomes available.

Chapter 11

PAY ATTENTION TO INTERVENER SURVIVAL

UTILIZE SELF-RELAXATION SKILLS

These five steps can be used almost anywhere and at any time. They were adapted from some of the work done in this field by Doctor Edward S. Rosenbluh. During this total relaxation, your mind remains alert. As long as you do not do the steps for longer than twenty minutes, you are not likely to fall asleep. When you are finished, you will feel relaxed and fresh. Experienced relaxers even talk of a "natural high" produced without drugs.

When time or circumstances do not permit following the whole program, you may do parts of it. It can be done with your eyes open or shut. It can be done for short periods of time. It can even be done in a meeting, as a passenger in a car, during breaks or downtime, and during other appropriate or private times. You will feel more refreshed and alert even after a short session than if you had remained tense the entire time.

Step One: Sit or lie in a comfortable position. Allow the weight of all parts of your body to be supported. Lean your head forward if sitting, or back if lying down.

Step Two: Close your eyes and relax all parts of your body. Feel your feet getting heavy and relaxed, then your ankles, knees, hips, mid-section, hand, arms, shoulders, neck, jaw, eyes, forehead, and even your tongue. Feel each part of your body, in succession, starting with your feet, become heavy, relaxed and comfortable.

Step Three: Begin to concentrate on your breathing. Observe it with your mind as it slowly goes in and out. During each exhale, say the word, "One," to yourself, e.g., inhale, exhale, "One," inhale, exhale, "One," and so on.

Step Four: The word "One" will help keep meaningful thoughts from your mind. Do not worry if fleeting thoughts come in and out of focus. Concentrate on breathing and on "One."

Step Five: Continue for 20 minutes. Do this once in the morning and once in the evening, as needed and as possible. Do these steps anytime you feel tense. You may check the clock periodically. Because of digestion, which might interfere, it would probably be best to avoid total relaxation for about two hours after eating. If you feel your hands getting warmer, this is okay. Such sensations often accompany total relaxation. Sometimes, it even helps to think about your hands and arms getting warmer after Step Two.

UNDERSTAND STRESS MANAGEMENT

Signs and Symptoms of Stress and Burnout

- High resistance to doing one's job or responding to a deployment.
- A pervasive sense of failure.
- Anger and resentment.
- Guilt and blame.
- Discouragement and indifference.
- Negativism.
- Isolation and withdrawal.
- Feelings of tiredness and exhaustion.
- Frequent clock-watching and wanting to leave assignments early.
- Extreme fatigue after an assignment.
- Loss of positive feelings even when helping others.
- Resistance to helping others.
- Inability to concentrate.
- Feelings of being immobilized.

- Cynicism.
- Sleep disturbances.
- Self-preoccupation.
- Use of tranquilizers or other medications in order to cope with situation.
- Frequent minor illnesses, colds and flus.
- Headaches.
- Gastrointestinal disturbances.
- Rigidity and inability to change even when needed or directed to do so.
- Suspicion and paranoia.
- Excessive drug use.
- Marital conflict.
- Family conflict.
- Free-floating anxiety.
- Tunnel vision.
- Increasing feelings of helplessness.
- High absenteeism.

Stress Management

- Eliminate stressor foods and substances.
- Get sufficient rest and sleep.
- Exercise regularly. Exercise is a very good stress damper. All exercise should be within any limitations directed by the intervener's physician.
- Be willing to accept the "givens" in your life. The "givens" are what is at the moment.
- Assess abilities realistically.
- Schedule time for fun.
- Schedule time for "dreaming."
- Schedule recreation time.
- Find positive nurturing for yourself.
- Set realistic goals.
- Consider choices and "responseabilities."
- Seek help if needed and seek it early.

Dr. Leviton's "50" Steps to Proactive Stress Management Before and During Deployment

- Clear job descriptions.
- Clear interview processes.
- Delegating.
- Realistic task assignments.
- Realistic responsibilities.
- Realistic expectations.
- Knowledge of the "big picture."
- Responding rather than reacting.
- Effective planning.
- Consistency.
- Perception of reliability.
- Order.
- Efficiency.
- Support.
- Structure.
- Accurate information.
- Valued creativity.
- Open communication lines.
- Accessibility.
- Use of a person's name.
- Awareness of environment in which working.
- Encouraging input.
- Clear directions.
- Directions that cannot be misunderstood.
- Feedback.
- Perception of fairness.
- Encouraging self-development.
- Providing a safe and secure work environment.
- Supportiveness.
- Lack of defensiveness.
- Identification and reduction of stressors.
- Awareness of indicators of stress.
- Realistic goals.
- Encourage networking with peers.
- Teach and model conflict resolution.
- Continuous, realistic and effective evaluations.
- Acknowledge the need for humor.
- Set appropriate climate for over all organization.
- Recognition that most people want to feel commitment, challenge and control.

DEVELOP PERSONAL SURVIVAL SKILLS

All interveners have an optimal level of stress for that individual. To keep stress from becoming distress, it is important that we have the right amount of stress for the proper duration. Nutritional stress can be as problematic and debilitating as can emotional stress. The end results can be the same regardless of the cause.

1. Introspection may assist you in becoming aware of yourself and of the power that you have over your own body.
2. Everything that you put into your mouth in the way of food affects, in some way, your brain, lungs, heart and other areas of your body.
3. You determine, to a great extent, how your body will function by what you put into it. This is true day-to-day and also during a deployment.
4. How you care for your body will determine how well it will function.
5. The human body is generally self-supporting. If we take care of it, put the right things in and dispose of the wrong things and the waste, our body will usually work very well.
6. Natural energizers or "natural highs" can be produced by a well-functioning body and mind.
7. Disaster interveners cannot care effectively for victims until we care enough about ourselves to take care of our bodily and mental functions.
8. How we take care of our own bodies and minds has a direct effect on our abilities to assist others.
9. To be helpful, we must remain effective. Effectiveness as interveners is related to many things including continual self-care. This should not be overlooked.
10. The complete elimination of stress is not possible.
11. Elimination of all stress is not even desirable. A certain amount of stress in our life keeps us alert, and aids us in our daily life.
12. Stress can be either "good stress" or "bad stress." The reduction of bad stress should be our goal.
13. We cannot escape stress, but we can make it work for us rather than against us.
14. All people do not react to stress in the same way.

15. Emotional and physical stress will vary.
16. Stress will attack the "weakest" part of our body and may seem to concentrate there.
17. A responsible nutritional regimen can assist in our resistance to high stress.
18. If we bombard ourselves with stressor food, the result may be additional, nonproductive stress (see Figure 11.1).
19. The starting point is to become aware of stressor foods and substances to which we may be subjecting ourselves.
20. Understand that nutritionally-produced stress may interfere with your effectiveness when attempting to help others.
21. Nutritionally-produced stress may also interfere with your own ability to deal with the surrounding stress present during a disaster. If you cannot handle the stress, what might that mean for your interventions with others?
22. Stressor foods and substances might include the following:
    a. Refined sugars and foods that contain refined sugar. These are found all around us, and in about everything that we generally eat.
    b. Refined and processed carbohydrates and starches. A little goes a long way depending on its source.
    c. Caffeine. Some may experience "addiction" to caffeine-rich products and hence a sense of withdrawal when they try to cut back. Caffeine may be present in many foods, drinks and in over-the-counter drugs.
    d. Artificial sweeteners are generally felt by many to be safe and non-stress producing. This may not be so. Additionally, the chemicals in these sweeteners often have no nutritional value.
    e. Monosodium glutamate or MSG may be found in many tenderizers and pre-packaged meats, to mention a few.
    f. Cigarettes have a long history of doing bad things to our bodies. They are often the self-medication of choice for some during high-stress encounters.
23. Stressor foods in combination or individually can have a direct effect on body chemistry. Elevations may be seen in cholesterol, triglycerides, uric acid and can cause serious fluctuations in blood sugar levels.
24. Our brains are sensitive to changes in body chemistry. What we

put in or what we leave out can have direct and major effects on the brain and this can affect the rest of our bodily functions.

25. Avoid approaching this area as a "nice to know, but it doesn't affect me" scenario. It is vital to know and it will affect you and your ability to function during high stress situations. What you don't know can hurt you, and in the case of the disaster intervener, can hurt others.

26. Encouraging sufferers to pay attention to nutritional factors will go better if you have experience doing the same.

27. The following may be signs of a poor diet:
    a. Irritability.
    b. Poor sleep habits.
    c. Poor sleep patterns.
    d. Excessive fatigue.
    e. Frequent illnesses.
    f. Poor elimination patterns.

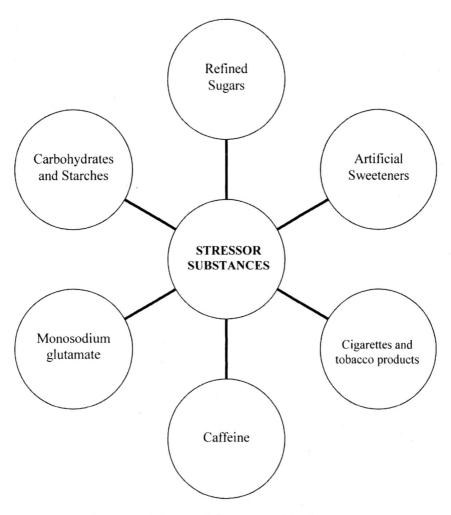

Figure 11.1. Stressor Substances and the Intervener.

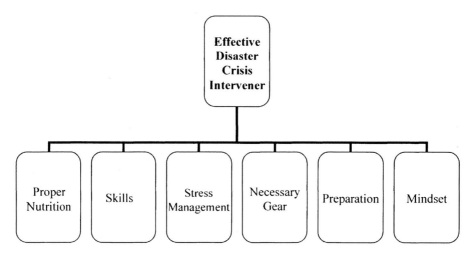

Figure 11.2. Effective Disaster Crisis Intervener includes this and more.

Chapter 12

LEARN AND UTILIZE EFFECTIVE
COMMUNICATION SKILLS

Before a problem can be managed effectively, the disaster intervener must know what the problem is. Often, more than one problem is present in a given situation. Disaster scenarios may bring out old emotional wounds as well as those caused instantly. When this occurs, the following questions can be asked to determine the priority for intervention:

ASK THE RIGHT QUESTIONS

1. Which of the problems presented is of immediate concern? Which has the highest priority as evaluated by the intervener?
2. Which problem would prove most damaging if not dealt with immediately?
3. Which of the problems presented can be resolved the quickest?
4. Which problem must be dealt with before others can be handled?
5. What resources do I have at hand to handle the problems presented?
6. What are the barriers and obstacles currently present, or likely to be present, that will hinder problem solving?
7. Is there anything that must be done or changed now in order

---

Note: Some of the material in this chapter has been revised and adapted from James L. Greenstone, *The elements of police hostage and crisis negotiations: Critical incidents and how to respond to them* (Binghamton, NY: The Haworth Press, Inc., 2005).

to enhance problem management? Why do I want to change these things at the current time? Why not change them? Has anything occurred to necessitate the anticipated change? If not, why change?

Although it is necessary to answer the preceding questions, the disaster intervener/responder must be able to acquire the needed information quickly and accurately. While some of the information needed will come from external sources, the intervener will gather much that must be known from the victim directly. This means that the responder must listen actively to the victim's total message and give the person full concentration and undivided attention. Further, the intervener must sift through the victim's words to gain information and insight into the person's problems and views of those problems.

UNDERSTAND THE MESSAGES

Every communication from the disaster victim contains three messages:

1. **A content message.** This message provides information about what the sender believes, thinks or perceives the situation to be.
2. **A feeling message.** The feeling message conveys the nature and intensity of the sender's emotion about the current or related situations.
3. **A meaning message.** This concerns the behavior or situation that has generated the feeling.

Usually, the person who sends the communication implies, rather than explicitly stating, the behavior or situation that creates the feelings. The intervener must try to infer what the behavior or situation is.

UNDERSTAND THE NATURE OF DISTORTIONS

Doctor Edward S. Rosenbluh, a pioneer in the field of Crisis Intervention, explained that when another person communicates with you, distortions can occur in three main areas:

1. What the subject means to say.

2. What the subject actually says.
3. What you, as the disaster responder, believe that you hear.

BE EMPATHETIC

The key to effective listening is accurately hearing the feelings and meaning behind the content of any communication. This is often referred to as the skill of empathy. Empathy is the ability to enter the subject's world, and to reflect your understanding of this world, to the subject. Empathy contains two elements:

1. **Passive empathy.** This is the ability to hear the facts contained in the words and the feelings contained in the subject's body language, intensity and tone.
2. **Active empathy.** Active empathy refers to the ability to reflect this understanding to the other person in a manner that generates warmth, trust and a willingness to be open. This is often a difficult skill for novice responders and the more experienced alike. Practice, practice, practice. The tendency is to take the usual approach and deal only with surface facts. Not being able to get below the surface of these facts will reduce the effectiveness of the intervener in bringing the situation to a successful conclusion and assisting the victim. Now go back and read the previous sentence again.

NEVER ASSUME

Sometimes a victim will make a statement that the intervener does not fully understand. At other times, the victim's words and nonverbal behavior may not agree. At such a point, the intervener must focus on the misunderstanding and try to clarify the statement made prior to continuing with the intervention. Interveners must not assume that they understand what the victim means. The intervener must find out and know what the victim means. Conversely, two people can have very different experiences, and relate these experiences similarly. Interveners must be sure that they know precisely about what the victim is talking. To do so, the intervener must:

1. Inquire to clarify vague or ambiguous statements.
2. Be sure that the victim and the intervener are talking about the same thing at the same time.

CLARIFY STATEMENTS

1. Repeating key words
   a. Repeat key words or phrases that the victim uses.
   b. Focus on a specific word or phrase that is not clearly understood. This may cause the victim to clarify the meaning.
   c. Encourage the victim to explain in more detail.
   d. Be careful using this technique. Repeating can sound insincere.
   e. Parroting may make the victim distrustful of, or uneasy with, the responder.
   f. This is a useful tool when used cautiously.
2. Restatement
   a. Rephrase what the victim says as a way of encouraging them to clarify meaning.
   b. Restatement may cause the victim to talk more about areas of their life or situation that is most pressing.
   c. Encourages the victim to provide more detail.
   d. The additional information gained using this technique will help the intervener to understand what the victim is thinking and feeling.
3. The direct method
   a. Very effective.
   b. Admit that you are confused or puzzled about the victim's statement.
   c. Ask the victim for clarification.
   d. Explain that this clarification will result in better understanding on your part.
   e. Lets the victim know that the intervener is interested in what is being said.
4. Asking Questions
   a. Simple way to get a clearer idea of the victim's meaning.
   b. Ask questions.
   c. Ask simple questions.

d. Ask one question at a time. This is suggested unless the asking of multiple questions is done for a specific purpose.
e. Ask open-ended questions to gain information.
f. Ask closed-ended questions to pinpoint specific items. Especially effective when the intervener is fairly sure what additional information is needed.

KNOW WHEN AND HOW TO ASK QUESTIONS

1. Can be used to obtain accurate information if done correctly.
2. Probably necessary and often helpful.
3. Pace of questions must be considered so as not to raise the victim's stress level, unless this is desired.
4. Bombarding with questions can confuse and frustrate the victim, and even, at times, the intervener.
5. Allow sufficient time for the victim to answer the questions posed.
6. Ask in a nonthreatening, and nonaccusatory tone.

DEAL EFFECTIVELY WITH SILENCE

The intervener/responder will often encounter silence both while dealing with crisis disaster victims. Knowing how to handle the silence is very important. For some crisis interveners, silence is deadly. It need not be.

1. Do not assume that silence means that nothing is happening.
2. Learn to be comfortable with your feelings of being uncomfortable.
3. Use silent moments to listen more carefully for relevant information in the background.
4. Handle silence by being silent.
5. Pay attention to what the victim is "not saying."
6. Why have they not said it?
7. What significance does this silence have in the overall scenario?
8. If the silence persists, you may want to reassure the victim that you are still there and ready to listen if they want to talk.

9. After you reassure the victim, remain quiet.
10. Insert information, or empathy into silence only as actually deemed necessary.
11. Sometime, persistent silence can be broken by the intervener carrying on both sides of the conversation as though the victim were responding. The victim may reenter the conversation just to find out what is going on. This technique requires practice and can be very effective.

RESPOND TO THE VICTIM IN AN EFFECTIVE WAY

Responding to another person's feelings is a delicate process. In gathering information from victims, interveners must handle feelings with care and concern. If the intervener wants the victim to continue to talk about facts pertinent to the problem, the intervener cannot judge, use logic, or attempt to give advice. If things were reversed, and someone did that to you, how open would you probably be to sharing your innermost feelings with them? The individual's feelings must be legitimized. The goal is to increase communications rather than to shut them off.

EFFECTIVELY COMMUNICATE

1. Learn and practice to listen effectively.
2. Strive to hear fully what the victim is saying, and what they might be really saying. It takes practice.
3. If possible, depending on the situation, maintain appropriate eye contact.
4. Let the victim speak freely. Do not short-stop.
5. Try to comprehend what the victim is saying even if it sounds garbled or strange.
6. Listen for both feelings and content.
7. Paraphrase the victim's statements to gain clarification.
8. Ask for clarification when necessary. Do not interrupt unless you must to avoid a misunderstanding.
9. Do not let your own feelings get in the way of understanding what the other person is trying to say.

10. Respond in a descriptive manner.
11. Do not be evaluative in your responses in order to avoid defensiveness from the victim.
12. Remember that "rightness" or "wrongness" may not be the issue.
13. Effective communications is not a contest. Unfortunately, some crisis interveners think that it is and that they must "out-communicate" the victim. The "win or lose" mentality is actually inappropriate here.
14. Learn all that you can about the other person's thoughts and feelings.
15. Let the victim know some things about you, if appropriate. Self-disclosure is not always appropriate. However, revealing certain nonsensitive things about your self may help put the other person at ease. It may make the intervener seem more nearly human.
16. Use descriptive statements and reveal your reactions to the other person, as needed.
17. Use your own feelings, as warranted. Do not be afraid of this.
18. Note that feelings are important in communicating, and that they are always present.
19. Practice expressing your own feelings. It is not as easy as one would think. Sometimes, it is especially difficult for crisis interveners.
20. Take responsibility for your feelings.
21. Use communications messages to the victim that begin with "I" rather than "You." Those beginning with "I" tend to reduce the threat to the other person. Also, use "I" rather than "We" when talking to the victim. This reinforces your attempt to help, makes the current interaction appear more personal.
22. Use descriptive statements that contain feelings.
23. Be clear and specific about your feelings.
24. Be sure to do an assessment of needs—all needs that may present themselves.
25. Consider the needs of all involved.
26. Address issues over which the victim has actual control.
27. Avoid being judgmental or critical. Avoid preaching.
28. Be sure that your responses to the subject are timely.
29. Deliver responses at the time that they are most important.

30. Deliver responses as soon as possible after the behavior that requires a response.
31. Do not use old or saved concerns as a weapon.
32. Assess whether the other person is ready to handle your responses at this time.
33. Discuss emotional issues with as much privacy as possible.
34. Practice, practice, practice communications skills to develop the greatest effectiveness. Sounds easy, but it is hard. Requires work to develop.
35. During conversations with victims, keep in mind the following:
    a. Listening is basic to successful communications.
    b. Listening requires responsiveness.
    c. Listening encourages expression.
    d. Listening enables the listener to know more about the speaker.
    e. Listening allows exploration of both feelings and content.
    f. Listening helps establish trust between subject and negotiator.
    g. Listening allows greater accuracy of communications.
    h. Listening requires practice and is not always easy to learn.
    i. Listening includes listening for content, feelings, and for points-of-view.
    j. Listening lets the intervener relax.
    k. Attitudes and feelings may be conveyed nonverbally.
36. When you listen, remember to do the following:
    a. Attend to verbal content.
    b. Attend to nonverbal cues.
    c. Hear and observe.
    d. Attend to the feelings expressed by the victim.
    e. Do not think about other things when you are listening to the subject. Hard to do? That is why it is a good idea to intervene with a partner. Let that person attend to everything else except the actual intervention.
    f. Do not listen with only "half an ear."
    g. Become attuned to the speaker's verbal and nonverbal messages.
    h. Note any extra emphasis the speaker places on certain words.
    i. Notice the victim's speech patterns and recurring themes.

BE AWARE OF NONVERBAL MESSAGES

1. Nonverbal messages may be conveyed in the following ways. Watch and listen carefully. How many of these can be discerned over the telephone?
   a. Sighing.
   b. Flipping through papers.
   c. Wincing.
   d. Looking around or up and down.
   e. Smoking.
   f. Chewing gum.
   g. Yawning.
   h. Tapping a finger or foot.
   i. Frowning.
   j. Displaying nervousness.
   k. Avoiding eye contact.
   l. Saying nothing.
   m. Making jerky gestures.
   n. Dressing sloppily.
   o. Blinking rapidly.
   p. Constantly looking at a clock or watch.
   q. Acting bored.
   r. Showing favoritism.
   s. Being drunk.
2. Nonverbal cues that may indicate openness include:
   a. Uncrossed legs.
   b. Open hands.
   c. Unbuttoned coat.
   d. Hands spread apart.
   e. Leaning forward.
   f. Being willing to speak of more personal things.
   g. Appearing to be accepting of the negotiator.
3. Nonverbal cues that may indicate defensiveness:
   a. Fists closed.
   b. Arms crossed in front of individual.
   c. Legs crossed.
   d. One leg over the chair arm.
   e. Being very matter-of-fact in conversations with the negotiator.

    f. Rejecting the negotiator.

    g. Abruptly hanging up the telephone.

4. Nonverbal cues that may indicate cooperation:
   a. Opening his or her coat.
   b. Tilted head.
   c. Sitting on the edge of the chair.
   d. Eye contact.
   e. Hand-to-face gestures.
   f. Leaning forward.
   g. Being willing to bargain.
   h. Keeping an agreement once reached.
   i. Making relevant suggestions.
   j. Making realistic suggestions.

5. Nonverbal cues that may indicate evaluating:
   a. Head tilted.
   b. Chin stroking.
   c. Looking over glasses.
   d. Pacing.
   e. Pinching the bridge of the nose.
   f. Asking for clarification.
   g. Repeating conditions or instructions.
   h. Asking if the crisis intervener can protect him or her.

6. Nonverbal cues that may indicate readiness:
   a. Hands on hips.
   b. Leaning forward.
   c. Confident speech patterns.
   d. Moving closer to another person involved.

7. Practice these skills.

8. Now, go back and practice some more. My experience tells me that the first things to fail in almost any stressful situation, including disaster scenarios, are the communications skills. All of us believe that we are communicators. Some are and some are not. Whether one is a good communicator or not depends on the skills that they learn and are then willing to use again and again.

Chapter 13

PLAN AND PREPARE INTERVENER EQUIPMENT

Having the right equipment, at the right time, at the right place and in the right hands is crucial to the success of any intervention during a disaster. This includes psychosocial interventions. Disaster interveners must be tactically as well as technically proficient with their equipment and their skills, as well as their own personal survival skills. Making this occur in an effective way requires planning and careful preparation before a disaster strikes and one is called to assist. Waiting until the last minute, or failing to take seriously this preparation can and will compromise the intervener's effectiveness and ultimate helpfulness.

The following is provided as suggestions for personal equipment that may be needed by the intervener:

ASSEMBLE THE 24-HOUR PACK

The 24-hour pack is for immediate response and to sustain you for the initial 24 hours of deployment.

1. Hat.
2. Rain gear.
3. Sturdy clothing selected for the disaster environment and weather.
4. A uniform if mandated by your agency.
5. Sturdy boots or shoes.

6. Extra clothing.
7. Extra underwear.
8. Driver's license.
9. Money.
10. Credit cards.
11. Passport, if necessary.
12. Emergency phone numbers.
13. Snacks and/or energy bars.
14. Eye protection.
15. Ear protection.
16. Leather work gloves.
17. Flashlight and batteries.
18. Knife.
19. Hand sanitizer.
20. Sanitary napkins.
21. Personal first aid supplies:
    a. Band-Aids.
    b. 2x2" gauze pads.
    c. 3x3" gauze pads.
    d. Betadine pads.
    e. Moleskin.
    f. Small roll of gauze.
    g. Triangular bandage.
    h. Antibiotic ointment.
22. Professional supplies based on your profession or job on-site.
23. Pens.
24. Notebook.
25. Disposable gloves.
26. Creature comforts as space and weight permit.

ASSEMBLE THE 72-HOUR PACK

The 72-hour pack is for extended deployment and to sustain you past the initial 24-hour period.

1. Extra clothing or uniforms.
2. Shorts.
3. T-shirts.
4. Tennis shoes.

5. Extra boots.
6. Shower shoes.
7. Bandanna.
8. Underwear.
9. Socks.
10. Swimwear.
11. Casual attire as appropriate.
12. Long johns.
13. Wool sweater or sweatshirt.
14. Warm coat or jacket.
15. Wool socks.
16. Cold weather boots.
17. Wool cold weather cap.
18. Mess kit of some sort to include plate, cup and bowl.
19. Knife, spoon and fork set.
20. Meals Ready to Eat (MRE's) if available.
21. Several bottles of water.
22. Water purification tablets or other purification items.
23. Razor blades.
24. Shaving cream.
25. Toothpaste.
26. Toothbrush.
27. Toilet paper.
28. Bar soap.
29. Shampoo.
30. Hand lotion.
31. Deodorant.
32. Comb and/or brush.
33. Medications in at least a 2-week supply or more depending on specific deployment.
34. Foot care items to include powders and moleskin.
35. A head lamp for use as a second light source.
36. Extra batteries and bulbs for whatever appliances brought with you.
37. Matches or disposable lighter. Matches should be in a water-proof container.
38. Dust mask.
39. Safety mask.
40. Goggles or safety glasses. If you wear glasses, be sure ahead of

time that your goggles will accommodate the glasses.
41. Tape.
42. Safety pins.
43. Sewing kit.
44. Towels.
45. Wash cloth.
46. Fifty feet of 550 parachute cord.
47. Large trash bags.
48. Nail clippers.
49. Bandage shears.
50. Chargers for cell phones and computers.
51. Immunization record.
52. Medical record as needed.
53. Laundry bag.
54. Sunglasses.
55. Ziploc baggies.
56. Felt tip markers.
57. Trail mix.
58. Sunscreen.

ASSEMBLE AND MAINTAIN INTERVENER GEAR

This is the professional equipment and materials that you will need to do your job as a crisis intervener. What you include will vary depending on your anticipated job, the type of disaster, and overall circumstances. Plan on an austere environment with little or nothing to be provided to you. It is important that when you arrive at your assignment, that you can proceed without undue delay. With this in mind consider the following to be included in your disaster intervener deployment bag:

1. Pencils.
2. Pens.
3. Markers.
4. Tape.
5. Stapler and extra staples.
6. Paper.
7. Instructional handouts and reading materials for victims.
8. Professional guidelines and manuals.

9. Copy of your professional liability insurance, if applicable.
10. A copy of this book.
11. Copies of professional certificates and qualification cards.
12. Facial tissue.
13. Snack items to sustain you on the job.
14. Crisis intervention guidelines.
15. Guidelines specific to the agency for which you are responding.
16. Folding stool or chair.
17. Cellular phone.
18. Personal hygiene items that may be needed on the job and away from your 24-hour or 72-hour packs.
19. Masking tape.
20. Thumbtacks and pushpins.
21. Hand puppets.
22. Toys and dolls.

KEEP PERSONAL EQUIPMENT READY TO GO

Remember: Keep deployment equipment and gear within arm's reach. Be ready to go.

DEVELOP "PACKS" AND "PACKETS"

1. Go-Packs consist of basic medical supplies that you may need immediately upon arrival after deployment.
   a. Prepare packs to take with you.
   b. Do not assume that basic supplies and instruments will be available from other sources after deployment. Most times, they will not.
   c. Include those things that you will need to accomplish a basic and primary response to those who require care.
   d. Package items so that they can withstand a harsh environment.
   e. Package in such a way as to protect instruments from water, excessive cold or heat and the like.
   f. As possible, carry the go-pack in your pocket(s) or day bag.
2. Go-Packets are made up of the paperwork that you will need

on-scene to document and respond to your job.
   a. Make multiple copies.
   b. Do not plan on having copy machines available or working.
   c. As strange as it may sound today, take some carbon paper along with you.
   d. Package so as to avoid temperature extremes or water damage.
   e. Plastic zipper bags of various sizes work well here.
   f. Include writing and marking implements in your packets. They may not be available on-scene.
   g. Keep your Go-Packets with you.

Chapter 14

REMEMBER THESE THINGS WHEN RESPONDING TO A DISASTER

Responders can be victims; victims can be responders. Either way, it is important to attend to your personal and family needs if you are to be able to devote your time and energy to helping others. The following is very basic information. It is provided here so that it will not be forgotten in the rush to deploy during a disaster. While this information could apply to anyone, disaster responders should take this very seriously. Don't wait. Go ahead and begin your planning and preparation now. Most will wait. You should not. Because you have much more about which to be concerned, get the basics relating to your and your family's personal well-being arranged and keep it that way. The importance of peace of mind is hard to measure. What we do know is that it will make you more helpful and effective in the field.

KNOW WHAT HURRICANE ALERTS MEAN

1. A hurricane watch means that hurricane conditions are possible in a specified area usually within 36 hours.
2. A hurricane warning means that hurricane conditions are expected in the specified area within 24 hours.

Note: Some of the material in this chapter is adapted and modified from information provided by the Federal Emergency Management Agency, the American Red Cross, the Mormon Church and Clorox Bleach.

PREPARE A PERSONAL EVACUATION PLAN

1. Ahead of time, make a decision about where you would go if you had to evacuate. Consider several places in case one of your choices becomes unavailable.
2. Keep the telephone numbers of your evacuation choices.
3. Maintain a road map of your locality.
4. Listen to the radio, weather channels and broadcasts of the NOAA.
5. If and when advised to evacuate by competent authority, or if you feel threatened, leave immediately.

WHEN EVACUATING BE SURE TO TAKE THE FOLLOWING WITH YOU

1. Medications and medical supplies (medications must be kept in original prescription bottle or container)
2. Bedding or sleeping bags and pillows
3. Extra clothing
4. Bottled water
5. Extra batteries
6. Flashlight
7. Battery-operated radio
8. First Aid kit
9. Car keys
10. Maps related to your locality or to the locality to which you are traveling
11. Driver's license
12. Social Security card
13. Tax records
14. Proof of residence
15. Insurance policies
16. Deeds
17. Other documents that you determine you may need

ASSEMBLE A DISASTER SUPPLIES KIT

Include the following:

1. Essential and required prescription medications; extra if available
2. Canned food and appropriate can opener
3. Water; it is recommended by some that you have available approximately three gallons of water per person when evacuating
4. Protective clothing
5. Rain wear
6. Sleeping bags
7. Special items that are needed for the elderly, infants, toddlers and those who are disabled members of the family
8. Instructions how to turn off your electricity
9. Instructions how to turn off your gas
10. Instructions how to turn off your water

PREPARE FOR HIGH WINDS

1. Install hurricane shutters on your window.
2. If you do not have shutters, use one-half-inch plywood on your window.
3. Pre-drill the plywood so that you can put them up quickly.
4. Install anchors for the plywood.
5. Remove damaged limbs from trees to make them more resistant to wind.

KNOW WHAT TO DO WHEN A HURRICANE WATCH IS ISSUED

1. Get up-to-date weather information from weather channels on television and radio.
2. Listen to NOAA Weather Radio.
3. Prepare to bring lawn furniture and outdoor decorations inside.
4. Bring in trash cans.
5. Get ready to bring in hanging plants.

6. Prepare to cover all windows.
7. Taping windows may not prevent breaking.
8. Fill the gas tank on the car that you will be using to evacuate.
9. Recheck tie-downs for manufactured homes.
10. Check batteries to be sure that they are functional.
11. Stock up on canned food.
12. Be sure you have necessary first aid supplies.
13. Check medications.
14. Check water supply.

KNOW WHAT TO DO WHEN A HURRICANE WARNING IS ISSUED

1. Listen to the advice of officials.
2. When local officials tell you to leave, evacuate.
3. Complete all preparation activities.
4. If not evacuating, stay inside and away from windows.
5. Understand that the "calm eye" of the storm does not mean that the storm is over.
6. Wind occurring after the "calm eye" can be very destructive. Prepare for this.
7. Be alert for tornadoes.
8. For a tornado, stay toward the center of your house in a room or closet with no windows. A bathroom may be protective.
9. Stay away from flood waters.
10. When encountering flooded roads, turn around. Go a different way.
11. If your car or current area is flooding, leave your car and climb to higher ground for safety.

KNOW WHAT TO DO WHEN THE HURRICANE IS OVER

1. Keep abreast of continuing weather activity by staying tuned to radio and television.
2. If you evacuate, return home only when local officials determine it is safe to do so.
3. Inspect your home for damage.

4. Use flashlights instead of candles if possible.
5. Be aware of downed power lines. Avoid them.
6. Inspect all food before consuming. If in doubt, don't.
7. Observe chainsaw safety if using this tool.
8. Observe generator safety. Read the manual.
9. Understand how to treat polluted water in multiple ways. There is a lot of information about this on the Internet.
10. Do not drink contaminated water.

LEARN TO SHELTER IN PLACE

1. Evacuation may not always be possible or advisable. If that is the case, knowing how to shelter-in-place wherever you are is important.
2. Understand that if you shelter-in-place, you may be on your own for a period of time. Preparation is a must.
3. Learn about the types of disaster likely to occur in your area.
4. Learn the warning signals and what they mean.
5. Find out and prepare for animal care during a disaster.
6. Plan for the elderly or disabled if that is your circumstance.
7. Find out about existing disaster plans at work-sites, schools, day-care centers and other places where members of your family may be at the time of a disaster.
8. Create a family disaster plan.
9. Discuss and teach the plan to your family members.
10. Share the responsibilities among and between family members. Do so according to age and ability.
11. Pick a place to meet after a disaster.
12. Pick an alternate meeting site also.
13. Be sure that each family member knows the family home address and telephone numbers.
14. Determine a nonfamily friend to act as a contact point for your family members post-disaster. This may be an out-of-state friend. All family members should know this contact telephone number and know to call this person if they are separated from the family.
15. Repeat your discussion about what to do during and after a disaster. Do this at regular intervals to insure learning and com-

pliance.

16. Inventory your shelter-in-place location, probably your home, for possible hazards that could present themselves during a disaster. Common household items, appliances and fixtures could become dangerous and cause injury and damage if winds are strong or water is high. Look for these potential hazards and look for ways to mitigate them.
17. Post emergency telephone numbers and be sure that all know when and how to use them.
18. Teach children how to call 9-1-1 or other medical assistance.
19. Each family member should know how to turn off utilities.
20. Be sure that you have adequate insurance coverage.
21. Obtain and learn to use fire extinguishers.
22. Install and regularly check smoke detectors.
23. Assemble disaster supplies. Periodically reassess these supplies and replace outdated or damaged items.
24. Take a course in Cardiopulmonary Resuscitation and first aid. Practice these skills.
25. Determine escape routes from your home.
26. Determine escape routes from each room of your home.
27. Work with neighbors regarding plans to assist each other as needed.

PROTECT YOUR VALUABLES

1. Move things to a safe place that may be damaged by wind, water, collapse, etc.
2. Move electronic equipment to higher levels in your home.
3. Wrap items in blankets, burlap, sheets, etc., as needed.
4. Make a visual and written record of household possessions.
5. Record model and serial numbers of possessions.
6. If you have sufficient warning of an impending disaster, you may want to consider storing your valuables elsewhere.
7. You will need, and should take with you, the following if you leave your home. Put them in a suitable container prior to the advent of the disaster. Consider containers that are easy to carry. Multiple containers that are lighter may be better than one heavy container. Consider the capabilities of those who may

need to do the carrying:
a. Flashlight(s)
b. Extra batteries
c. Battery-powered radio and/or television
d. First aid kit
e. Personal medical items:
   • Prescription medications in original bottles
   • Copies of your prescriptions
   • Eyeglasses and prescription
   • Extra eyeglasses
   • Required medical appliances
f. Three-day supply of food and water:
   • Bottled water. Quantity recommendations vary. However, one gallon of water per person per day is a good formula. This may need to be increased depending on physical conditions, disabilities and age.
   • Foods that do not require refrigeration or cooking
g. Items required by infants, children and the elderly or disabled
h. Changes of clothing for each family member
i. Sleeping bag or the like for each member of your family
j. Blankets
k. Checkbook
l. Cash
m. Credit cards
n. Maps of the area
o. Vital Documents:
   • Driver's license or personal identification
   • Social Security card
   • Proof of residence in the form of a deed or lease
   • Insurance policies
   • Birth certificates
   • Marriage certificates
   • Negotiable certificates such as stocks and bonds
   • Wills and deeds
   • Copy of recent tax returns
p. Hygiene supplies for each family member
q. Shovel and other tools that may be needed and useful
r. Liquid bleach to treat drinking water (Learn how to do this.)

There are sites online that will tell you how.
s. Matches in a waterproof container
t. Manual can opener
u. Current photographs of each child, parents and spouses
v. Keys to where you may be going, if possible and extra car keys

ASSEMBLE THE ADULT KIT

Have these items ready to go on short notice.

1. Blanket
2. Ground cloth
3. Small tent
4. An alert whistle
5. One change of clothing
6. 2 changes of socks
7. 2 pair of work gloves
8. Cap
9. Rain gear
10. Clean-up wipes
11. Lightweight jacket
12. Personal hygiene items
13. Drinking cup
14. Plate, bowl and utensils
15. Medications
16. Small first aid kit
17. Snacks that will not turn bad over a period of time
18. Women should bring personal protection items
19. Food and water for three days
20. A carrier for this gear such as a backpack

ASSEMBLE THE TODDLER KIT

Have this kit ready to go on a moment's notice.

1. Blanket
2. Ground cloth

3. Diapers as needed
4. Several changes of clothing
5. Several changes of socks
6. Rain poncho
7. Jacket
8. Small plastic bags for soiled clothing
9. Drinking cup
10. Plate, bowl and eating utensils
11. Baby wipes
12. Wash cloths
13. Small towel
14. Toothbrush and toothpaste
15. Band Aids and a topical antibiotic
16. One or two toys to play with
17. Several books to read
18. Snacks appropriate to age of child
19. Food and water for three days
20. A carrier for this gear such as a backpack

ASSEMBLE THE BABY KIT

Have these items packed and ready to go on a moment's notice.

1. Blanket
2. Diapers
3. Several changes of clothing
4. Cans of ready-made formula
5. Bottles for formula
6. Cereal and small bowl
7. Fruit in jars
8. Spoon and bib
9. Washcloths and small towel
10. Small plastic bags for soiled diapers
11. Baby carrier
12. Rocking seat
13. Toys appropriate to age of baby
14. Extra plastic sandwich baggies
15. Baby shampoo

16. Baby oil
17. Baby powder
18. Diaper rash ointment and/or powder
19. A carrier for this gear such as a backpack

ASSEMBLE THE TEEN KIT

This kit should be ready on a moment's notice.

1. Blanket
2. Ground cloth
3. Two changes of clothing
4. Two changes of underwear
5. At least two changes of socks
6. Rain gear
7. Lightweight jacket
8. Sweatshirt
9. Work gloves
10. Cleanup wipes or washcloths
11. Small towel
12. Drinking cup
13. Plate and bowl
14. Eating utensils
15. Personal hygiene items
16. Journal or notebook
17. Pencils and pens
18. Books to read or games to play
19. Band Aids and a topical antibiotic
20. Snacks that will not spoil
21. Small tent for privacy
22. For female teens, bring personal protection as needed
23. Food and water for three days
24. A carrier for this gear such as a backpack

ASSEMBLE THE PET KIT

This kit should be immediately available to help care for household pets.

1. Pet collar
2. Leash
3. Identification tag
4. Shot records
5. Papers related to your pet
6. Photograph of pet
7. Kennel/pad
8. Water
9. Bowl
10. Pet food
11. Wipes to clean animal
12. Shampoo/conditioner
13. Stress reducers. Check with your veterinarian
14. Pain relief that can be given to animals. Do not give aspirin to cats
15. Sulfodene 3-way ointment
16. Treats
17. Toys
18. Brush
19. Comb

BE ABLE TO PURIFY WATER

Boiling Is Best

Short of using a very high-quality water filter, this is the most reliable method for killing microbes and parasites. Bring water to a rolling boil and keep it simmering for at least several minutes. Add one minute of boiling to the initial 10 minutes for every 1,000 feet above sea level. Cover the pot to shorten boiling time and conserve fuel.

Liquid Clorox Bleach

In an emergency, think of one gallon of Regular Clorox Bleach as 3,800 gallons of drinking water. Store these directions with your emergency bottle of Clorox Bleach.

First, let water stand until particles settle. Pour the clear water into an uncontaminated container and add Regular Clorox Bleach.

2 drops of Regular Clorox Bleach per quart of water
8 drops of Regular Clorox Bleach per gallon of water
1/2 teaspoon Regular Clorox Bleach per five gallons of water

Mix well. Wait 30 min. Water should have a slight bleach odor. If not, repeat dose. Wait 15 min. Sniff again. Keep an eyedropper taped to your emergency bottle of Clorox Bleach, since purifying small amounts of water requires only a few drops. If water is cloudy, double the recommended dosages of Clorox Bleach.

Don't pour purified water into contaminated containers. In lieu of steaming hot water, sanitize water jugs and dishes with a little Clorox Bleach. Mix 1 tablespoon Regular Clorox Bleach with one gallon of water. Always wash and rinse items first, then let each item soak in Clorox Bleach Sanitizing Solution for 2 minutes. Drain and air dry (Only use Regular Clorox Bleach (not Fresh Scent or Lemon Fresh). To insure that Clorox Bleach is at its full strength, replace your storage bottle every three months).

REVIEW NUTRITION TIPS

1. Water is essential; often food is not.
2. Healthy people can survive for an extended period of time on half their usual food intake if their activity is greatly reduced.
3. A person can exist without any food for many days.
4. Food can be rationed except for children and those who are pregnant.
5. If water is in short supply, avoid eating those things that increase thirst.
6. Canned foods are usually a good choice during disasters as they may not require cooking or refrigeration. Check the information on the cans.
7. Stock enough food for at least two weeks on your own. A good way to do this is to gradually increase the basic foods already on your shelves.
8. Periodically inspect all stored food for spoilage. Replace immediately as needed.

9. Use tight-seal containers for open food as needed.
10. Keep food covered at all times.
11. Use foods before they go bad. Replace with fresh supplies.
12. Mark food containers with date acquired. Change food when expired.
13. Eat at least one well-balanced meal per day when under disaster circumstances.
14. During a disaster, drink enough water to enable your body to function properly.
15. Two quarts of water per day per person is recommended.
16. More water may be needed to sustain those who are ill, elderly or with other medical or physical conditions.
17. Take in enough calories to allow you to perform whatever work is necessary.
18. Stockpile adequate vitamin supplements and take recommended dosage during a disaster to assure sufficient nutrition.
19. Become aware of the shelf-life of all foods in your stockpile. Rotate and replace as indicated.

Chapter 15

ATTEND TO PUBLIC HEALTH CONCERNS

It took this author some reflection to realize that much of disaster intervention is concerned with public health matters. This may be true for responders throughout their tour. But, certainly, once the basic emergency care is given and the immediate life-threatening issues are managed, the concerns must be far-reaching with regard to public health. It is not enough to give first aid, or in this case emotional first aid. The attention to those ongoing events that may create additional emergencies, degrade the help already provided, or prevent future care, must not be overlooked or taken for granted.

The story of the "pump handle" may be illustrative.

The London, England of the mid nineteenth Century was inundated by an epidemic of cholera. Little was understood about the origin of the disease or what was needed to stop it. At this same time, Doctor John Snow attempted to solve this pressing problem. He charted the outbreaks of the disease and determined that clusters of those contracting the disease occurred around community water wells. Even without community authority, and at least 30 years before there was adequate understanding of the disease of cholera and how disease was spread, Doctor Snow removed the pump handles from these community water pumps. Virtually within days, the spread of the disease diminished.

1. Pay attention to the existence of "pump handles," or those elements related to the causation of current or future medical or psychological problems.
2. Find the pump handles early and eliminate them. Keep looking for them.

3. Recognize that managing psychosocial trauma is about managing public health issues as well.
4. Determine what procedural, environmental and personal practices compromise the overall health of victims.
5. Regardless of professional discipline, embrace public health issues as part of your overall intervention responsibilities.
6. Look at the connections between emotional health, physical health and societal health.
7. Consider the following basic areas:
   a. Hand washing
   b. Hand sanitizing
   c. Trash removal
   d. Bedding removal
   e. Isolation procedures
   f. Public health education
   g. Preventative medical and psychological issues
   h. Immunizations of victims
   i. Immunizations of interveners
   j. Personal protective equipment, fitted and current
8. Maintain personal protective equipment appropriate to the encountered situation.
9. Prepare for personal safety.
10. Attend to personal health issues even while responding to others.
11. Develop a working knowledge of public health law.
12. Think public health before, during and after your deployment.
13. Work closely with your public health officers and staff.
14. Keep public health authorities advised of potential health concerns, threats and hazards.
15. Pay attention to risk assessments.
16. Perform your own risk assessment as needed.
17. Remember that your crisis intervention does not end until the pump handles are found and removed. Always look for and be aware of the pump handles. It will make better your life and the lives of those you are attempting to help.
18. Public Health issues encompass all disaster responses. See Figure 15.1.
19. Ask questions about public health and to public health workers.
20. Remember that most disasters are public health emergencies.

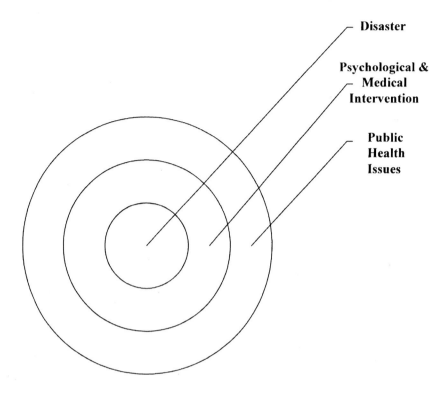

Figure 15.1. Public Health Issues Encompass All Disaster Responses.

Chapter 16

UNDERSTAND THE ROLE AND FUNCTION OF THE DISASTER MENTAL HEALTH PROFESSIONAL

W hile it may be true that some people, even disaster responders, may have difficulty seeking out the services of a mental health professional, these services can be vital to the intervener. This awareness can be achieved by understanding the role and purpose of the disaster psychologist or counselor, the pre-disaster training done by this professional, by understanding the rules of engagement, and the importance attached to such services by the responder. Lip-service to this aspect of disaster response is not enough. It must be embraced by all who are involved in disaster work. This will happen only if psychological services are perceived as safe and beneficial. The responsibility for this acceptance is shared by the mental health professional and by the disaster responder. In order to be helpful, we must remain effective. As Doctor Rosenbluh implied, if we do not take the care of ourselves seriously, we could compromise our effectiveness.

The role of the disaster mental health professional may well be tied to four major areas. These include teaching, responding and assisting, providing crisis intervention direct services, referral as needed and follow-up during and post disaster. These will be detailed below followed by an example of mental health professional qualifications as viewed by the National Disaster Medical System. This is to provide a possible model that may be useful in mental health team development as well

Note: Some of the material in this chapter has been adapted from the *National Disaster Medical System Handbook*, Washington, D.C.

as an indicator of what current federal Disaster Medical Assistance Teams have established as standards.

TEACH BEFORE THE DISASTER

1. Educate your team and/or other responders about what to expect psychologically from a deployment.
2. Develop and explain the procedures to be followed for trauma stress countermeasures.
3. Help team members to understand the purpose of your role in disaster response both from the standpoint of direct services delivery and psychological force protection. While physical force protection is a little better understood as a way of safeguarding persons and property, psychological force protection, sometimes called force protective medicine, is not as well understood. Protection at this level often means attempting to ameliorate problems in their beginning stages and before they interfere with, or degrade, a responder's ability to perform. It also means getting help to those responders who need it when they need it.
4. Explain the rules and exceptions of confidentiality.
5. Develop and explain the way in which psychological services can be obtained post-disaster deployment.
6. Discuss the issues of Standard of Care versus Sufficiency of Care in disaster scenarios.
7. Discuss the dangers and threats to be encountered and how to mitigate them if possible. Sometimes, knowledge is the key.
8. Educate about the legal aspects of disaster response both from the responder and victim perspective.

RESPOND AND ASSIST DURING THE DISASTER

1. Make all preparations needed for being ready and able to respond if called to work a disaster scenario.
2. Respond only if alerted and deployed.
3. Be willing to assist in areas of disaster relief other than your particular field.
4. Assisting in other areas will bring you into contact with victims and responders that may need your assistance.

5. Be available.
6. Take good care of yourself. Your effectiveness with victims or responders may depend on it. Do not overextend.
7. Be where you need to be.
8. Do not wait for victims in need or responders in need to come to you. If they do not, go to them.
9. Perform threat assessments as needed. Inform appropriate leadership of psychological threats and psychological status.
10. Remember that your responsibilities may include updating team leaders, providing professional assistance and crisis intervention to responders as needed, and providing direct services to disaster victims.

PROVIDE CRISIS INTERVENTION

1. Remember that persons in crisis, victims or responders, want to talk to someone; but they will not talk to just anyone.
2. Do not "play" at Crisis Intervention. If you do not know what you are doing, get someone in there who does. Do not make the mistake of believing that a good therapist is also always a good crisis intervener. Could be, but not necessarily.
3. Provide crisis intervention if trained to do so.
4. Be ready and willing to act as the back-up source for trained interveners who are assisting others. Mental health professionals often do very well in these circumstances. Those not formally trained as mental health providers, but who are trained in disaster intervention, often do better than their professional counterparts in crisis situations. Therapists often want to do therapy. Crisis interveners do not have that burden.
5. Remember that disaster scenarios are often not the best place for therapy. That may need to come later. Experience tells me that if we do a good job providing crisis intervention, the need for therapy later may be greatly reduced.

REFER FOR TREATMENT AS NEEDED

1. While effective crisis intervention in the field may obviate the need for referral, be ready with authoritative referral sources as needed.

2. Be sure that it is possible for the person referred to actually utilize the referral source. Follow-up may be needed as indicated below.
3. Find substantial referral sources early on in your deployment. Usual sources may not be available during a disaster.
4. Assist the person in getting to the referral source. Do a physical hand-off if at all possible.
5. Responders may have access to post-deployment assistance by virtue of their particular team membership. Find out pre-deployment or at least very early-on in the deployment.
6. Update referral sources often.
7. Be sure that you are familiar with the services offered by your sources.
8. Check that your sources understand the particular needs of victims referred to them.
9. A good referral source during normal times may not be an adequate source for victims of disaster. Check this out.
10. Assist other crisis interveners with referral choices and procedures.
11. Do not underestimate the importance of in-place and validated referral sources. An otherwise effective intervention can fail because the referral was not handled properly.

FOLLOW-UP AS POSSIBLE

1. Follow-up to check if victims and/or responders actually obtained help from the referral source.
2. Follow-up may not always be possible and is harder to do sometimes than it might at first seem.
3. Check to see the current status of those referred.
4. Make additional referrals as needed if the initial referral failed for any reason.
5. If the failed referral is for reasons of access, try to remedy this if you can.

BE FAMILIAR WITH NATIONAL DISASTER MEDICAL SYSTEM (NDMS) QUALIFICATIONS FOR MENTAL HEALTH PROFESSIONALS

Below are examples of qualifications for mental health professionals at various governmental service levels.

Mental Health Specialist, GS-101-11

This position is organizationally located in the Office of Emergency Preparedness, Office of Public Health and Science, Office of the Secretary. The Department of Health and Human Services is the primary agency for the Emergency Support Function (ESF) #8, "Health and Medical Services," under the Federal Response Plan (FRP). The Office of Emergency Preparedness is the headquarters for the National Disaster Medical System (NDMS) and, in that capacity, supports the planning, organization and development of medical response teams of NDMS. The disaster medical response teams, i.e., primary care, specialty, and others, are a basic element in the personnel component and can be expanded to a clearing-staging unit while other teams are preparing for activation. Health care providers and medical support personnel are recruited from local communities to serve national needs in the event of disasters or other major emergencies requiring extraordinary medical services.

The incumbent of this position serves as a Mental Health Specialist of the disaster medical response team/ specialty/ or other and is responsible for planning and implementing mental health services for disaster victims and their families. He or she also:

- Works under the direction of the Mental Health Officer and assists in the planning and implementation of mental health services for disaster victims and their families.
- Collaborates with local mental health programs and services in implementing and coordinating mental health services for disaster victims including children and their families. Identifies technical assistance and support mechanisms within the state, city or town to respond to the immediate crisis.
- Identifies appropriate interventions and prevention services techniques and counseling for early identification of victims at

risk of mental health and related problems. Consults with team members, local mental health workers and family members to identify needed clinical testing and evaluation procedures. Provides for and arranges professional assistance and consultation regarding treatment planning and other intervention efforts.

- Evaluates mental health services available in local areas and installs networks for crisis intervention and assistance. Develops professional resource networks for provision of integrated multi-disciplinary services to disaster victims. Initiates special efforts to develop resources to serve the special needs of infants and children during disaster situations.
- Must possess a license or registration as a professional mental health worker in a state, the District of Columbia, the Commonwealth of Puerto Rico, or a territory of the United States.
- Possesses a certification in emergency social work or mental Health Association or equivalent, which is desirable.
- Performs other duties as assigned.

Psychologist, GS-180-13

This position is organizationally located in the Office of Emergency Preparedness, Office of Public Health and Science, Office of the Secretary. The Department of Health and Human Services is the primary agency for the Emergency Support Function (ESF) #8, "Health and Medical Services," under the Federal Response Plan (FRP). The Office of Emergency Preparedness is the headquarters for the National Disaster Medical System (NDMS) and, in that capacity, supports the planning, organization and development of medical response teams of NDMS. The disaster medical response teams, i.e., primary care, specialty, and others, are a basic element in the personnel component and can be expanded to a clearing-staging unit while other teams are preparing for activation. Health care providers and medical support personnel are recruited from local communities to serve national needs in the event of disasters or other major emergencies requiring extraordinary medical services.

The incumbent of this position serves as a Mental Health Officer of the disaster response team/ specialty/ or other and is responsible for planning and implementing mental health services for disaster victims and their families, as well as disaster response personnel working on-site of the disaster or major emergency. This person:

- In collaboration with local mental health programs and services, implements and coordinates mental health services for disaster victims including children and their families. Identifies technical assistance and support mechanisms within the state, city or town to respond to the immediate crisis.
- Identifies appropriate interventions and prevention techniques and counseling for early identification of victims and responders at risk of mental health and related problems. Consults with team members, local mental health workers and family members to identify needed clinical testing and evaluation procedures for disaster victims. Provides for and arranges professional assistance and consultation regarding treatment planning and other intervention efforts.
- Evaluates mental health services available in local areas and installs networks for crisis intervention and assistance. Develops professional resource networks for provision of integrated multidisciplinary services to disaster victims. Initiates special efforts to develop resources to serve the special needs of infants and children during disaster service.
- Monitors incident stress levels of team members and implements stress reduction measures as necessary.
- Keeps abreast of programs and services in the field of mental health especially in the areas of stress management and crisis intervention.
- Must possess a license or registration as a professional psychologist in a state, the District of Columbia, the Commonwealth of Puerto Rico, or a territory of the United States. Has experience in dealing with incident stress situations is essential.
- Performs other duties as assigned.

The incumbent works under the broad direction of the Team Leader in charge of the Clearing-Staging Unit (CSU) and assists in the planning and implementation of activities related to mental health services for disaster victims and their families. Work is reviewed in terms of meeting the overall objectives of the disaster mission.

Supervisory Mental Health Specialist, GS-101-14

This position is organizationally located in the Office of Emergency Preparedness, Office of Public Health and Science, Office of the Secretary. The Department of Health and Human Services is the primary agency for the Emergency Support Function (ESF) #8, "Health and Medical Services," under the Federal Response Plan (FRP). The Office of Emergency Preparedness is the headquarters for the National Disaster Medical System (NDMS) and, in that capacity, supports the planning, organization and development of medical response teams of NDMS. The disaster medical response teams, i.e., primary care, specialty, and others, are a basic element in the personnel component and can be expanded to a clearing-staging unit while other teams are preparing for activation. Health care providers and medical support personnel are recruited from local communities to serve national needs in the event of disasters or other major emergencies requiring extraordinary medical services.

The incumbent of this position serves as the Family Assistance Division Supervisor and is responsible for coordinating, providing, and exchanging information between the activities of the morgue and the families of deceased disaster victims, including next of kin notifications, autopsies, and disposition of victims remains. In addition:

- Coordinates the location of, and sets up the Family Assistance Center (FAC) with the approval of local and NDMS mortuary authorities.
- Establishes and supervises the FAC activities, including operating procedures, counseling, and the kind and level of mental health workers required to staff the FAC.
- Ensures discretion and confidentiality among staff of all verbal and written documentation concerning the deceased, next of kin, and family members.
- Directs the work of staff members in collaborating with the Medical Examiner/Coroner during notification of positive identification to the next of kin. Ensures the exercise of professional judgment in obtaining ante mortem information from the next of kin of deceased to the Medical Examiner/Coroner.
- Supervises the work of professional mental health workers (e.g., social workers, psychologists, mental health counselors) engaged

in the work of the FAC. The grades of the mental health staff range from GS-11 to GS-13. Selects employees for vacant FAC positions; trains employees; hears and resolves complaints; recommends annual performance evaluations; etc.

- Represents the Operations Section Chief in dealing with local and state officials, the public, and visitors from other Federal organizations.
- Prepares reports and required documents in accordance with supervisor instructions.
- Extensive knowledge of NIIMS/ICS is required.
- Counseling skills and the ability to manage subordinates in stressful work environments is required.
- Extensive knowledge of FAC methods to deal with families of disaster victims is required.
- Performs other duties as assigned.

The incumbent works under the broad direction of the Operations Section Chief and plans, develops and implements activities relative to family assistance services for disaster victims and their families. Work is reviewed in terms of meeting the overall objectives of the disaster response mission.

Chapter 17

UNDERSTAND STANDARD OF CARE UNDER NORMAL CIRCUMSTANCES VERSUS SUFFICIENCY OF CARE DURING DISASTER SITUATIONS

This is a topic that is the subject of much controversy and debate in professional circles. The reasons may be obvious to most. Traditionally, health care responders are trained and held to the standard of care of their profession when rendering aid. Nothing less is acceptable. Even the public understands this and demands this high level of care; even under disaster conditions. Medical professionals run scared of litigation and liability exposure.

Disasters pose a countertestimony to the training that most receive. With overwhelming numbers of victims, and supplies that may never be adequate under such circumstances, the care mandated must be first aimed at those who can benefit the most from it. Additionally, it must reach the greatest numbers possible of such victims. All necessary care may not be possible to render to all victims of a disaster. And, it cannot be rendered to those who will not survive even with such care. These are less-than-ideal circumstances and we must be prepared to provide less-than-ideal care when that is necessitated and mandated by conditions. In so doing, survival potential may be enhanced for those with the greatest opportunity to survive. This is not advocacy for not giving the best care possible to all affected. It is meant to suggest that we must respond realistically to the circum-

Note: Some of the material in this chapter has been adapted from D. Isch, Director of Ethics, Personal Communication, May 8, 2006.

stances under which we may find ourselves working.

1. Usual standard of care may not be possible to achieve within a disaster scenario.
2. Understand the application of sufficient care.
3. Expect the standard to shift from Standard of Care to Sufficiency of Care. Sufficient care is the best care that we can give under the current circumstances with the resources at hand. It may be less than optimal.
4. Adjust your mindset to this eventuality.
5. Recognize that people will die.
6. Now, recognize it again; this time at the level of your gut or feelings.
7. Sufficiency of care may need to be the standard of care in a disaster.
8. Expect Sufficiency of Care to be the standard under most disaster situations. If the circumstances are better, great. Just do not expect them to be.
9. Plan for this mentally as well.
10. Plan for the eventuality emotionally as well as intellectually.
11. Discuss the concept with other responders pre-incident.
12. Remind each other during the incident.
13. Provide Standard of Care, when possible.
14. Understand that the Standard of Care may not be possible.
15. Work this out for yourself before being deployed.
16. Allow for your feelings about this and for your resistance to it. None of us are currently trained this way.
17. Discourage self-blame of others.
18. Resist blaming yourself.
19. Seek professional help early to resolve difficult issues, as you need such help.
20. Remember, that in disasters, needs will outweigh resources.
21. Remind yourself that all of your available resources must provide the greatest good for the greatest numbers of people.
22. Recognize that you cannot eliminate all suffering, and that some people will suffer despite your best efforts.
23. Also, remind yourself that critical need resources must be allocated to those having the best chance of benefiting from them.
24. In our best professional judgment, we will often have to make

these decisions.

25. Learn how to manage and comfort those who will die.
26. Remember that helping those who are already dying to do so with dignity is an important aspect of our care for them.
27. Help the greatest number by providing what you have to offer.
28. Resist the guilt that results from not accepting this.
29. Prepare yourself to surrender the standard when necessary and to provide care that is at least sufficient under the existing circumstances.
30. Allow this to be "okay" under these circumstances.
31. Recognize that it is okay because you are prevented from giving a higher level of care because of the totality of the circumstances, not due to your own lack of knowledge and skill.
32. Avail yourself of the current information on protective laws that shield health professionals from civil and criminal litigation and liability exposure. (See Chapter 18 in this book for assistance.)
33. Remember that the goal for each of us is not to "get over" what we feel. That is an impossible task. The realistic goal is to find ways to "get past" what has happened and what we feel, and find ways to get on with life. We try to teach this to victims. We need to learn it to help ourselves.
34. Learn to accept limits. Many will find this very hard. Consider the limits of your circumstances and your personal limitations. The ability to do this may vary from culture to culture. Consider your culture and what it says to you about handling limitations.
35. Expect the moral traces of remorse as you think about your experience. Sometimes it presents as a "twinge" when you remember what happened and what you did or were not able to do.

Chapter 18

KNOW THE LEGAL ASPECTS OF DISASTER CRISIS INTERVENTION

Probably the last things disaster crisis interveners want to concern themselves with are the legal ramifications of what they are about to do. However, the importance of this area of responder preparation and training should never be underestimated. In today's world, it has been noted that, "No good deed goes unpunished." A little pessimistic? Perhaps. On the other hand taking time to protect yourself, your livelihood, and your professional reputation is worth the time spent. If you are aware of the legal underpinnings of your profession and the related ethical guidelines, and you do the things you usually do, you will probably be okay. In the alternative, disaster situations create change in the way we see things and may have to do things. Other chapters in this book speak more of this. Knowledge of the law and legalities may help you when faced with difficult decisions. Here will be discussed some of the legalities and the structure of the law that surrounds interveners. Taken together, this material is not exhaustive. If you are going to work in this field, take some time to stay aware of new legislation and new laws that may become available. Become aware of what is changing, current and relevant.

1. The chaos of disasters increases the need to see victims as human beings.
2. Demonstrate honest respect for all victims and sufferers.
3. Avoid intervening outside the limits of your training. Do what you are licensed or certified to do.
4. Consider your preexisting duty to intervene, consider carefully

whether you want to perform an intervention.

5. Do not cease to intervene once you have started.

6. Discontinue your intervention only if you are relieved by someone with greater skill than your own.

7. Good Samaritan laws may or may not relate to the types of intervention in which you may be involved. Find out before you get started.

8. Contact a competent attorney and discuss concerns about your legal exposure relevant to your intervention.

9. Confidentiality of all information you obtain about a crisis victim is sacrosanct. Understand the exceptions to this rule and when to use them.

10. All you say and do with a victim should be documented if at all possible. This may assist you later if you or your procedures are challenged.

11. Update your training and credentials as required. Keep copies of your credentials with you at all times.

12. If in doubt about a victim's consent, obtain the victim's consent before you assist with the crisis.

13. Emergency circumstances may not allow for actual consent by the victim. If this is the case, you may be able to proceed under the concept of implied consent. During such circumstances, do only what is absolutely necessary to effectively intervene or rescue.

14. Disaster scenes are often crime scenes. Respect crimes scenes. If you cannot avoid doing so, note exact locations of whatever is moved so that later you can give such information to proper authorities.

15. Avoid searching the personal effects of a victim or sufferer. If you must search, have one or two witnesses present to observe your actions.

16. You may be required to report to the authorities certain information. Requirements vary from state to state. (For example, child abuse must be reported in most states.)

17. There are legal procedures in all jurisdictions for admissions for psychiatric care. Usually admissions are categorized as either voluntary or involuntary. Be aware of these requirements. In the field, you may need this information.

18. Even during a disaster, exercise care when operating a motor

vehicle. Usually there is no immunity from observing of motor vehicle laws or from legal responsibility for vehicular accidents or property damage.

19. All disaster victims have a right to privacy. Be respectful of this during your interventions.

20. Minor sufferers require the permission of one of their parents before you can intervene. If this is not possible, you may be able to proceed under the doctrine of implied consent, as you would with an adult.

21. With victims, openness and honesty is usually the best policy.

22. Consider the risks and safeguards to be applied before proceeding with your attempts to assist. Ask yourself, "Why am I doing this now?"

23. Know your Crisis Intervention skills, and the laws that may apply to what you will be doing.

24. Remember that liability exposure can be affected by both acts of commission and acts of omission.

25. A sufferer has the right to refuse your intervention. If they refuse you, back off unless you can proceed under some other acceptable theory. Ie. Implied consent.

26. Gain the victim's permission before entering a crisis victim's domain, dwelling, or office. Know when the laws of your locality permit you to enter without permission.

27. If you are the director or supervisor of a Crisis Intervention agency, be sure all interveners and hotline workers are properly trained, certified and practiced in disaster intervention.

28. Within Crisis Intervention agencies, develop specific, understandable policies and procedures that clearly regulate and illustrate how intervention is to be performed.

29. Disaster and nondisaster policies and procedures may not be the same. As an agency director or supervisor, adhere to agency policy in effect during a disaster and insist that interveners do likewise.

30. Incorporate agency policies and legal issues, disaster and-nondisaster into the training of crisis interveners.

UNDERSTAND LEGAL FRAMEWORK FOR DISASTER RESPONSE

1. The local jurisdiction's power to act comes from the 10th Amendment of the United States Constitution: "*The powers not delegated to the United States by the Constitution, nor prohibited by it to the States, are reserved to the States, respectively, or to the people.*"
2. In a disaster, legitimately, some civil rights may be subjugated to the public welfare.
3. The "Police Power" during times of disaster may extend to:
   a. Establishing curfews
   b. Ordering evacuations
   c. Closing buildings and businesses
   d. Suspending liquor sales
   e. Suspending firearms sales
   f. Closure of roads
   g. Going into or out of a disaster scene
   h. The use of public and/or private equipment and other items necessary for the disaster response
4. The mission of the Federal Emergency Management Agency, or another group following FEMA, is, "To reduce the loss of life and property and to protect our nation's critical infrastructure from all types of hazards through a comprehensive, risk-based, emergency management program of mitigation, preparedness, response and recovery."
5. The Stafford Act grants to the President of the United States the authority to direct any federal agency to:
   a. Utilize its authorities and resources.
   b. To do this with reimbursement or without reimbursement.
   c. 42 United States Code 5170a(1). Support State and local efforts during times of disaster.
   d. 42 United States Code 5170b(a)(1) and (2). Provide food, medicine, federal equipment, facilities, personnel and other provisions for use or distribution.
   e. 42 United States Code 5170b(a)(3)(B). Direct federal agencies to provide search and rescue assistance, emergency medical care and emergency shelter to disaster victims.
   f. 42 United State Code 5170b(c)(1). State Governors to request that the President of the United States direct the Se-

cretary of Defense to utilize the resources of the Department of Defense to assist in responding to a federal disaster.

6. Health care workers serving as disaster responders during times of local, state and national disasters may face special legal issues that should be recognized and addressed by the federal government and by the states.

7. Liability exposure by all health care workers should be examined and a personal determination made regarding willingness to accept this risk. At the end of the day, each professional remains responsible for their own actions. While this is generally accepted during nondisaster times, such exposure may change during unusual circumstances.

8. Sovereign Immunity may offer some protection. This is a doctrine precluding the institution of a suit against the sovereign [government] without its consent. Though commonly believed to be rooted in English law, it is actually rooted in the inherent nature of power and the ability of those who hold power to shield themselves.

9. Federal Preemption. This provides that if the federal government assumes control over a special situation such as a disaster, as a power granted to it by the United States Constitution, the states can do nothing to stand in the way of the federal government or do anything to frustrate its purpose.

10. Good Samaritan Laws and Doctrines. These vary from state to state and in their inclusion of health care responders. Each responder should know the Good Samaritan statutes in their jurisdiction. Although sometimes widely assumed that these particular doctrines will protect disaster responders, this may not be so and has not been widely tested. Check to be sure. If they work in your jurisdiction when responding to a disaster, the protection will be from civil liability. Criminal liability is not protected.

11. Each intervener should investigate the specific state laws applicable to your particular profession. One profession's rules or applicable laws may not apply to your work. Know before you go.

12. Each intervener should become knowledgeable of federal laws, regulations, House and Senate Bills, etc., designed to assist and to protect disaster responders. Some of these current at the time

of this writing are included in Appendix Three of this book.
13. Become aware of the National Emergency Management Assistance Compacts and other similar measures. This Compact addresses use of mutual assistance between states and the liability exposure and responsibility during such instances. These are often referred to as an EMAC and even exist internationally in some cases.

The following is provided in order to amplify the information presented above. Below is a representative sample of some of the laws that have emerged over several years that speak to various disaster-related issues including professional liability. This is not an exhaustive listing and new laws have been developed since this writing. Important to remember here is that disaster responders/interveners need to know the law and how it affects them when and after they deploy. The most often-asked question to this author relates to liability exposure for those practicing under state professional licensure. Much has been done in various states to address this. Much needs to be done. Several Federal Bills have been advanced and should be followed to assess their eventual relevance to your specific needs. If you have a chance, take a course in Public Health Law. They are offered in various locales. Some reference to Public Health Laws is made in the material presented below. No matter how diligent this author, all areas of the law, nor all of the laws on point can be presented here. Also, be aware of the work in this particular area being done by The Centers for Law and the Public's Health at both Georgetown University and Johns Hopkins University. The advancing project of developing the Emergency System for Advance Registration of Volunteer Health Professionals, known as ESAR-VHP, is vital to answering and solving the issues of credentialing. Take some time and find out about these endeavors. A useful website is www.publichealthlaw.net. I have included laws, etc., from my state. Be sure to check the laws in your own state. On deployment is not the time to be unsure about where you stand in these matters. Also, see http://www.govtrack.us.

SUMMARY OF STATUTORY PROVISIONS AFFECTING THE LIABILITY OF PROVIDERS IN A PUBLIC HEALTH EMERGENCY

Statute/Law	*Who is covered?*	*Immunity from what?*
Sovereign immunity under U.S. Constitution, 11th Amendment	State agency or individual sued in official capacity	Immune from liability for damages and/or from lawsuit
Official immunity	State or local government employee or official sued in individual capacities	Immune from personal liability for negligence
Government Code § 421.061, Civil Liability	• Officer or employee of state or local agency performing a homeland security activity, or • Volunteer performing homeland security activity at the request or under the direction of an officer or employee of state or local agency	Considered members of state military forces. Members of such forces are not civilly liable for an act performed in the discharge of duty under Government Code § 431.085
Civil Practice and Remedies Code § 79.003, Disaster Assistance	Person giving care, assistance or advice with respect to the management of an incident: • that is a disaster (man-made or natural) and • in which the care, assistance or advice is provided at the request of local, state, or federal agencies	Immune from civil liability for act or omission
Health and Safety Code § 81.007, Limitation on Liability	Private individual performing duties in compliance with orders or instructions of TDH or a health authority issued under Communicable Disease Prevention and Control Act, Health and Safety Code, Chapter 81	Not liable for death of or injury to person or for damage to property
Civil Practice and Remedies Code, Section 74.151, Liability for Emergency Care	Person who in good faith administers emergency care	Not liable in civil damages for act performed during the emergency

Statute/Law	Who is covered?	Immunity from what?
Civil Practice and Remedies Code, Section 74.152, Unlicensed Medical Personnel	Person not licensed or certified in the healing arts who in good faith administers emergency care as emergency medical service personnel	Not liable in civil damages for act performed
Title 42 United States Code, Chapter 139, Volunteer Protection, §§ 14501-14505	Volunteer of a nonprofit organization or governmental entity	Not liable for harm caused by an act or omission of the volunteer on behalf of the organization or entity
Civil Practice and Remedies Code, Chapter 84, Charitable Immunity and Liability Act of 1987	Volunteer health care provider who is serving as a direct service volunteer of a charitable organization	Immune from civil liability for any act or omission resulting in death, damage or injury to a patient
Title 42 United States Code, Section 233(p) as found in the Homeland Security Act of 2002, Public Law 107-296, Section 304	*Covered person* includes health care entities; drug and vaccine manufacturers; qualified persons who administer the countermeasure; or officials, agents, or employees of any of these persons. "Qualified" means that the person is authorized under the law of the state to administer the countermeasure.	• A *covered person* shall be deemed to be an employee of the Public Health Service with respect to liability arising out of administration of a *covered countermeasure* against smallpox to an individual during the effective period of a *declaration by the Secretary* of the U.S. Department of Health and Human Services. • A *covered countermeasure* means a substance that is used to prevent or treat smallpox or vaccinia immune globulin used to control or treat the adverse effects of vaccinia inoculation. The substance must be specified in the declaration.

Statute/Law	Who is covered?	Immunity from what?
Title 42 United States Code § 239 added by Public Law 108-20, Smallpox Emergency Personnel Protection Act of 2003	Person injured, directly or indirectly, by administration of smallpox countermeasures including: • Health care worker and emergency responder, or • Individual injured by accidental vaccinia inoculation through contact	Provides a "no fault" source of benefits and compensation for reasonable and necessary medical treatment reimbursement, certain lost employment income, lump sum death payment, and lost wages death benefit
Civil Practice and Remedies Code, Chapter 108, Limitation of Liability for Public Servants	• Public official, • State employee or officer, • Physician or psychiatrist who was performing services under a contract with any state agency, • Officer, volunteer, or employee of local government (county, city, district, political subdivision of state), • Physician providing emergency or post-stabilization services to patients in local government hospital, or • Employee of municipal hospital management contractor	Caps personal liability of public servant for damages arising from personal injury, death, or deprivation of right, privilege, or immunity or property damage resulting from act or omission by the public servant
Civil Practice and Remedies Code, Chapter 104, State Liability for Conduct of Public Servants	Act or omission in the scope of duties on behalf of a state agency by: • State employee or officer, or • Physician or psychiatrist who was performing services under a contract with any state agency	State will indemnify covered person for: • Negligence; • Deprivation of a right, privilege, or immunity secured by the constitution or laws of this state or the United States; or Indemnification in best interests of state as determined by AG

Statute/Law	Who is covered?	Immunity from what?
Civil Practice and Remedies Code, Chapter 102, Tort Claims Payments by Local Governments	• Officer, volunteer, or employee of local government (county, city, district, political subdivision of state), or • Employee of municipal hospital management contractor	Local government may pay damages (indemnify) for negligent act or omission in course and scope of employment
Civil Practice and Remedies Code; Chapter 101, Texas Tort Claims Act	Act addresses liability of governmental unit (state or political subdivision or municipal hospital management contractor) for wrongful act or omission or negligence of officer or paid employee (not volunteer or independent contractor) acting within scope of employment for property damage, personal injury, or death caused by motor vehicle or condition or use of tangible or real property	Act provides that filing suit under the Act against a governmental unit constitutes an irrevocable election by the plaintiff and immediately and forever bars any suit or recovery by the plaintiff against any individual employee of the governmental unit regarding the same subject matter
The Emergency Management Assistance Compact (EMAC) Health and Safety Code §778.001, Article VI	"Officers or employees of a party state rendering aid in another state pursuant to this compact…." A party state is a state, which has ratified EMAC and agreed to lend assistance to another state.	"Tort liability." Specifically: covered persons "shall be considered agents of the requesting state for tort liability and immunity purposes; and no party state or its officers or employees rendering aid … shall be liable on account of any act or omission in good faith on the part of such forces while so engaged or on account of the maintenance or use of any equipment or supplies in connection therewith."

Note: Prepared by Texas Department of Health, Office of General Counsel, April 20, 2006.

The statutes above are described in summary form with many provisions omitted. The actual statute and relevant case law should always be consulted for application in a particular situation. This document is not meant to substitute for the advice of an attorney.

This chart does not describe all statutes that generally (1) protect a governmental or other entity as opposed to employees, officers, or volunteers or (2) apply to tort liability or medical malpractice. The omission of these statutes does not imply they are unimportant or irrelevant. Consultation with an attorney is appropriate to determine the application of other statutes.

The Center for Law and the Public's Health

CDC just released several checklists. They include some good information and sum up a lot of the issues. The checklists are shown below as well as the websites where they can be found:

1. Public Health Emergency Legal Preparedness Checklist: Civil Legal Liability and Public Health Emergencies. The Center for Law and the Public's Health at Georgetown and Johns Hopkins Universities. December 2004.
    http://www.publichealthlaw.net/Resources/ResourcesPDFs/Checklist%203.pdf
2. Public Health Emergency Legal Preparedness Checklist: Interjurisdictional Legal Coordination for Public Health Emergency Preparedness. The Center for Law and the Public's Health at Georgetown and Johns Hopkins Universities. December 2004.
    http://www.publichealthlaw.net/Resources/ResourcesPDFs/Checklist%201.pdf
3. Public Health Emergency Legal Preparedness Checklist: Local Government Public Health Emergency Legal Preparedness and Response. The Center for Law and the Public's Health at Georgetown and Johns Hopkins Universities. December 2004.
    http://www.publichealthlaw.net/Resources/ResourcesPDFs/Checklist%202.pdf

Federal Law: Volunteer Protection Act of 1997

The purpose of the Volunteer Protection Act of 1997 is to promote the interests of social service program beneficiaries and taxpayers and to sustain the availability of programs, nonprofit organizations, and governmental entities that depend on volunteer contributions by reforming the laws to provide certain protections from liability abuses related to volunteers serving nonprofit organizations and governmental entities.[1] Two types of organizations can qualify as nonprofit organizations. The first kind of nonprofit organization is an organization which is described in section 501(c)(3) of the Internal Revenue Code of 1986 and exempt from tax under section 501(a) of the Code and which does not practice any action which constitutes a hate crime.[2] The other type of nonprofit organization is a not-for-profit organization which is organized and conducted for public benefit and operated primarily for charitable, civic, educational, religious, welfare, or health purposes and which does not practice any action which constitutes a hate crime.[3] A volunteer is an individual performing services for a nonprofit organization or a governmental entity who does not receive compensation (other than reasonable reimbursement for expenses) or any other thing of value in lieu of compensation in excess of $500 per year. This term includes those serving as director, officer, trustee, or direct service volunteer.[4]

This law provides that no volunteer of a nonprofit organization or governmental entity shall be liable for harm caused by an act or omission of the volunteer on behalf of the organization or entity if the volunteer meets four requirements. First, the volunteer must have been acting within the scope of the volunteer's responsibilities in the nonprofit organization or governmental entity at the time of the act or omission. Next, if it is required or appropriate, the volunteer must have been properly licensed, certified, or authorized by the appropriate authorities for the activities or practice in the State in which the harm occurred, where the activities were or practice was undertaken within the scope of the volunteer's responsibilities in the nonprofit organization or governmental agency. Third, the harm may not have been caused by willful or criminal misconduct, gross negligence, reckless misconduct, or a conscious, flagrant indifference to the rights or safety of the individual harmed by the volunteer. And finally, the harm may not have been caused by the volunteer operating a motor vehicle, vessel, aircraft, or other vehicle for which the State requires the operator or the owner of the vehicle, craft, or vessel to possess an operator's license or maintain insurance.[5]

This law explicitly limits the punitive damages that may be awarded against a volunteer. Punitive damages may not be awarded against a volunteer in an action brought for harm based on the action of a volunteer acting within the scope of the volunteer's responsibilities to a governmental agency or nonprofit organization unless the claimant establishes by clear and convincing evidence that the harm was proximately caused by an action of such volunteer which constitutes willful or criminal misconduct, or a conscious, flagrant indifference to the rights or safety of the individual harmed.[6] This law does not create a cause of action for punitive damages and does not preempt or supersede any Federal or State law to the extent that such law would further limit the award of punitive damages.[7]

A further limitation of liability exists for noneconomic loss. Noneconomic losses are nonpecuniary losses of any kind or nature.[8] In any civil action against a volunteer, based on an action of a volunteer acting within the scope of the volunteer's responsibilities to a governmental entity or a nonprofit organization, the liability of the volunteer for noneconomic loss shall be determined as follows.[9] Each defendant who is a volunteer shall be liable only for the amount of noneconomic loss allocated to that defendant in direct proportion to the percentage of responsibility of that defendant for the harm to the claimant with respect to which that defendant is liable. The court shall render a separate judgment against each defendant.[10] For purposes of determining the amount of noneconomic loss allocated to a defendant who is a volunteer, the trier of fact shall determine the percentage of responsibility of that defendant for the claimant's harm.[11] However, there are exceptions to the limitation for noneconomic losses. The limitation on the liability of a volunteer for noneconomic losses does not apply to any misconduct that constitutes a crime of violence or act of international terrorism for which the defendant has been convicted in any court. The limitation also does not apply to misconduct that constitutes a hate crime, or misconduct that involves a sexual offense for which the defendant has been convicted in any court. Also, misconduct for which the defendant has been found to have violated a Federal or State civil rights law is not subject to the liability limitation for noneconomic loss. Finally, the limitation does not apply to misconduct where the defendant was under the influence of intoxicating alcohol or any drug at the time of the misconduct.[12]

This law, however, does not affect any civil action brought by any nonprofit organization or any governmental entity against any volunteer of such organization or entity.[13] Furthermore, this law does not affect the liability of any nonprofit organization or governmental entity with respect to harm caused to any person.[14]

It is very important to note that this law preempts State laws to the extent that such laws are inconsistent with this law, except it shall not preempt any State law that provides additional protection from liability relating to volunteers or to any category of volunteers in the performance of services for a nonprofit organization or governmental entity.[15] The state of Texas provides additional protection of this kind for volunteers providing services for nonprofit organizations.

Texas Law: Charitable Immunity and Liability Act of 1987

The purpose of the Charitable Immunity and Liability Act of 1987 is to encourage volunteer services and maximize the resources devoted to delivering these services by reducing the liability exposure and insurance costs of charitable organizations and their employees and volunteers.[16] The Act provides physician volunteers immunity for performing nonemergency care for certain charitable organizations.

Five categories of organizations fall within the definition of a "charitable organization." The first class of charitable organizations are those that are exempt from federal income tax under Section 501(a) of the Internal Revenue Code of 1986 by being listed as an exempt organization in Section 501(c)(3) or 501(c)(4). Generally, these are organizations that are organized and operated exclusively for charitable, religious, prevention of cruelty to children or animals, youth sports and youth recreational, neighborhood crime prevention or patrol, fire protection or prevention, emergency medical or hazardous material response services, educational purposes, or is organized and operated exclusively for the promotion of social welfare by being primarily engaged in promoting the common good and general welfare of the people in a community.[17]

The second category includes any bona fide charitable, religious, prevention of cruelty to children or animals, youth sports and youth recreational, neighborhood crime prevention or patrol, or educational organization organized and operated exclusively for the promotion of social welfare by being primarily engaged in promoting the common good and general welfare of the people in a community, so long as it meets six additional requirements. The additional requirements include: the organization is organized and operated exclusively for one or more of the above purposes; it does not engage in activities which are not in furtherance of the purpose or purposes; it does not participate or intervene in any political campaign of any candidate for public office; it dedicates its assets to achieving the stated purpose or purposes of the organization; the organization does not allow inurement to the benefit of any group, shareholder, or individual; and it normally receives more that one-third of its support in any year from private or public gifts, grants, contributions, or membership fees.[18]

The third set of charitable organizations is made up of homeowners associations as defined by Section 528(c) of the Internal Revenue Code of 1986, or is exempt from federal income tax under Section 501(a).[19]

The fourth charitable organization is a volunteer center, as defined by Government Code Section 411.126.[20]

Finally, the fifth listed charitable organization is a local chamber of commerce that meets certain requirements.[21]

A volunteer is a person rendering services for a charitable organization who does not receive compensation in excess of reimbursement for expenses incurred. This includes a person serving as a director, officer, trustee, or direct service volunteer, including a volunteer health care provider.[22] There are eight types of health care providers that may be volunteer health care providers, provided they are either licensed or retired and eligible to provide health care services under the law of this state. These include physician assistants, registered nurses (including advanced nurse practitioners), vocational nurses, pharmacists, podiatrists, dentists, dental hygienists, and optometrists or therapeutic optometrists.[23]

A volunteer, including one who is serving as an officer, director, or trustee of a charitable organization, is immune from civil liability for any act or omission that results in death, damage, or injury if the volunteer was acting in the course and scope of his duties or functions.[24] A volunteer health care provider who is serving as a direct service volunteer of a charitable organization is immune from civil liability for any act or omission resulting in death, damage, or injury to a patient if the volunteer meets three requirements. First, the volunteer commits the act or omission in the course of providing health care services to the patient. Second, the services provided are within the scope of the license of the volunteer. And finally, before the volunteer provides the health care services, the patient, or if the patient is a minor or is otherwise legally incompetent, the patient's parent, managing conservator, legal guardian, or other person with legal responsibility for the care of the patient signs a written statement that acknowledges both that the volunteer is providing care that is not administered for or in expectation of compensation and the limitations on the recovery of damages from the volunteer in exchange for receiving the health care services.[25] No signed acknowledgment is required if the patient is incapacitated or the patient is a minor or is otherwise legally incompetent and the person responsible for the patient is not reasonably available.

However, a volunteer is liable to a person for death, damage, or injury to the person or his property proximately caused by any act or omission arising from the operation or use of any motor-driven equipment to the extent insurance coverage is required by Chapter 601 of the Transportation Code and to the extent of any existing insurance coverage applicable to the act or omission.[26]

Also, the liability of nonhospital charitable organizations and their employees for damages based on an act or omission is limited to money damages of $500,000 for each person and $1,000,000 for each single occurrence of bodily injury or death and $100,000 for each single occurrence for injury to or destruction of property.[27] These liability limitations do not apply to a health care provider unless the provider is a federally funded migrant or community health center, is a nonprofit health maintenance organization created and operated by a community center, or the provider usually provides discounted services at or below costs based on the ability of the beneficiary to pay.[28] Also, these limitations do not apply if the charitable organization does not have liability insurance coverage in the amount of at least $500,000 for each person and $1,000,000 for each single occurrence for any act or omission resulting in death or bodily injury and $100,000 for each single occurrence of injury to or destruction of property.[29] Note that the insurance requirement does not apply to volunteers.[30]

The limitations and immunities found in this Act do not apply in some situations. First, they do not apply to an act or omission that is intentional, willfully negligent, or done with conscious indifference or reckless disregard for the safety of others.[31] This Act also does not limit the liability of an organization or its employees or volunteers if the organization was formed substantially to limit its liability under this law.[32] Also, this law does not apply to organizations formed to dispose, remove, or store hazardous waste, industrial solid waste, radioactive waste, municipal solid waste, garbage, or sludge as defined under state and federal law.[33] Finally, this law does not apply to a governmental unit or employee of a governmental unit.[34] However, state sovereign immunity may provide protection to governmental units and their employees.

Good Samaritan Law: Liability for Emergency Care

The Texas Good Samaritan Law limits the civil liability of persons administering emergency care in good faith at the scene of an emergency or in a health care facility. The law limits the civil liability of these persons unless their actions are willfully and wantonly negligent. This protection does not apply to care administered for or in expectation of remuneration (but being legally entitled to remuneration is not determinative), or by a person who was at the scene of the emergency because he or a person he represents as an agent was soliciting business or seeking to perform a service for remuneration. Also, the limited civil liability is not available for a person whose negligence was a producing cause of the emergency for which care is being administered.[35]

Emergency medical service personnel who are not licensed in the healing arts who administer emergency care in good faith are not liable in civil damages for an act performed in administering the care unless the act is willfully or wantonly negligent. This limit of liability applies regardless of whether the care is provided for or in expectation of remuneration.[36]

The limited civil liability provided by the Good Samaritan law is an affirmative defense. This means that after a lawsuit is filed, the physician must prove that the law provides protection. So, although the physician may be protected from liability, he will still bear the financial burden of defense.

Under the Charitable Immunity and Liability Act, physician volunteers may be immune from civil liability in providing nonemergency medical services as a volunteer health care provider. In order to assure that the immunity will apply, physicians should verify that they are working for a charitable organization, within the scope of their employment and license, and obtain written consent from the patient, when feasible.

Furthermore, a physician may be immune from civil liability in providing emergency medical services. The Good Samaritan Law was intended by the legislature to provide physicians broad immunity when administering uncompensated emergency care.

Texas House Bill 9

House Bill 9 gives the governor the duties of directing Texas homeland security, developing a statewide homeland security strategy, and allocating and reviewing homeland security grants and funding. The bill creates the Critical Infrastructure Protection Council as an interagency advisory entity administered by the governor and authorizes the governor to appoint additional special advisory committees composed of representatives from state and local agencies and nongovernmental entities not represented on the council. It establishes a Texas Infrastructure Protection Communications Center, administered by the Department of Public Safety (DPS), and makes the DPS the repository for multi-jurisdictional criminal intelligence information related to homeland security. The bill modifies eligibility for the Texas State Guard and establishes the role of the guard in homeland security and community service activities. It requires pharmacists to report unusual incidents or trends that might suggest bioterrorism or serious disease outbreaks, and adds emergency medical service personnel, peace officers, and firefighters to those required to report suspected cases of reportable diseases. Confidentiality provisions relate to critical infrastructure, security systems, risk and vulnerability assessments, encryption codes and security keys, weapons construction and assembly, reports to the federal government on acts of terrorism and related criminal activity, and the tactical plans, staffing requirements, and contact numbers of emergency response providers. Other provisions address issues of liability relating to the performance of homeland security activities. The bill establishes September 11 as Texas First Responders Day to honor Texans who assist others in emergencies.

Senate Bill 513

Senate Bill 513 amends the Civil Practice and Remedies Code to provide that, under certain conditions, a person is immune from civil liability for an act or omission that occurs in giving care, assistance, or advice relating to the management of a man-made or natural disaster when help is requested by an authorized governmental authority and the person is not compensated for the help.

Special Needs Plan

The Texas Government Code, Chapter 418, known as the Texas Disaster Act of 1975, applies during a state of disaster and the following recovery period. Several provisions are pertinent to the ability of state and local government to address medical special needs. The provisions include the following:

§ 418.015. EFFECT OF DISASTER DECLARATION. An executive order or proclamation declaring a state of disaster: (1) activates the disaster recovery and rehabilitation aspects of the state emergency management plan applicable to the area subject to the declaration; and (2) authorizes the deployment and use of any forces to which the plan applies and the use or distribution of any supplies, equipment, and materials or facilities assembled, stockpiled, or arranged to be made available under this chapter or other law relating to disasters.

   (a) The preparedness and response aspects of the state emergency management plan are activated as provided by that plan.

   (b) During a state of disaster and the following recovery period, the governor is the commander in chief of state agencies, boards, and commissions having emergency responsibilities. To the greatest extent possible, the governor shall delegate or assign command authority by prior arrangement embodied in appropriate executive orders or plans, but this chapter does not restrict the governor's authority to do so by orders issued at the time of the disaster.

§ 418.016. SUSPENSION OF PROCEDURAL LAWS AND RULES. The governor may suspend the provisions of any regulatory statute prescribing the procedures for conduct of state business or the orders or rules of a state agency if strict compliance with the provisions, orders, or rules would in any way prevent, hinder, or delay necessary action in coping with a disaster.

§ 418.017. USE OF PUBLIC AND PRIVATE RESOURCES. The governor may use all available resources of state government and of political subdivisions that are reasonably necessary to cope with a disaster.

(a) The governor may temporarily reassign resources, personnel, or functions of state executive departments and agencies or their units for the purpose of performing or facilitating emergency services.

(b) The governor may commandeer or use any private property if the governor finds it necessary to cope with a disaster, subject to the compensation requirements of this chapter.

§ 418.018. MOVEMENT OF PEOPLE. The governor may recommend the evacuation of all or part of the population from a stricken or threatened area in the state if the governor considers the action necessary for the preservation of life or other disaster mitigation, response, or recovery.

(a) The governor may prescribe routes, modes of transportation, and destinations in connection with an evacuation.

(b) The governor may control ingress and egress to and from a disaster area and the movement of persons and the occupancy of premises in the area.

§ 418.171. QUALIFICATIONS FOR RENDERING AID. A person who holds a license, certificate, or other permit issued by a state or political subdivision of any state evidencing the meeting of qualifications for professional, mechanical, or other skills may render aid involving the skill in this state to meet an emergency or disaster. This state shall give due consideration to the license, certificate, or other permit.

Liability

Immunity (protection) from liability or limitation on liability exists under a variety of federal and state laws that apply to certain types of persons in certain situations. Statutes and relevant case law should always be consulted for application to a particular situation.

The following is a brief list of laws that may apply to preparation and response under this appendix. The list does not describe all criteria that must be met in order for the stated provision to apply.

- Government Code, Section 421.061, Civil Liability (protects state or local agency officer or employee or a volunteer under a state or local agency employee or officer performing homeland security activity)
- Government Code, Section 421.062, Liability under Interlocal

Contract (protects state or local agency furnishing homeland security activity under contract)

- Civil Practice and Remedies Code, Section 79.003, Disaster Assistance (protects person giving care, assistance or advice in management of disaster at request of governmental agency)
- Title 42 United States Code, Chapter 139, Volunteer Protection, Sections 14501-14505 (protects volunteer of nonprofit or governmental entity)
- Civil Practice and Remedies Code, Chapter 84, Charitable Immunity and Liability Act of 1987 (protects volunteer health care provider serving charitable organization)
- Civil Practice and Remedies Code, Section 74.151, Liability for Emergency Care (protects person administering emergency care in good faith)
- Civil Practice and Remedies Code, Section 74.152, Unlicensed Medical Personnel (protects person administering emergency care without expectation of remuneration)
- Civil Practice and Remedies Code, Chapter 108, Limitation of Liability for Public Servants (limits liability of state or local government employee or officer, physician under contract with state, or volunteer of local government)
- Civil Practice and Remedies Code, Chapter 104, State Liability for Conduct of Public Servants (state indemnifies state employee or officer or a physician under contract with state)
- Civil Practice and Remedies Code, Chapter 102, Tort Claims Payments by Local Governments (local government may indemnify its officers, employees, or volunteers)
- Health and Safety Code, Section 81.007, Limitation on Liability (protects private individual performing duties per orders of state of local health authority under communicable disease law)
- Sovereign immunity under the United States Constitution, 11th Amendment protects state agency or individual
- Official immunity protects state or local government employees or officials.

Liability Issues for the Medical Reserve Corps

See MRC website <u>www.medicalreservecorps.gov</u>

The U.S. Government, health profession organizations, and volunteer organizations are fully aware of this concern. It must be kept in mind, however, that in our federal system of government, tort law is primarily a state responsibility. All states have some form of "good Samaritan legislation," although this legislation is limited in its protections. The Volunteer Protection Act ("VPA") (codified at 42 U.S.C. § 14501 et. Seq.) provides qualified immunity from liability for volunteers and, subject to exceptions, preempts inconsistent state laws on the subject, except for those that provide protections stronger than those contained in the VPA.

Under the VPA, a volunteer of a nonprofit organization or governmental entity is immune from liability for harm caused by an act or omission on the part of the volunteer working on behalf of the organization or entity if: (1) the act or omission was within the scope of the volunteer's responsibilities within that organization or entity; (2) if required, the volunteer was properly licensed, certified, or authorized by the appropriate state authorities for the activities or practice giving rise to the claim; (3) the harm was not caused by "willful or criminal misconduct, gross negligence, reckless misconduct, or a conscious flagrant indifference to the rights or safety of the individual harmed by the volunteer;" and (4) the harm was not caused by the volunteer's operation of a motor vehicle, vessel, aircraft, or other vehicle for which the state requires the operator to possess a license or to maintain insurance.

The VPA defines a volunteer as "an individual performing services for a nonprofit organization or a governmental entity which does not receive compensation (other than reasonable reimbursement or allowance for expenses actually incurred); or any other thing of value in lieu of compensation, in excess of $500 per year...."

The VPA is helpful because it provides baseline legal protection amidst a wide variety of state laws. Nonetheless, because the VPA's protections are not absolute, each MRC Unit should consult with an attorney from its state for a more detailed analysis of the law's protections and limitations.

A number of health profession organizations as well as the U.S. Congress are examining the issue of appropriate liability protection for health providers during public health emergencies.

Texas Court, Legislature Strengthen Good Samaritan Law (Robbins, 2003)

Doctors who provide care in emergencies with no intention of seeking payment will have an easier time claiming the protection of the state's Good Samaritan statute under a recent Texas Supreme Court ruling and a change in the law that takes effect on Sept. 1.

On June 26, the high court held unanimously in *McIntyre v. Ramirez, et al.* that a person claiming the Good Samaritan defense provided under Texas Civil Practice and Remedies Code § 74.001 must prove that he "would not ordinarily receive or ordinarily be entitled to receive payment under the circumstances in which the emergency care was provided." The decision reverses a 2001 decision by Austin's 3rd Court of Appeals that a physician failed to prove conclusively that he was entitled to protection under the statute.

Written by Justice Dale Wainwright, the state Supreme Court's opinion in *McIntyre* included an English lesson. Although the adverb "ordinarily" appears only before the verb "received" in TCPR § 74.001(d), "ordinarily" modifies both "received" and the verb phrase "be entitled to receive," Wainwright wrote for the court.

"Of all the lawsuits in my 23 years as a lawyer, this is the most important one I've ever handled," says James Ewbank, attorney for Doctor Douglas K. McIntyre, an obstetrician sued for negligence in connection with neurological injuries an infant allegedly suffered during a complicated birth.

Ewbank, a shareholder in Austin's Ewbank and Byrom, says the opinion will encourage doctors to respond to emergencies in their specialties.

Laurie Higginbotham, an attorney for plaintiff Debra Ramirez, says the decision – although it addresses an issue of first impression – is moot because of a change the Legislature made in the law.

However, Ewbank says the decision is important. "It reiterates that the Legislature has a strong policy of encouraging doctors to respond to emergencies without fear of being sued," he says. "The legislative change is sort of belt and suspenders."

Higginbotham, an associate with Austin's Whitehurst, Harkness, Ozmun and Brees, says the decision is disappointing. The court essentially ruled that any doctor other than a patient's attending physician does not have a standard for care for emergency treatment provided in a hospital, she says.

"Our position all along has been there is a big difference between a doctor providing emergency care in a ditch along the side of the road and a doctor providing emergency care in a hospital. The court has said there is no difference," Higginbotham says.

Summary of Pandemic and All Hazards Preparedness Act

The United States Senate has passed a bill related to Public Health Preparedness. The Pandemic and All Hazards Preparedness Act (S.3678) became law on December 9, 2006 and established an "all-hazards" approach to public health preparedness, rather than focusing exclusively on acts of bioterrorism. Below you will find a summary of the provisions in the bill that are most pertinent to local public health departments.

The bill codifies much that is already existing or planned practice with respect to the CDC cooperative agreement program that provides funds to state and local health departments to support preparedness. In addition, it establishes penalties for states (and the three direct urban grantees) that fail substantially to meet performance benchmarks or that exceed carryover limits that the Secretary of Health and Human Services would establish. There is a strong emphasis on performance measurement and fiscal accountability and a new requirement for a state match beginning in 2009 (which would include in-kind contributions).

The bill establishes a modest new federal public health workforce program, in the form of grants to states that establish state loan repayment programs for public health professionals who go to work in state or local health departments that provide services to health professional shortage areas or areas at risk of a public health emergency. It is important to note, however, that this new program would not be implemented until Congress appropriated new funds for it and a state established a loan repayment program. The bill also officially authorizes the Medical Reserve Corps in order to provide for an adequate supply of volunteers in the case of a public health emergency.

The bill also opens the hospital preparedness program (which it moves organizationally from the Health Resources and Services Administration to a new Assistant Secretary for Preparedness and Response) to direct funding by HHS of partnerships that could include a group of hospitals and a state or local health department, rather than passing all the funding through the state.

The bill codifies into law the requirement for local concurrence with state spending allocations that has existed for several years in the CDC cooperative agreement guidance. It also requires activities undertaken under both CDC and the hospital preparedness cooperative agreement programs to be consistent with the activities of local health departments and local emergency plans. This reflects NACCHO's consistent advocacy for the proposition that public health response to a disaster takes place in the context of local emergency management plans.

The bill ensures some additional local flexibility in spending preparedness funds by explicitly permitting their use to pay salary and expenses for any health department personnel carrying out preparedness activities, even if that is not their primary assignment. NACCHO proposed and advocated strongly for this provision. The bill also requires states to coordinate with local public health departments, the Cities Readiness Initiative and local emergency plans when determining the activities to be carried out.

The bill creates an Advisory Committee on At-Risk Individuals and Public Health Emergencies and requires that recipients of state and local public health grants include preparedness strategies in their plans to address the medical and public health needs of at-risk individuals in the event of a public health emergency.

The bill requires HHS to establish a "near real-time" electronic nationwide public health situational awareness capability through an interoperable network of systems to share data and information to enhance early detection of, rapid response to, and management of infectious disease outbreaks and other public health emergencies. This network will be built upon systems that are already in place for this purpose.

The bill allows for the creation of a vaccine tracking program to track the distribution of federally purchased influenza vaccine in an influenza pandemic that would be dependent on manufacturers, wholesalers and distributors choosing to participate. The bill also encourages information exchange between public health officials and manufacturers, wholesalers and distributors regarding the distribution of seasonal influenza vaccine. It reflects CDC's current activities in this area.

The bill authorizes Centers for Public Health Preparedness based at accredited schools of public health. Centers for Public Health Preparedness are required to develop a competency-based training program to train public health practitioners. The bill also requires Centers for Public Health Preparedness to collaborate with state, local or tribal public health departments to create materials or trainings on public health preparedness and response for use in educating the general public.

The full text of the bill can be found by searching for S. 3678 at www.thomas.loc.gov.

Credentialing Issues

Below is the response to several issues relating to credentialing of professionals serving in the Texas Military Forces. In studying these responses, it may be possible to shed additional light in this overall area of concern.

In regard with privileging for medical professionals, can a medical professional practice, while on State Active Duty (SAD), in another state? This applies to the current situation with the EMAC.

According to the Emergency Management Assistance Compact (EMAC), Public Law 104-321, Article V, Whenever any person holds a license, certificate, or other permit issued by any state party to the compact evidencing the meeting of qualifications for professional, mechanical, or other skills, and when such assistance is requested be the receiving party state, such person shall be deemed licensed, certified, or permitted by the state requesting assistance to render aid involving such skill to meet a declared emergency or disaster, subject to such limitations and conditions as the governor of the requesting state may prescribe by executive order or otherwise.

My opinion: The medical personnel who are on SAD are required to be properly licensed in their home state. These personnel are also periodically required to provide evidence of their credentials to their state JFHQ (Joint Forces Headquarters) for credentialing, usually on an annual basis. According to this statute, a medical professional on state active duty, so long as they are properly licensed and privileged in their home state, is able to practice in a state that has requested assistance through the EMAC. The EMAC would indeed protect medical professionals. To read it otherwise would be to eviscerate one of the primary resources needed and contemplated by the EMAC. This would also include our medics.

When medical personnel on SAD are practicing out of the state, while in compliance with the EMAC, how are they covered for malpractice?

According to the Emergency Management Assistance Compact (EMAC), Public Law 104-321, Article VI, Officers or employees of a party state rendering aid in another party state rendering aid in another state pursuant to this compact shall be considered agents of the requesting state for tort liability and immunity purposes; and no party state or its officers or employees rendering aid in another state pursuant to this compact shall be liable on account of any act or omission in good faith. The statute further states that good faith in this article shall not include willful misconduct, gross negligence, or recklessness.

A medical professional, acting in goof faith, is protected from prosecution for tort liability by the tort claim act of the state that is receiving aid under the EMAC, so long as they are acting in good faith, and not acting with willful misconduct, gross negligence, or recklessness. Because they are considered state agents, they would be defended by the state in any tort action (theoretically).

Who pays workmans compensation for soldiers who are on SAD and working in another state under the EMAC?

Article VIII of the Emergency Management Assistance Compact (EMAC), Public Law 104-321, states that each party state shall provide for the payment of compensation of compensation and death benefits to injured members of the emergency forces of that state and representatives of diseased members of such forces in case such members sustain injuries or are killed while rendering aid pursuant to this compact, in the same manner and on the same terms as if the injury or death were sustained within their own state.

If a soldier is on SAD and working in another state under the EMAC, and this Soldier becomes injured or ill, then according to this text, the Soldier would seek workmans compensation benefits in their own state, and not the state where the injury occurred. Correct. I'm unsure whether the requesting state would be required to compensate the sending state for these costs, but that issue is irrelevant to your question. The state that the soldier belongs to provides the benefits.

Texas Medical Rangers

Texas State statutes related to the Texas State Guard Medical Brigade (Medical Reserve Corps)

REFERENCE: TEXAS GOVERNMENT CODE

http://www.capitol.state.tx.us/statutes/docs/GV/content/htm/

BENEFITS and protection authority, while on State Active Duty orders See § 431.017. STATE MILITIA)

CIVIL LIABILITY and immunity while on State Active Duty orders, and Homeland Security funding issues. See 421.061 & § 421.072 (from House Bill 9, May 2003). (HOMELAND SECURITY)

DISCIPLINE, Commander Non-Judicial Punishment & more severe discipline. See § 432.021 through § 432.036. (TEXAS CODE OF MILITARY JUSTICE)

FEDERAL SERVICE of State Guard Members is precluded. See § 431.058. (STATE MILITIA)

EXEMPTION from civil arrest while on State Active Duty status. See § 431.086. (STATE MILITIA)

INCORPORATION of TMR Groups requires unit activation orders from the TAG See § 431.036. (STATE MILITIA)

MILITARY JUSTICE, deserter apprehension, AWOL, missing movement, disrespect, contempt, etc. See § 432.130 through § 432.167, § 432.012 through § 432.014. (TEXAS CODE OF MILITARY JUSTICE)

MILITARY LEAVE, 15 days paid each federal FY, for State employees, authorization. See § 431.005 & § 431.006. (STATE MILITIA)

PAY provisions and limitations. See § 431.082. (STATE MILITIA)

SPECIAL FUND authority. See § 431.014. (STATE MILITIA)

STATE ACTIVE DUTY status, at the call of the Governor, paid and additional if a state employee. See § 431.052 & § 431.0825 & § 431.111. (STATE MILITIA)

STATE AWARDS for service and valor. See § 431.131 through §

431.137. (STATE MILITIA)

STATE EMERGENCIES, calling on state military forces, support to civilian authorities. See § 433.005. (STATE OF EMERGENCY)

TEXAS STATE GUARD, statutory provisions. See § 431.051 & § 431.052. (STATE MILITIA)

NOTES

1. 42 U.S.C.A. §14501(b).
2. 42 U.S.C.A. §14505(4)(A).
3. 42 U.S.C.A. §14505(4)(B).
4. 42 U.S.C.A. §14505(6).
5. 42 U.S.C.A. §14503(a).
6. 42 U.S.C.A. §14503(e)(1).
7. 42 U.S.C.A. §14503(e)(2).
8. 42 U.S.C.A. §14505(3).
9. 42 U.S.C.A. §14504(a).
10. 42 U.S.C.A. §14504(b)(1).
11. 42 U.S.C.A. §14504(b)(2).
12. 42 U.S.C.A. §14503(f)(1)(A)-(E).
13. 42 U.S.C.A. §14503(b).
14. 42 U.S.C.A. §14503(c).
15. 42 U.S.C.A. §14502(a).
16. Tex Civ Prac & Rem Code Ann §84.002.
17. Tex Civ Prac & Rem Code Ann §84.003(1)(A).
18. Tex Civ Prac & Rem Code Ann §84.003(1)(B).
19. Tex Civ Prac & Rem Code Ann §84.003(1)(C).
20. Tex Civ Prac & Rem Code Ann §84.003(1)(D).
21. Tex Civ Prac & Rem Code Ann §84.003(1)(E).
22. Tex Civ Prac & Rem Code Ann §84.003(2).
23. Tex Civ Prac & Rem Code Ann §84.003(5).
24. Tex Civ Prac & Rem Code Ann §84.004(a).
25. Tex Civ Prac & Rem Code Ann §84.004(c).
26. Tex Civ Prac & Rem Code Ann §84.004(d).
27. Tex Civ Prac & Rem Code Ann §84.005 and 84.006.
28. Tex Civ Prac & Rem Code Ann §84.007(e).
29. Tex Civ Prac & Rem Code Ann §84.007(g).
30. Tex Civ Prac & Rem Code Ann §84.007(g).
31. Tex Civ Prac & Rem Code Ann §84.007(a).
32. Tex Civ Prac & Rem Code Ann §84.007(c).
33. Tex Civ Prac & Rem Code Ann §84.007(d).
34. Tex Civ Prac & Rem Code Ann §84.007(f).

35. Tex Civ Prac & Rem Code Ann §74.151.
36. Tex Civ Prac & Rem Code Ann §74.152.

Chapter 19

KNOW HOW TO DO PSYCHOLOGICAL TRIAGE

UTILIZE THE CRISIS INTERVENTION TRIAGE SYSTEM

What is Triage?

Triage comes from the Old French word "Trier" which means to "Sort." It is a process of separating sufferers by symptoms and priority for treatment.

Why Triage?

Disaster situations require that available care be allocated first to the most sufferers who can benefit from such care and the, often limited, resources available at the time. It is a way of establishing a priority for care on the likelihood of a victim benefiting from immediate care. In this author's opinion, a triage system for disaster mental health must be a simple process that can be accomplished with limited training and performed quickly. It should also be done without sacrificing the dignity of the victim while at the same time making critical decisions about who will get scarce care and who will have to wait or get no real care at all. It is a basic tenet of psychological triage that it be performed on victims who have received needed medical care or who may have been screened medically and/or require no medical care. This system has been developed to be similar to triage systems used in

Note: A special note of gratitude for the help on this section given by Doctor Sharon Leviton, Author and Crisis Intervention Specialist, and Karen Ray, Psychology Doctoral Student at Capella University.

137

emergency medicine. Probably, it is most closely linked to the M.A.S.S. Triage System promulgated by the National Disaster Life Support Foundations and American Medical Association in its Basic and Advanced Disaster Life Support courses.

The Disaster Crisis Intervention Triage System can be used by:

A. Experienced disaster mental health and crisis intervention personnel in the course of their work with traumatized victims of disaster.
B. Mental health workers less familiar with disaster crisis intervention techniques but desiring to assist.
C. Inexperienced volunteers who receive "Just-in-time" training in the Disaster Crisis Intervention Triage System.

Following in this chapter you will:

1. Understand the basic overview of the four levels of triage.
2. Study the characteristics of each psychological level.
3. Understand the characteristics across all categories.
4. See the triage card to be attached to the victim.
5. See the triage card to be used by triage person.
6. Read the guidance concerning the proper use of triage card system.
7. Review the crisis intervener qualifying questions.
8. Utilize the triage checklists to perform triage.
9. Know the questions to develop the needed information to complete the triage process.

UNDERSTAND THE BASIC OVERVIEW OF THE FOUR LEVELS OF TRIAGE

The Disaster Crisis Intervention Triage System consists of four levels of triage. This is similar to many of the emergency medical triage systems.

Minimal Level

Few indicators of crisis. Upset and/or experiencing effects of psychosocial trauma with few or no indicators of crisis, as indicated by some of the following:

1. Coherent thought processes
2. Able to make personal care decisions
3. Upset or crying but obviously in control of self
4. Able and willing to discuss experience
5. No violent acting-out behavior
6. May want to help others
7. Re-triage may be needed

Immediate Level

Must be seen and attended to now! In crisis as indicated by some of the following:

1. Becoming more and more depressed
2. Out-of-structure (control issues)
3. Acting-out behavior
4. Difficulty following instructions
5. Poor decision making
6. Yelling and screaming

Delayed Level

Can wait. Must be re-triaged. Very upset but obviously coping to some degree as indicated by some of the following:

1. Some withdrawal
2. Some confusion
3. No acting-out behavior
4. Intact decision making
5. Expression of concerns and desire to talk to someone

Extreme Level

Return to these only when others are assisted. May need to re-triage later as time and resources permit. These will require long-term support or psychotherapy and are not likely to respond to crisis intervention techniques as indicated by some of, but not limited to, the following:

1. Chronic mental illness without appropriate medications
2. Totally unresponsive to inquiries

3. Communication shut-down
4. Unable to do anything for self
5. Custodial care probably required

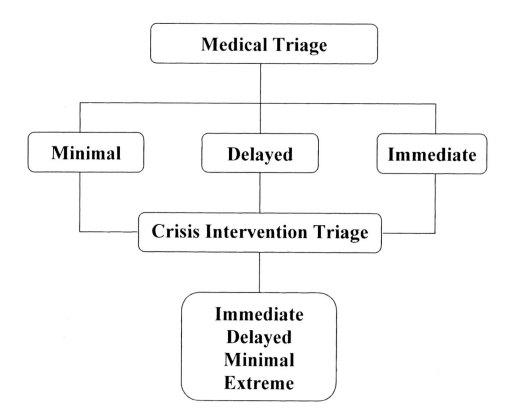

Figure 19.1. Crisis Intervention Triage System.

STUDY THE CHARACTERISTICS OF EACH PSYCHOLOGICAL LEVEL

1. **IMMEDIATE** – treat now. They can benefit instantly from immediate crisis intervention. This is what they look like:
   Attitude and General Behavior – Extremely upset, hyperactive, defiant, angry, overwhelmed, preoccupied, mistrustful, scared, limited self-control.
   Mental Activity – Self-absorbed, illogical, irrelevant, difficulty expressing complete thoughts, generally coherent.

Emotional Reactions – Euphoric or depressed, apprehension, fear, labile, generally appropriate affect.

Thoughts – Some trouble forming clear thoughts, fearful, shut down.

Orientation – Clear sensorium.

Fund of General Knowledge – Appropriate to age and education, some production difficulties at the outset.

Suicidality – Thoughts may be present.

Insight – Limited.

2. **DELAYED** – treat as soon as I can. They can wait a while although best in a group. These can benefit from crisis intervention, but are not suffering to the same extent as the IMMEDIATEs. This is what they look like:

Attitude and General Behavior – Upset, basically in control of self, mild mistrust, talkative, may make light, nervous giggle.

Mental Activity – Accessible, worried, concerned about situation and that of others, compliant.

Emotional Reactions – Appropriate to the situation, anxiety, moderate fear, moderate depression.

Thoughts – May have difficulty accessing clear thoughts, may catastrophize, concern about others, wants to help self and others, may intellectualize situation and their response, stream of thoughts may be less than adequate to maintain a conversation.

Orientation – Sensorium clear in all three realms of time, person and place.

Fund of General Knowledge – Appropriate to age and education.

Suicidality – May have some fleeting suicidal ideations, denies suicidal desires.

Insight – Some, but still limited, less limited than those in IMMEDIATE category.

3. **MINIMAL** – treat later. They can get along on their own for now. These may not be in crisis, but could be headed in that direction. Probably will do fine with support and even with utilization as a volunteer to assist you in helping or monitoring others. Just because they look okay initially, does not mean that they might not experience crisis later. Pay attention to this group but put them to work if they are willing. If not, check on them occasionally as resources allow. This is what they look like:

Attitude and General Behavior – Presents well, could appear calm or preoccupied but in control of self, compliant and cooperative, responsive to inquiries, positive attitude.

Mental Activity – Accessible, coherent and relevant, alert and appropriately talkative.

Emotional Reactions – Appropriate affect, mild depression, mild fear, some anxiety, emotionally stable.

Thoughts – Within normal limits, relates to others easily, engages in conversation and is easily understood, maintains appropriate stream of thoughts.

Orientation – Well oriented in all spheres.

Fund of General Knowledge – Appropriate.

Suicidality – No suicidal ideation.

Insight – Appropriate to age, education and current experience.

4. **EXTREME** – Will not benefit from the help available at this time or requires more assistance than resources allow. Are so bad off or mentally disturbed that attempts to help them would require hours of time and personnel needed elsewhere, and the benefit to the patient would be minimal or nonexistent. Attempts to treat these would be after all of the above groups have been helped. This is what they look like:

Attitude and General Behavior – Disheveled and untidy, limited cooperation, mistrustful, suspicious, antagonistic, motor retardation or hyperactivity, perseveration.

Mental Activity – Self absorbed or inaccessible, circumstantial, flight of ideas, underproductive, mute, irrelevant, incoherent, illogical, blocking.

Emotional Reactions – Elation, exhilaration, depression, emotional instability, incongruity of thought content, ambivalence, emotional deterioration.

Thoughts – Delusions, hallucinations, paranoid ideations, grandiose ideas, autistic thinking, unreal ideas.

Orientation – Limited orientation in three spheres.

Fund of General Knowledge – May be appropriate.

Suicidality – Suicidal ideations may be present, prior suicidal behavior, plan of suicide clear, means of suicide clear.

Insight – May be nonexistent.

Also, ask about a previous diagnosis or treatment and medications related to mental health problems. Probably, there will be positive responses to at least some of these inquiries.

REMEMBER: People in crisis could appear mentally ill and those who are mentally ill could be in crisis. Differentiation is crucial. Generally, if a person in crisis is removed from the source of the crisis, or if the crisis situation is removed from the person in crisis, the crisis will subside substantially. This is not true for a person who is mentally ill. The mental illness may be exacerbated or diminished by removal, but the mental illness continues.

UNDERSTAND THE CHARACTERISTICS ACROSS ALL CATEGORIES

Attitude and General Behavior

1. IMMEDIATE – Extremely upset, hyperactive, defiant, preoccupied, mistrustful, scared, limited self control.
2. DELAYED – Upset, basically in control of self, mild mistrust, talkative.
3. MINIMAL – Presents well, preoccupied but in control of self, compliant and cooperative, responsive to inquiries, positive attitude.
4. EXTREME – Disheveled and untidy, limited cooperation, mistrustful, suspicious, antagonistic, motor retardation or hyperactivity, perseveration.

Mental Activity

1. IMMEDIATE– Self absorbed, illogical, irrelevant, difficulty expressing complete thoughts, generally coherent.
2. DELAYED – Accessible, worried, concerned about situation and that of others, compliant.
3. MINIMAL – Accessible, coherent and relevant, alert and appropriately talkative.
4. EXTREME – Self absorbed or inaccessible, circumstantial, flight of ideas, underproductive, mute, irrelevant, incoherent, illogical, blocking.

Emotional Reactions

1. IMMEDIATE – Euphoric or depressed, apprehension, fear, labile, generally appropriate affect.
2. DELAYED – Appropriate to the situation, anxiety, moderate fear, moderate depression.
3. MINIMAL – Appropriate affect, mild depression, mild fear, some anxiety, emotionally stable.
4. EXTREME – Elation, exhilaration, depression, emotional instability, incongruity of thought content, ambivalence, emotional deterioration.

Thoughts

1. IMMEDIATE – Some trouble forming clear thoughts, fearful, shut down.
2. DELAYED – May have difficulty accessing clear thoughts, may catastrophize, concern about others, wants to help self and others, may intellectualize situation and their response, stream of thoughts may be less than adequate to maintain a conversation.
3. MINIMAL – Within normal limits, relates to others easily, engages in conversation and is easily understood, maintains appropriate steam of thoughts.
4. EXTREME – Delusions, hallucinations, paranoid ideations, grandiose ideas, autistic thinking, unreal ideas.

Orientation

1. IMMEDIATE – Clear sensorium.
2. DELAYED – Sensorium clear in all three realms of time, person and place.
3. MINIMAL – Well oriented in all spheres.
4. EXTREME – Limited orientation in three spheres.

Fund of General Knowledge

1. IMMEDIATE – Appropriate to age and education, some production difficulties at the outset.
2. DELAYED – Appropriate to age and education.

3. MINIMAL – Appropriate.
4. EXTREME – May be appropriate.

Suicidality

1. IMMEDIATE – Thoughts may be present.
2. DELAYED – May have some fleeting suicidal ideations, denies suicidal desires.
3. MINIMAL – No suicidal ideation.
4. EXTREME – Suicidal ideations may be present, prior suicidal behavior, plan of suicide clear, means of suicide clear.

Insight

1. IMMEDIATE – Limited.
2. DELAYED – Some, but still limited, less limited than those in IMMEDIATE category.
3. MINIMAL – Appropriate to age, education and current experience.
4. EXTREME – May be nonexistent.

SEE THE TRIAGE CARD TO BE ATTACHED TO THE VICTIM

```
NAME                    LAST 4 SS#


4 - EXTREME                     }  BLACK

To: CARE          Location:
- - - - - - - - - - - - - - - - - - - - -

1 - IMMEDIATE                   }
                                }  RED
To: CRISIS        Location:     }
INTERVENTION
- - - - - - - - - - - - - - - - - - - - -

2 - DELAYED                     }
                                }  YELLOW
To: GROUP         Location:     }
- - - - - - - - - - - - - - - - - - - - -

3 - MINIMAL                     }
                                }  GREEN
To: REST AREA OR  Location:     }
ASSIST ___R ___A
```

Figure 19.2. Triage Card that will be attached to victim. Attach a duplicate carbonless copy for triage person to keep. Children's victim tags should be attached to child's back.

SEE THE TRIAGE CARD TO BE USED BY TRIAGE PERSON

Figure 19.3. Triage Card to be used by Triage Person (Side One).

Crisis Intervention Qualifying Questions

(Deliver in a calm and reassuring manner)

1. Are you hurt? Have you seen medical?

   If yes to the first question and have not seen medical, refer to medical. If yes to the first question and have seen medical, continue with questions.

   If no to the first question: Do you currently take any medications? If so, what, and for what reason?

   If for medical issue...refer to med unit.

   If for psychological reason:

   If they have meds with them and seem stable, continue questioning.

   If they do not have meds with them, assess stability, find out when next dosage due and tag DELAYED, IMMEDIATE or EXTREME as further evaluated.

2. How are you doing with all of this?

   Pay attention to what they are saying and to how they are saying it. Also pay attention to what they are not saying. In addition, look for eye contact, nervousness, frustration, anger levels, body language, voice tone, pitch and pacing.

3. Are you feeling depressed? Suicidal? REMEMBER they MUST say they are or are not suicidal, if not ASK).

4. Have you ever gone through something like this before?

5. Do you have family or friends here?

Figure 19.4. Triage Card to be used by Triage Person (Side Two).

READ THE GUIDANCE CONCERNING PROPER USE OF TRIAGE CARD SYSTEM

1. After initial triage, additional re-triage will be necessary as treatment is provided to one group and as conditions change and become emergent.

2. The group initially classified as DELAYED will become the IMMEDIATEs after the initial IMMEDIATE group has been assisted.

3. Pay attention to those triaged as MINIMAL. Re-triage this group as needed.

4. Re-triage the EXTREMEs when IMMEDIATEs and DE-LAYEDs have been given emotional first aid.

5. Those triaged initially as MINIMAL need basic care. Crisis intervention in a group setting may work for some. Basic individual attention will work better for others. MINIMAL does not negate the need for assistance.

6. Enlist help in triage from those with limited clinical skills and from volunteers given "just-in-time" training. While these may not be able to provide ongoing crisis intervention, they can be trained on-site to do effective triage. At first, this may require some supervision by those more experienced in triage.

7. Basic crisis intervention skills may be taught to novices on-site as needed and as practical.

8. At times, the best crisis interveners are those without professional clinical training who receive specific practical crisis intervention instruction.

9. Use those available and willing to provide crisis intervention. Supervision and direction must be provided and followed in order to remain effective.

10. MINIMALs may be able to assist in the intervention process on an individual basis once assessed.

11. While doing crisis intervention, always be aware of latent or emergent medical conditions that may require immediate attention. Refer and escort to medical attention as needed. Medical first; crisis intervention second . . . as a general rule.

12. The triage card system consists of two cards: One for the Triage Person and the other to be attached to the victim once triaged. Both cards are shown. See Figures 19.2–19.4.

13. Side One of the Triage Person Card, contains information that the triage person can use along with the information in triage categories also presented. See Figure 19.3.

14. Side One of the Triage Person Card is for the use of the triage person only and is not shown to the victim. Clinical findings may be put on this card and is retained by the triage person.

15. Side Two of the Triage Person Card contains the specific questions asked by the triage person in order to begin and to conduct triage. See Figure 19.4.

16. The Victim Tag consists of the original tag and a copy. A carbonless copy system is recommended. Carbon can be used between the card and another card or paper as appropriate.

17. Once completed by the Triage Person, the Victim Tag is attached to the Victim. Preference should be given to attaching the Victim Tag directly to the victim's body rather than to their clothing. Clothing may be taken off thus increasing the possibility of losing the tag.

18. Children's Victim Tags should be secured to the back, or on the back, of the child as possible. This may help avoid having the tag torn off. A little creativity may go a long way here. How do you get the tag on their back? Perhaps put the tag on a lanyard or string as you might do with adult victims. Then rotate the string so that the tag in on the child's back. A small piece of tape may secure the tag to the back of the child's clothing, but will not cause the tag to be lost if the child is undressed.

19. A usual spot for attaching triage tags to the body is to attach the tag to a piece of string placed around the victim's neck. If this is not possible or practicable, consider on the wrist, arm or even the leg. The tag could be taped directly to the body surface if required. In unusual circumstances, consider writing on the person's forehead with a marker or lipstick. If you utilize this approach, the system provides a number from one to four indicating the triage categories: 4 = EXTREME; 3 = MINIMAL; 2 = DELAYED; and 1 = IMMEDIATE. Put the number and an indicator of the location of the victim. This will serve until something better can be used. Remember that the information about the victim should stay with the victim and be transported with the victim. Therefore victim information should be attached to the victim.

20. Only the information asked for on the Victim Tag should be provided.

21. The Victim Tag copy should be retained by the Triage Person and attached to the Triage Person's tag for that victim.

22. Note that the Victim Card contains the name of the victim and only the last four digits of his or her social security number.

23. The information on the Victim Card provides several items relating to each victim. A concerted effort has been made in this system not to provide any information which might contribute to further upsetting the victim or exacerbating the problems already experienced.

24. On the EXTREME segment, if this has been determined the category of the instant victim, it states that the person is to be taken "To: Care" and a location is provided. In this instance "To Care" means that the victim is to be placed in a custodial care area until such time as they can be re-triaged. If they have their own medications with them, they can be encouraged to self-medicate as they usually do, or with assistance. If it is possible to obtain needed psychotropic medications from the medical resources, do so. The location of the custodial care area should be noted on the card in the appropriate space. All three tags below this category should be torn off of the tag along the serrations. If no serrations, cut or tear off the bottom three sections leaving only the EXTREME tag attached to the person. The victim should be escorted carefully to the custodial care area.

25. On the IMMEDIATE segment, if this has been determined the category of the instant victim, it states that the victim is to be taken to "Crisis Intervention" and a location blank is provided. This person will receive care first and once triaged, should be immediately escorted to an active crisis intervener or mental health professional who will attend to them immediately. It could be that the triage person may have to give some care at the moment of triage and then pass the victim to a caregiver not involved directly in triage. Note the location to which the IMMEDIATE victim is taken. Detach, cut or tear off the two triage category tags left below the IMMEDIATE tag. At this point the top tag will read EXTREME and the second, or primary, tag will read IMMEDIATE.

26. If the triage category has been determined to be DELAYED, this should be noted on the proper segment of the triage tag by the triage person. DELAYED victims will be seen for care after IMMEDIATEs have received care. On this segment, the victim is directed "To Group," and a location indicator is provided as with the others. "To Group" means that this person will be escorted to an area containing other DELAYED victims and provided the opportunity for group interaction and group crisis intervention. This will be provided by a crisis intervener or mental health professional not otherwise involved in triage. Be sure to detach the triage tag segment below DELAYED prior to attaching the tag or escorting the victim.

27. If determined that the current victim is to be placed in the MINIMAL category, additional options are possible. MINIMAL sufferers have experienced the incident trauma, but manifest obvious coping skills that they are using to cope. If this is the triage determination, consider the possibility of asking those coping better to assist in performing triage under your or some other triage person's supervision. Make the request only an option that they can choose or not at their discretion. If they do not choose to assist with triage, suggest that they try to rest and relax and that they will be seen as soon as possible. These will be seen after the DELAYED category. On the MINIMAL segment of the triage tag, is indicated either R for REST or A for ASSIST in the appropriate section. If assisting with triage is their choice, indicate the triage location. If the choice of the victim is to rest, indicate the location of the rest area and escort them to that location as needed and as appropriate. A person in this category may make other choices for themselves. However, this becomes a matter of their personal responsibility. If this is the triage level selected for this person, leave the entire tag intact and attach to the person or child as mentioned above.

28. Do the best you can to insure that the triage tags remain with the respective victim. One person should not hold the tags for multiple people. The information contained should be available to those who will come later to treat or to re-triage.

29. When moving among victims, notice the presence or absence of triage tags. If no tag is observed, inquire. If the person requires aid or needs to be triaged, make sure that this happens.

30. Triage must always be seen as an ongoing process rather than a one-time event. Triage persons should remain active and look for the need to re-triage a victim into a different category based on need or available resources.

31. Triage categories will change as primary victims receive care. Be alert for this. The last expenditure of intervention resources should be to those in the EXTREME triage category. They will become the next IMMEDIATE category after all others have been helped and to the degree that resources are available.

32. A Reminder: Be sure to retain the copy generated on the Victim Triage Tag. Attach the victim tag to the victim and attach the copy to the respective Triage Person's card for that victim. Maintain these for future reference.

33. Another reminder: Triage persons should pay close attention to changes in the mental status of victims which may necessitate a triage category change. Category changes will be necessitated as higher priority categories are treated and released or re-categorized.

REVIEW THE CRISIS INTERVENER QUALIFYING QUESTIONS:

(Deliver in a calm and reassuring manner.)

1. Are you hurt? Have you seen medical?
   If yes to the first question and have not seen medical, refer to medical. If yes to the first question and have seen medical, continue with questions.
   If no to the first question: Do you currently take any medications? If so, what, and for what reason?
   If for medical issue . . . refer to med unit.
   If for psychological reason:
   If they have medications with them and seem stable, continue questioning.
   If they do not have medications with them, assess stability, find out when next dosage due and tag DELAYED, IMMEDIATE or EXTREME as further evaluated.
2. How are you doing with all of this?

Pay attention to what they are saying and to how they are saying it. Also pay attention to what they are not saying. In addition, look for eye contact, nervousness, frustration, anger levels, body language, voice tone, pitch and pacing.

3. Are you feeling depressed? Suicidal? REMEMBER they MUST say they are or are not suicidal, if not ASK).
4. Have you ever gone through something like this before?
5. Do you have family or friends here?

UTILIZE THE TRIAGE CHECKLISTS TO PERFORM TRIAGE

IMMEDIATE

☐ *Attitude and General Behavior* – Extremely upset, hyperactive, defiant, preoccupied, mistrustful, scared, limited self control.
Comments:

☐ *Mental Activity* – Self absorbed, illogical, irrelevant, difficulty expressing complete thoughts, generally coherent.
Comments:

☐ *Emotional Reactions* – Euphoric or depressed, apprehension, fear, labile, generally appropriate affect.
Comments:

☐ *Thoughts* – Some trouble forming clear thoughts, fearful, shut down.
Comments:

☐ *Orientation* – Clear sensorium.
Comments:

☐ *Fund of General Knowledge* – Appropriate to age and education, some production difficulties at the outset.
Comments:

☐ *Suicidality* – Thoughts may be present.
Comments:

☐ *Insight* – Limited.
Comments:

DELAYED

☐ *Attitude and General Behavior* – Upset, basically in control of self, mild mistrust, talkative.
Comments:

☐ *Mental Activity* – Accessible, worried, concerned about situation and that of others, compliant.

Comments:

☐ *Emotional Reactions* – Appropriate to the situation, anxiety, moderate fear, moderate depression.

Comments:

☐ *Thoughts* – May have difficulty accessing clear thoughts, may catastrophize, concern about others, wants to help self and others, may intellectualize situation and their response, stream of thoughts may be less than adequate to maintain a conversation.

Comments:

☐ *Orientation* –Sensorium clear in all three realms of time, person and place.

Comments:

☐ *Fund of General Knowledge* – Appropriate to age and education.

Comments:

☐ *Suicidality* – May have some fleeting suicidal ideations, denies suicidal desires.

Comments:

☐ *Insight* – Some, but still limited, less limited than those in IMMEDIATE category.

Comments:

MINIMAL

☐ *Attitude and General Behavior* – Presents well, preoccupied but in control of self, compliant and cooperative, responsive to inquiries, positive attitude.

Comments:

☐ *Mental Activity* – Accessible, coherent and relevant, alert and appropriately talkative.

Comments:

☐ *Emotional Reactions* – Appropriate affect, mild depression, mild fear, some anxiety, emotionally stable.

Comments:

☐ *Thoughts* – Within normal limits, relates to others easily, engages in conversation and is easily understood, maintains appropriate stream of thoughts.

Comments:

☐ *Orientation* – Well oriented in all spheres.

Comments:

☐ *Fund of General Knowledge* – Appropriate.

Comments:

☐ *Suicidality* – No suicidal ideation.
Comments:

☐ *Insight* – Appropriate to age, education and current experience.
Comments:

EXTREME

☐ *Attitude and General Behavior* – Disheveled and untidy, limited cooperation, mistrustful, suspicious, antagonistic, motor retardation or hyperactivity, perseveration.
Comments:

☐ *Mental Activity* – Self absorbed or inaccessible, circumstantial, flight of ideas, underproductive, mute, irrelevant, incoherent, illogical, blocking.
Comments:

☐ *Emotional Reactions* – Elation, exhilaration, depression, emotional instability, incongruity of thought content, ambivalence, emotional deterioration.
Comments:

☐ *Thoughts* – Delusions, hallucinations, paranoid ideations, grandiose ideas, autistic thinking, unreal ideas.
Comments:

☐ *Orientation* – Limited orientation in three spheres.
Comments:

☐ *Fund of General Knowledge* – May be appropriate.
Comments:

☐ *Suicidality* – Suicidal ideations may be present, prior suicidal behavior, plan of suicide clear, means of suicide clear.
Comments:

☐ *Insight* – May be nonexistent; Also, ask about a previous diagnosis or treatment and medications related to mental health problems. Probably, there will be positive responses to at least some of these inquiries.
Comments:

KNOW THE QUESTIONS TO DEVELOP THE NEEDED INFORMATION TO COMPLETE THE TRIAGE PROCESS

1. "All of you here, please give me your attention so that we can get you the help you need.

2. "Have you received the medical care you needed?" (Yes). If *no*, refer to medical triage. Escort as needed and as possible.

3. "Those who need immediate medical care or medications, please move over here so that we can get you the care you need."

4. Look for: Very distraught, screaming and yelling. Out of control or out of structure. Panic, unable to care for self effectively, illogical thinking, reacting to the disaster even though currently safe. Incoherent speech. (No). If *yes*, separate to alternate location. Tag IMMEDIATE.

5. Tell them "Please come with us. We are going to help you now."

6. If "no" to number 4, go to number 7.

7. Not screaming or yelling, but showing 1000 yard stare, crying, sobbing, wandering, autism, confusion. (No). If *yes*, these are DELAYED. Keep this group together and monitor. Reassure as a group.

8. Keep families together if at all possible.

9. Provide needed information about the situation and resources to the remaining group.

10. Remaining group accepts information as helpful. If *yes*, with limited symptomology, these are MINIMAL.

11. Enlist the aid of those willing MINIMALs to assist with other patients. Train them to triage as needed. Use them to help in other needed areas as their abilities and talents allow.

12. If no, information is not accepted as helpful, and displayed are symptoms of mental illness or chronic mental disabilities, these are EXTREME. Place away from others and do a custodial monitor of these.

13. DELAYED becomes the next IMMEDIATE after IMMEDIATE are helped.

14. MINIMALs become IMMEDIATE after the DELAYED are helped.

15. The EXTREME become the IMMEDIATE after all others have been helped and if resources are still available. They may require custodial care during this time.

16. Triage is an ongoing process that must be done continually. It is not a one-time procedure. Ongoing triage may change the grouping originally established.

17. Those with Medically Unexplained Symptoms (MUPS): These are sometimes inappropriately called the "Worried Well." These individuals should be taken seriously and guided toward an area where they can associate with other MUPS and have someone with whom to speak within that area. Individuals with MUPS are suffering as are others who are victims of a disaster. They have a right to be worried and they have developed symptoms that may need to be addressed either medically or psychologically. Pay due attention to this group. Do not disregard them as nonsufferers. That would be a mistake.

Summary and Epilogue

This system is a work in progress. It should be treated accordingly and improved upon as appropriate. There are many other systems of triage available. Some are better than others and more or less confusing and complicated. This author believes that the key is simplicity and specificity. This system involves two triage cards. The purpose of the two cards is that the victim/sufferer card has nothing on it concerning the condition of the victim. This was done thoughtfully in order to avoid creating additional problems or concerns for the victim, while at the same time directing them to appropriate care and care locations within whatever situation the triage person may find themselves. It is a card with a duplicate copy attached to be torn off and then attached to the Triage Person's evaluation card. This card can be serrated between categories and the nonapplicable categories detached. This is seen with other triage systems. The Triage Person's evaluation card is two-sided. Side one provides the triage categories with explanatory information to aid proper assessment. Side two contains the specific questions to be asked, and actions to be taken, to actually perform the triage, or to re-triage as needed.

Chapter 20

UNDERSTAND THE DANGERS OF DISASTER RESPONSE

It is likely that if you respond to a disaster you will find one uncertainty followed by another. And, this will continue throughout your involvement. Part of this uncertainty will be the danger that surrounds you. In a 2006 Gallup Poll of 1005 people, and published in *U.S.A. Today* August 9, 2006, we live in a "jittery world." Seventy-six percent of people view the world today as a more dangerous place than they did at other times in their life. Eighty-three percent of women and 67 percent of men saw our world as more dangerous. The standard of error was +/- 3 percentage points. With that said about relatively normal, nondisaster times, consider the following.

Your entry into a disaster situation as a responder carries with it the almost certainty of danger. Danger to yourself and danger to those with whom you may work. How you prepare for this now may well affect your survival under these circumstances. I have heard some who say that the key is to, "Suck it up; get over it; and move on." There may be some truth to that philosophy, but it is not enough. Neither are the "pollyanna" approaches of, "I can handle anything," or "I'm sure everything will be okay," or "Someone else will take care of that." We may need to adjust our mindset about danger before the fact just as we have discussed doing in other related areas such as standard-of-care. Not to do so, leaves us unduly vulnerable. The danger will be real and so must our preparations be reality based.

1. Understand the danger going in. Do not be surprised by it. If you do not want the danger, stay out. There is no disgrace in

that decision.
2. Plan for the worst.
3. Accept the dangerous nature of what you do.
4. Adjust your mindset to the reality of the almost certain danger.
5. What you do is dangerous and you will be in danger at various times.
6. Avoid platitudes when thinking about responder danger.
7. If needed, get help to accept the dangerous nature of your disaster work.
8. Discuss your concerns with significant others.
9. Get out of disaster work if you are unable to adjust to the eventualities. Disaster work is not for everyone. There is no disgrace in that. Your life and health, both physically and psychologically, are more important ultimately.
10. Not everyone can do this type of work.
11. Do not ignore this part of your disaster preparedness.
12. Do not make light of this issue. No one is immune.
13. Prepare yourself to take care of yourself under foreseeable, and even unforeseeable, circumstances.
14. Prepare–Prepare–Prepare.
15. Mindset–Mindset–Mindset.
16. Mental preparation comes through, (1) Training; (2) Acceptance of what could be encountered; (3) Considering the "If . . . Then" possibilities; (4) Playing the, "What if . . ." game; and (4) Flexibility and the recognition that change will be constant.
17. Consider the terrain in which you will be operating.
18. Take weather into account in your planning.
19. Avoid "siren psychosis." Prepare for the noise and the turmoil. You may have to work under these conditions.
20. Drive responsibly.
21. Plan–Plan–Plan.
22. Protect yourself and protect your team.
23. Remember that disasters are unsafe, uncertain and unpredictable.
24. Expect things to happen suddenly, unexpectedly and arbitrarily. This is true for disaster victims also. Crises often occur in this way.
25. Disaster = Danger.
26. Different disasters = different dangers.

27. Danger will always be present regardless of the disaster.
28. You must prevent yourself from becoming a disaster victim and from going into crisis because of your reaction to the danger factors.
29. Perception of danger depends on personal, professional and past experiences and exposures.
30. Handling of danger effectively may well depend on how you have handled dangerous situations in the past.
31. Self awareness becomes important to understanding your feelings regarding danger and to effectively dealing with danger during a disaster.
32. Prepare for, and to give end-of-life care to patients or victims you may encounter.
33. Expect deaths. In a disaster neither you nor anyone else can save everyone.
34. As needed and appropriate, speak with a disaster mental health specialist. Establish the relationship both for now and for later.

Chapter 21

EXPLORE THE UTILIZATION OF STATE DEFENSE FORCES: UNIFORMED MEDICAL RESERVE CORPS FOR DISASTER MEDICAL AND PSYCHOSOCIAL RESPONSE

The following may serve as a model for the utilization of State Military Forces as a Uniformed Medical Reserve Corps during a response to man-made and natural disasters. The medical, psychosocial and public health aspects of this utilization are key to the effectiveness of such a response. The organization of a state-wide medical reserve corps, organized along the lines of their civilian, county-based, counterparts, allows for a broader response capability. The military organization contributes the command and control element often missing in civilian medical reserve corps. The ability to deploy quickly, for extended periods, and to relate within the military framework as medical and support professionals is the key to overall success. The quotations from those with whom this contingent worked, seems to tell the main story about the value added.

"The stormy waters of Louisiana crashed against the sturdy shores of Texas." This quote from the Dallas Chief Medical Officer, Raymond Fowler, M.D., set the stage for what happened after Hurricane Katrina and Hurricane Rita in 2005, and for what follows here. Doctor Fowler went on to say that one-third of all those transported out of Louisiana were received by his service. Treatment was given to more than eight thousand patients in the first two week period. There were no fatalities and no adverse outcomes. And the Texas Medical Rangers of the Texas State Guard were an integral and pervasive part of making this happen.

The Texas State Guard was organized by Congressional passage of the state defense force statutes in 1940. The tradition of the Texas State Guard dates to the Republic of Texas in 1835. The Texas Medical Rangers have been established for only about 3 years. They were first organized within the Texas State Guard 10 March 2003 with the Headquarters in San Antonio, Texas. The northern area command was organized 27 March 2004. Texas Medical Rangers are a Uniformed Medical Reserve Corps developed much like their civilian counterparts. A major difference is the military structure and organization. Whereas civilian medical reserve corps are organized along county lines, the uniformed medical reserve corps is organized on a state-wide basis.

Deployment

The Texas Medical Rangers were first called to State Active Duty and deployed in the wake of Hurricane Katrina. They were again deployed shortly thereafter to respond to the effects of Hurricane Rita. This mandatory deployment of state military forces lasted for several weeks for each deployment.

The Rangers augmented the emergency medical care operations at the Dallas Convention Center, at Dallas Reunion Arena and established the Disaster Hospital site in Tyler, Texas. Heretofore, an untested good idea, the Rangers provided on-site medical and support assistance to evacuees and patients presenting for help. They provided roving medical patrols, on a twenty-four hour basis, to assess and reassess evacuees who might needs additional medical assistance. To their credit, several lives were saved by this procedure. They set up isolation areas to control disease, and instituted a hand-sanitizing program throughout their area of responsibility that actually prevented an epidemic. They worked continually for the Chief Medical Officer on the sites.

During the aftermath of Hurricane Rita, Texas Medical Rangers established and administered a Disaster Hospital provided for special needs patients evacuated from the South. An inspector from the Office of the Surgeon General of the United States said in her report that the hospital was a "best practices model. . . ." It was organized along the specifications of a field military hospital and, in so doing, was able to administer in an effective manner to hundreds in serious need of help. The military organizational ability of the uniformed medical reserve allowed this to happen flawlessly. Structure to the overall organization was provided where chaos may have prevailed.

Medical and Support

The Rangers brought many medical and support specialties to the assigned sites. These professionals included:

1. Physicians
2. Nurses
3. Physician Assistants
4. Psychologists and other Mental Health Professionals
5. Respiratory Therapists
6. Emergency Medical Technicians
7. Paramedics
8. Infection and Disease Control Specialists
9. Administration specialists
10. Logistics Personnel
11. Operations Officers
12. Command Staff Officers and Command Sergeants Major
13. Computer Operators
14. Force Protection Personnel
15. Laboratory Technicians

Significant Quotation

"Y'all's efforts controlled an epidemic." This quote from Doctor Fowler begins to spell out the value of the Texas Medical Rangers, Uniformed Medical Reserve Corps. An outbreak of dysentery was occurring when the Rangers arrived in Dallas. At the direction of the Chief Medical Officer, instituting a 100 percent hand-sanitizing program throughout the Dallas Convention Center and Dallas Reunion Area almost immediately brought an end to this potentially destructive outbreak.

The Numbers

Numbers of evacuees assigned to the various sites worked by the

Texas Medical Rangers at any one time were as follows:

Reunion Arena	7,649
Dallas Convention Center	12,659
Tyler Disaster Hospital	800

Illnesses and Conditions Treated

Illnesses treated included:

- Special needs
- Wound care
- 1 Baby delivered
- 2 Myocardial infarctions
- Diabetes
- Mental health problems
- Hypertension
- Diarrhea
- Heat injuries
- Asthma
- Respiratory illnesses in children
- Isolation for dysentery and vomiting
- Viral meningitis
- Injuries due to off-site fighting
- Tuberculosis
- HIV

Quotation

Doctor Fowler, the Chief Medical Officer in Dallas reported that, "The Urgent Care Clinic at Dallas Convention Center is seeing more patients in a 24-hour period than the Emergency Room at the county Parkland Hospital. Parkland sees 300 patients per day. The clinic at Dallas Convention Center is seeing 719 patients on average in a 24-hour period."

During this increase of patients at the convention center, no increase occurred in the patients seen in the Parkland Emergency Room when compared to both 2004 and 2005 figures. The implication for the Medical Rangers is that they contributed to developing the surge capacity that was so urgently needed.

Strength

Texas Medical Ranger strength included:

Medical in Dallas	30
Non-Medical in Dallas	20
Medical and Non-Medical in Tyler	23

Duties

Daily duties included:

- 2 Medic Team Roving Patrols (2 soldiers each team)
- 1 Team Isolation Management (2 soldiers)
- Laboratory assistance (1 soldier)
- Administrative (9 soldiers)

Over 6000 man-hours were worked.

Key Events

Key events occurring during the several deployments included:

1. Rangers worked with the chief county epidemiologist to effectively handle the diarrhea outbreak.
2. Rangers were assigned by the Chief Medical Officer, and administered mandatory hand-sanitizing for all residents and workers.
3. Roving teams of medics identified many patients with mental and physical needs that might have otherwise been overlooked.
4. Unsanitary conditions in the feeding lines were corrected.
5. Reorganized the feeding procedures to make them more efficient.
6. Designed and built an isolation and containment area to control a dysentery outbreak at the direction of the County Public Health Officers and the Chief Medical Officer.
7. Worked with officials of the Centers for Disease Control.
8. Recognized, treated and referred cases involving heat injuries to evacuees.
9. Found and returned several lost children.
10. Obtained help for evacuees identified with mental health is-

sues.

11. Reconnaissance of Reunion Arena residents.
12. Assistance to evacuees in the FEMA lines.
13. Evacuation of chest pain victim from assistance lines.
14. Identification of several critical diabetic patients.
15. Coordinated Tuberculosis control with Dallas County Health Department.
16. Shelter management.
17. Assisted individuals in obtaining identification cards.
18. Developed a Psychological Force Protection program.
19. Identified abandoned beds and public health problems.
20. Provided assistance to special needs and nursing home patients.

Deployment Events

There were three main roles that were filled by the Texas Medical Rangers at the Dallas Convention Center and at Reunion Arena. These three functions included providing roving medic teams, assessing public health needs for, and participating in, infection control, and staffing of the urgent care area.

Roving Medic Teams—Upon arrival at the convention center and after Colonel James L. Greenstone and Captain Mark Ottens had spoken with the Chief Medical Officer (CMO), roving medic teams were established throughout the convention center. These roving medic teams were found to be invaluable to the health and welfare of the population. They identified physical and mental health issues that would have undoubtedly gone unnoticed and led to less than desirable outcomes or even death. Some of the events that the medics discovered and cared for are as follows:

All roving teams early on in the deployment started immediately noticing patients with extreme mental disturbances that had not received care. They were able to assist these individuals many of whom allegedly had been sexually assaulted or witnessed terrible actions during their evacuation from Louisiana.

The roving team of First Lieutenant Richard Nessner and Sergeant Olivia Anderson identified a way to better route evacuees through the lunch line. This better organization allowed for the enforcement of proper hand hygiene to prevent disease proliferation.

The roving team of Technical Sergeant Lisa Bureau and Specialist

Terry Smith found food vendors in the convention center who were passing out food without hand hygiene in place and with no use of gloves. They immediately corrected the issue, and averted a problem.

When FEMA opened their registration line outside in the heat on a day with the heat index above 100 degrees, the roving team of First Lieutenant Mike Hudson and Major William Kaschub were sent to watch for heat injuries. Four evacuees had to be sent to the hospital for care due to heat injuries. Major Steve Sanderfer and Captain Mark Ottens were notified of the problem and took Gatorade and cold water to the line and convinced FEMA to move it inside where it was cooler.

The roving teams maintained surveillance of hand hygiene on the food line. On several occasions they professionally and immediately shut down the serving line when they found that hand hygiene principles were not in place. The lines were reopened when hand-sanitizing was established.

Technical Sergeant Lisa Bureau and Specialist Terry Smith attended an individual who, while in the FEMA line, started having chest pains. He was rapidly evacuated to a medical facility where emergency care could be delivered. It was later discovered that this gentleman had a heart attack.

Technical Sergeant Bureau and Specialist Smith on four separate occasions during the deployment identified patients who did not appear to be well. Upon further assessment these patients were found to have severely low blood sugar due to their poorly managed diabetes. Bureau and Smith are credited by the CMO for having saved the lives of these individuals.

Second Lieutenant Harold Timboe and First Lieutenant Richard Nessner noticed that evacuees were moving out of the convention center and had left their bedding behind. This was determined to be a public health hazard. A process for tagging and removing abandoned bedding and personal belongings was developed during a conference with the Chief Medical Officer. This process was then initiated by the medic teams to control a potential health hazard.

As the population of the convention center dwindled and the population at Reunion Arena increased, roving teams were sent to Reunion Arena to be the only medical teams that were on the floor to assess the needs of the population. They did have Dallas Fire Department on the scene to utilize as needed for evacuation of patients.

Public Health Issues

The public health needs of such a large number of people packed into a tight space were evident. The infection control aspect of dealing with the issues of having so many people fell to the medical personnel of the Texas Medical Rangers. An outbreak of infectious dysentery was well underway upon arrival of the Texas Medical Rangers. With the implementation of hand hygiene and infection control procedures, this potentially disastrous epidemic was prevented. The Chief Medical Officer, Doctor Fowler stated that, "The Texas Medical Rangers prevented an epidemic."

Major Carol Olivier and Sergeant DiAnna Jones upon their arrival, began to work with Doctor John Carlo, Chief Epidemiologist with Dallas County Health and Human Services, to do surveillance on the source of the outbreak of dysentery. The CDC epidemiologists arrived, and the Rangers were attached to them to continue the search for the source of the outbreak. It was determined early on that the source was most likely poor hand hygiene. A hand hygiene policy was placed into effect that required all persons entering and exiting any area of the convention center, food lines, and bathrooms to use alcohol based hand sanitizer. Within only a few days the epidemic was under control.

Major Olivier and Sergeant Jones, upon recommendation from the CDC, designed, built, and organized both an isolation and containment area for both pediatric and adult patients to prevent the spread of infectious dysentery and vomiting. This proved to be a highly efficient and effective way to prevent spread of disease in those persons already affected.

All of the Texas Medical Ranger staff maintained due diligence by monitoring and enforcing the hand hygiene policy throughout the deployment.

As a public health recommendation the Rangers identified trash and abandoned bedding that needed to be removed. They assisted in educating the population and removing these items as necessary.

Rangers provided the primary force for staffing of the adult and pediatric isolation area. Most of the civilian volunteers were not willing to go into this area. Texas Medical Ranger nurses, Emergency Medical Technicians, Paramedics, and doctors staffed this area 24 hours a day until its closure at the point that it was no longer needed.

Texas Medical Ranger staff was asked to maintain public health surveillance of Reunion Arena. This was done by sending teams of infection control specialists to that location to report back to the Chief Medical Officer with their findings.

Urgent Care

The urgent care area at the Convention Center was a highly functional area that saw patients 24 hours a day and 7 days a week. They averaged 719 patients a day and by the end of the deployment had seen more than 8000 patients. More than 300 patients were evacuated to the hospital. They helped to maintain the health of the population, and, as a result, there were no deaths or severe adverse events at the convention center. The Texas Medical Rangers augmented the civilian volunteer staff in this area.

Rangers provided the only Medical Technicians to staff the lab during the entire operation. They maintained the staffing in this area 24 hours a day until the clinic closed.

Nurses and Paramedics triaged patients continually.

There were Nurses, Paramedics, Physician's Assistants, and Physicians on duty in the Urgent Care from the Texas Medical Rangers to augment the civilian staff for virtually 24 hours of every day. For the last week of the deployment, after nearly all of the civilian volunteers left, Rangers provided the main force for staffing of this area.

Texas Medical Rangers found and treated, along with the civilian volunteer doctors, an infant that was suffering from infectious dysentery. This case was so severe that, according to the Chief Medical Officer, the infant was near death. Through quick treatment and fluid resuscitation this infant was saved.

Dignitaries

Several dignitaries visited Dallas Convention Center to witness the efforts, among others, of the Texas Medical Rangers. These included:

U.S. Surgeon General Richard Carmona
Mayor Laura Miller–Dallas
Mayor Nagin–New Orleans
Kathleen Blanco–Governor of Louisiana
Kay Bailey Hutchison–Senator from Texas

Pete Sessions–U.S. Congressman
Michael Levitt–Director of U.S. Department Health and
    Human Services
Major General Jerry Ragsdale–Commander, Texas Air National
    Guard
Major General Richard Box–Commander, Texas State Guard
Major General Charles Rodriguez–Texas Adjutant General
Colonel Cruz Medina–Task Commander, Texas Army National
    Guard
Colonel Raymond Peters–Chief of Staff, Texas State Guard
Command Sergeant Major Robert Smith–Texas State Guard

Operations

The Texas Medical Rangers at Dallas Convention Center, Dallas Reunion Arena and Tyler, Texas functioned in a highly organized manner. Shifts were staffed from 0800–2000 and 2000–0800 daily. There was an Officer-in-Charge and a Noncommissioned Officer-in-Charge for each shift. Brigadier General Scantlin, the North Texas Area Commander and the Deputy Commanding General of the Texas Medical Rangers held a daily briefing for anyone who wanted to stay abreast of the events and to address concerns of the previous day. Also, there was a daily meeting conducted for the Texas Medical Ranger's Command Staff with the Chief Medical Officer, Doctor Ray Fowler. This was done in order to stay abreast of medical concerns and events related to the treatment and housing of evacuees. A formation of Ranger personnel was held prior to each shift to inform every one of events and of the mission. This allowed the troops to be informed of conditions as they changed, and to give specific assignments.

In addition, Captain Robert Rainey served as the Psychological Force Protection/Protective Medicine Officer for the Texas Medical Rangers. As troops became overwhelmed with the burden of caring for thousands of evacuees who had lost everything, Captain Rainey maintained contact with them to assist as needed. As a result, morale and psychological injuries were minimal. Captain Leopold Celiz served as Physical Force Protection Officer-in-Charge to make sure that the belongings of personnel were protected at all times.

Command Staff Texas Medical Rangers

The Command Staff of the Texas Medical Rangers deployed in the North was composed of the following:

Brigadier General Marshall Scantlin–NORTEX Area Task Force Commander
CSM Bill Schaaf–Area Command Sergeant Major
COL James Greenstone–Deputy Area Commander–Medical
Command Sergeant Major Cecil Rickman–Deputy Area Command Sergeant Major–Medical
Major Steve Sanderfer–Acting Executive Officer
Captain Phil Vaughn–Personnel Officer
Lieutenant Colonel Paul Moore–Executive Officer
Captain Mark Ottens–Operations Officer
Captain Robert Rainey–Logistics Officer

Observations

There were several observations that were made to improve future deployments of the Texas Medical Rangers.

a. Deployment packets must be ready at all times.
b. Early meetings should be established with the Chief Medical Officer.
c. Medical Supplies should be available to augment medic supplies.
d. Communications must be established early and maintained with appropriate and sturdy communications equipment.
e. Texas Medical Ranger staff should be in place and ready to assist early on with the psychological effects of deployment.
f. For long deployments laundry and billeting must be arranged in advance.
g. Office supplies (Paper, Pens, Pencils, Computers, Printers, Projector, and Fax Machine) should be maintained on a stand-by basis to take care of required forms and reports.
h. Water-tight boxes need to be obtained to pack deployment gear in for easy access and transportation.

There have been many historical moments for the Texas Medical Rangers, Medical Reserve Corps (MRC), since it was first deployed for Hurricanes Katrina and Rita. Another major history-making event occurred in Tyler, Texas. A representative of the United States Public Health Service, from Surgeon General Carmona's office, visited the Tyler shelter. She told Dr. Luis Fernandez, Tyler Medical Response Group Commanding Officer, and the Disaster Hospital Commander, that this was not a "shelter" or even a "special needs shelter." It was truly a Disaster Hospital organized and run on the military medical scale and was a "best of practice model." The Texas Medical Rangers were an untested good idea prior to Katrina. They are now tested veterans who can augment a major disaster medical system. They are also capable of staffing and running a full-blown disaster hospital. What has been accomplished may well serve as the model for such disaster responses, at least according to the words of Doctor Carmona's representative. As a uniformed MRC, we have a lot of which to be very proud. Texas Medical Rangers will always go where they are needed and they will do whatever is necessary to accomplish the mission.

Chapter 22

UNDERSTAND THE RELATIONSHIP BETWEEN CRISIS INTERVENTION AND CRITICAL INCIDENT STRESS MANAGEMENT

Some confusion seems to exist about the relationship of Critical Incident Stress Management to Crisis Intervention. Are they the same? Are they different? Is one merely a specialized part of the other? And how do they both relate to the practice of the psychotherapy and psychoeducation? Many novices and those without well-grounded historical perspectives may benefit from added clarification of these issues. This will attempt to provide this clarity.

Introduction and Statement of the Problem

The discipline of Crisis Intervention has long suffered from its own identity crisis. Often confused with other specialty areas, it was subsumed as though it were the step-child of Psychology in particular and the social sciences in general. Neither is the venue of Crisis Intervention, and many, including Greenstone (1982, 1989), Leviton (1982), Rosenbluh (1986), Fowler (1989), and others have spent much of their individual and collective careers in the pursuit of clarification of this point. As noted by Doctor Sharon Leviton as early as 1979, "Crisis Intervention or Crisis Management, although firmly rooted in current and accepted psychological and social scientific theory, is a recognizable and distinct discipline unto itself."

With the advent, years ago, of current Critical Incident Stress Management theory and procedures (Mitchell, 1982, 1983), again the confusion among the new professionals in the field, as well as those without historical perspective in the field, rears its head only to add to the problems of this advancing field. Critical Incident Stress Management concepts are certainly not new in the overall history of stress management in this country and elsewhere.

Neither are the bases for Crisis Management. Thanks to current leaders such as Mitchell, in the former, and Bard, Rosenbluh, Resnik, Schneidman, Hafen, Fowler, Leviton and others, in the latter, modern theory and practice has emerged.

As this occurs, it seems prudent that we should attempt to define and to clarify the parameters of these two professional areas. Additionally, we should attempt to discern their relationship to those closely akin.

This writing will attempt to do just that, at least from the perspective of the author and his colleagues. Failure to do so has already, and may continue, to create confusion in the minds of those entering these fields. Additionally, it often occurs that the novice who fails to recognize the relationship of their activity to already established disciplines, may spend much wasted time, "re-inventing the wheel," as it were. Such massive expenditures of energy might better be spent advancing the established discipline to the benefit of all and to the satisfaction of the professionals involved.

Definitions and relationships, once established and understood, will reduce overall confusion. Also, it will reduce specific confusion about such things as:

1. Is Crisis Intervention a form of psychotherapy?
2. Is Critical Incident Stress Management a psychotherapeutic or psychoeducational process?
3. Is Critical Incident Stress Management a form of Crisis Intervention?
4. What is the role of the Peer Counselor in either Crisis Intervention or a Critical Incident Stress Debriefing?
5. Do mental health professionals do Crisis Intervention?
6. Are mental health professionals required for Critical Incident Stress Debriefing purposes?
7. Are mental health professionals required for Crisis Intervention procedures to be utilized?
8. Are both Crisis Intervention and Critical Incident Stress Management procedures designed each for separate or similar

groups? If so, when? If not, why not?

9. Should mental health professionals desist from their primary role while acting in the role of a debriefer or stress manager?

10. What is the relationship of Crisis Intervention to psychotherapeutic thought, Crisis Counseling, short term theory, group theory, and indeed, to the procedures advocated in Critical Incident Stress Management?

Historical Perspective

Crisis Intervention techniques are not a recent innovation. Crisis Intervention, in its broadest sense, dates back to man's earliest days. One person with a problem came to another person and was met with understanding, support, and active assistance rather than being rejected and possibly attacked for being viewed as weak. The term "crisis" came into Psychology from Medicine. Hippocrates used it for the sudden cessation of a state which was gravely endangering life, in contrast to the slow "lysis." Analogously, a crisis is thought of, in this context, as being a dramatic decision or coming to terms with mental conflict (Eysenck, 1972).

The movement for assisting individuals who have experienced crisis in their lives has existed since the beginning of this century. 1906 saw the development of National Save-A-Life League in New York and Suicide Centers in Chicago. However, credit for the development of modern Crisis Intervention theory, as known today, is given to Gerald Caplan and Erich Lindemann. Their work in the 1940s emphasized that an individual under great personal stress could be assisted in regaining the ability to function as he or she usually did through skillful third-party intervention. According to this concept everyone during the course of his or her life is susceptible to stress and tension. If this stress reaches unusual proportions, a person may experience crisis. During these times the person is particularly open to change, and if change occurs, it may be in a positive and productive direction or in a negative and nonproductive way. The quality and intensity of the stress are important considerations in knowing which direction the crisis victim will turn. The intervener's task is to help the individual avoid falling back on previous maladaptive or nonproductive coping mechanisms and thereby to use the crisis itself as a way of making significant development gains.

Crisis Intervention, as a field of study is a developing and emerging discipline. In its current modified form, it has precursors dating back to the 1930s and 1940s. Much of the credit for modern Crisis Intervention theory is generally given to Lindemann, Querido, and Caplan.

Lindemann (1944) focused his efforts on identifying the common mourning characteristics of individuals who lost loved ones and relatives in the 1943 Coconut Grove Club fire in Boston, Massachusetts. Lindemann's study supported the notion that there are several characteristics common to all individuals who experience acute grief, and that particular crises result in specific types of post-crisis behavior.

Querido (1968) developed a "psychiatric first aid service" in Amsterdam which provided support services to the police and hospitals. Querido screened admission to hospitals while also providing Crisis Intervention to those in need. A similar first aid approach was used with combat military personnel in World War Two and in the Korean War. Those personnel who were suffering from "combat fatigue" (temporary personality disintegration) were provided with warm food, sedation, and interpersonal support. Further, the support was provided as close as possible to the combat zone, which aided in providing speedy service to the victims, leading to a more rapid recovery time.

Several authors (Zusman, 1975; Schneidman, Farberow, and Litman, 1970; Lindemann, 1944) have indicated that failure to complete the grief process may precede a later psychiatric or psychosomatic illness. Caplan (1964) notes that an individual begins to make attempts to decrease or eliminate stress producing factors. In trying to eliminate or reduce the stress, the individual moves through several developmental phases. If the stress and accompanying feelings of guilt, fear and worthlessness are not reduced, then the person's personality may become involved in a major disorganization. As a result of this change, several ego-saving mechanisms will be utilized; namely, ag-gression, repression, withdrawal, or regression.

The work of Caplan and Lindemann indicated that an individual under emotional stress may require assistance. When stress reaches unusual proportions, the individual experiences crisis. During the crisis time, the individual is open to change. This change can be productive and positive, or it may be nonproductive and negative. The role of the intervener is to assist the crisis victim to avoid using maladaptive and nonproductive coping mechanisms. Further, the intervener must help the victim return to pre-crisis levels of functioning and to aid them in seeking the avenues for adequate coping skills as well as personal growth.

Programs designed to deal with human crises have existed in this country for many years. As a result of unusually high stress brought on by certain events that may occur without warning and in a sudden fashion, a person may experience an inability to cope with life in the way he or she would under more normal conditions. Rape, natural disasters, domestic disputes, child abuse and the like can each produce sufficient stress to create a crisis. Interested groups, lay persons, helping professionals and crisis-oriented agencies have sprung up to offer assistance in such situations.

Early studies of the victims of man-made disasters and families affected by wartime deaths set the stage for what has been emerging as the modern discipline of Crisis Intervention, or Crisis Management. As techniques developed, they were applied to many diverse fields, including law enforcement, penology, social science, business, religion and nursing. Many definitions of Crisis Intervention appeared, and as the term gained professional acceptance, books and papers were written under this popular heading, covering topics from psychotherapeutic techniques to short-term counseling. Yet Crisis Intervention was regarded as the stepchild to all other helping disciplines, such as sociology, psychology and psychiatry, while having little or no fixed and recognized place of its own. Few academic institutions addressed this particular area separately, and it was seen as part of some larger psychotherapeutic or counseling concern. It was thought that good counselors also made good crisis interveners; those who could handle day-to-day counseling sessions were assumed to be quite capable of intervening in emergencies and severe stress-related incidents.

Various mental health professionals, authors and theorists have placed much emphasis on providing immediate help to those individuals who are experiencing great distress in their lives. Private and community clinics were established to provide such care on a walk-in basis without the fixed appointment required in more traditional settings. The Benjamin Rush Center in Los Angeles and the New York Medical College-Metropolitan Hospital Center Walk-In Clinic both organized in 1967, were based on this concept. Such intervention centers concentrated on what could be done at that critical time when a person is in crisis to help the person return to his or her former level of pre-crisis functioning. If such assistance is available, the likelihood that the crisis victim will need subsequent psychotherapy due to prolonged maladjustment is reduced.

In addition to the development of crisis centers, there was a great increase in the use of the telephone as an effective means of crisis management, beginning in the 1950s with the opening of the Suicide Prevention Center in Los Angeles. The immediacy of crisis situations dictates the need for services to be delivered as soon as possible after the occurrence of the crisis. Hotline services can be as close as the telephone itself and are usually available 24 hours a day, seven days a week. The major reason for their proliferation since the 1950s was related not only to the ease and speed they supply in obtaining assistance, but also to the almost complete anonymity they provide to persons who call for help. As a rule the caller or crisis victim can obtain the complete services of the hotline without the need of self-identification. Suicide prevention centers, crisis intervention centers, drug abuse hotlines, venereal disease information centers and gay hotlines are only a few of the telephone services that have gained great popularity in this country.

Similar to the crisis hotline, teen and elderly assistance hotlines have also provided a special service to a particular population with particular problems. Teen hotlines were usually open during times when a teenager is most likely to call. Boston's Rescue, Inc. called its elderly members every day. The calls served several purposes. If no one answered the phone when the call was placed, a worker made a house visit immediately to check for any emergency that may have occurred. In addition, since the calls to senior citizens were made by other senior citizens, they have a social aspect, benefiting both the member and the caller. Such services are sometimes made available at no cost, while at other times agencies may require a fee from each participating member. Some crisis intervention hotlines opened their lines to those with general living problems, even though such problems may not as yet have escalated to crisis proportions. In this way a preventive aspect of crisis management was augmented.

Crisis Intervention and conflict management for police officers have also been a major area of concern. Because the police officer has often been the first line of response during such crises as domestic disputes, training was developed to assist the responding officer in providing skillful and immediate aid before such situations could deteriorate into violence and self-destruction. Studies made in the 1970s showed that more and more of a police officer's time was spent handling social, interpersonal-type problems and situations. A sample taken within the Miami Police Department for the year 1970 indicated that 61 percent of the calls answered were related to serviced-type requests rather than to criminal activity. These service requests included family disputes, neighborhood concerns of a noncriminal nature, juvenile problems, general disturbances and other crisis situations.

Traditionally, police officers have felt that responding to personal or psychological needs of a citizen was not part of "real" police work. While this notion is still held to some extent, more officers have begun to realize the relationship between such needs and "real" police work. Moreover, the greater confidence the public has in the ability of the police officer to handle personal crisis situations, the more they will trust the officer to deal with situations of a criminal nature. For some, the police officer is the first person they think to call when anything out of the ordinary happens. For others a policeman may be the only resource available. It has therefore become vital to supply human relations and Crisis Management skills to police officers during training and to reinforce these skills continually thereafter. Today's police academies are better in these areas than they were years ago; however, in most instances they must do more to increase the awareness of their graduates to the need for proficiency in these vital human need areas. The cop on the beat is not supposed to replace the psychologist or the social worker. He can, however, learn to be as effective in administering emotional first aid as he is in supplying physical first aid.

During the 1970s suicide prevention and other crisis intervention centers made extensive use of a new delivery system for responding to crisis situations: the nonprofessional or lay person. The nonprofessional volunteer may have contributed more than any other single source to the rapid development of crisis intervention services. According to some, little progress was made in the field of suicide prevention until the volunteer worker came into the picture. With the advent of such workers, persons who were suffering from acute crises in their lives could get help more quickly and efficiently than if the services had to be delivered by trained professionals.

The effectiveness of the nonprofessional has received a great deal of examination. From the Los Angeles Suicide Prevention Center comes what is known as "Litman's Law"; simply stated, the more severe the suicidal crisis is for a particular individual, the less need there is for a highly-trained professional to handle it. This is not to say that the trained professional does not handle such crises well. The implication is rather that the training and skills usually identified with the professional are not necessary to get the job done. It is more important, especially in the more serious cases, to show human concern, good judgment and a willingness to intervene immediately. In handling crises professionals may experience what has been described as a barrier that acts as a professional armor. This armor is developed during the professional training and is the way in which the professional may protect his or her own vulnerabilities. The essential difference between the professional and the nonprofessional is that while the professional may try to deal objectively with the problems presented, the volunteer is willing to deal subjectively, and perhaps to a better end in these particular situations. In the Crisis Intervention field, the volunteers may be the "real professionals."

Because the very nature of a crisis indicates that it is related to a present, here-and-now event in the victim's life, the customary delving into a person's psychology is for the most part unnecessary and even undesirable. Probing into the unconscious or into the childhood roots of the problems experienced may not be suitable or helpful to the victim who needs quick and, often, directed assistance. The training of the professional therapist is usually not aimed in this direction; therefore the therapist may not be able to offer the crisis victim the avenues needed at that particular time in his or her life. If the professional is unaccustomed to working in this mode, his delivery of services will suffer. In a sense, he cannot give that which he does not have. Years of dedicated training may not serve the therapist well or even at all under such circumstances. The professional may be asked to assume a role for which the nonprofessional is already better equipped. Because the nonprofessional is not likely to be influenced by the formal training of the therapist, they may be better able to function in crisis situations and to achieve quicker and more lasting results. To understand the need for utilizing the nonprofessional, it is important to see that just as psychopathological disorders may require a particular type of treatment that is best given by the trained psychologist or psychiatrist, the particular type of human disorder known as crisis may require a different and yet a no less-effective type of treatment, which the nonprofessional volunteer may be better equipped to handle.

Besides the many reasons why the nonprofessional worker may be better suited for the task of Crisis Intervention than the trained professional, in many crisis centers the volunteer has been the only person willing to take on the task of service delivery. In some cases professionals in the community have not been willing to provide the needed manpower and expertise to adequately staff crisis centers, hotlines and suicide prevention centers. As a result, the nonprofessional volunteer worker has stepped in to fill what was fast becoming a prominent void. While collaboration with professionals in the community is very important, someone has to supply the vital services, and in many cases that someone has been the volunteer.

In 1959, Friends, Inc. developed a program in Miami, Florida, that used the nonprofessional in interpersonal relationships relating to crises. This program clearly demonstrated the value of the volunteer. At about the same time, the Samaritans in England were providing crisis services internationally. The success of this program, whose fame spread throughout the United Kingdom, was also due to the skill and dedication of the nonprofessional, who was able and willing to extend himself or herself to whoever was in need.

We Care, Inc. formed in Orlando, Florida in 1965, served as an example of the effective use of the nonprofessional for many centers that followed soon after, including Brevard County Suicide Prevention Center. These centers set the standard for Lifeline in Miami as well as agencies of a similar nature in 19 cities and six states throughout the Southeast. The nonprofessional volunteer stood out as the primary agent in the crisis delivery system. Two surveys indicated that more than 80 percent of all crisis management programs utilized such volunteers to work directly with people who called the hotline numbers. In some instances, in which professionals were utilized during the initial formation of a Crisis Intervention or suicide prevention program, the professionals themselves soon began recruiting nonprofessionals to fill their jobs. Such a move clearly indicated the professional's recognition that the volunteer was able to respond better to a person in crisis. What also became apparent was that the professionally trained therapist or social worker was more valuable as a consultant or as a backup resource to those manning the phone.

In 1969, the Southern Indiana Chapter of the National Conference of Christians and Jews began a project in Louisville, Kentucky designed to provide training in community relations and Crisis Intervention. As it developed, the project gave professionals, paraprofessionals and nonprofessionals training and experience in techniques of Crisis Management that could prevent serious emotional upsets from becoming disastrous to the persons involved. Three years later an offshoot of this initial program was established to show that Crisis Intervention procedures and principles could be applied to any crisis situation. For example, the methods used by police officers could also be employed by crisis center counselors. The major proponents of this interdisciplinary approach were Doctor Edward S. Rosenbluh and Doctor James L. Greenstone, who began piecing it together in 1963 while at the University of Oklahoma; Lieutenant James E. Oney of the Louisville Division of Police; and Doctor Kent A. Rensin, a former police officer and high school administrator. It was at about this same time that Doctor Rosenbluh coined the term, "Emotional First Aid" to help describe the function and purpose of Crisis Intervention.

From these beginnings, the National Institute for Training in Crisis Intervention emerged. On a regularly scheduled basis, students of Crisis Management, regardless of professional credentials, could receive specific and expert training. The National Institute laid the groundwork in 1976 for the formation of the American Academy of Crisis Intervention. Crisis workers in all settings could now identify with their own organization rather than being subsumed as part of another group. The Southwestern Academy of Crisis Interveners formed in 1978 and aligned itself with the American Academy, although it remained separately incorporated. Subsequently, the National Training Conference for Crisis Intervention developed and offered graduated levels of training. Following the introduction of basic, intermediate and advanced levels of Crisis Management training, in 1980, a certification program was established to allow any crisis worker, who qualified, to be certified within his or her own discipline. All training adhered to the interdisciplinary concept that permits not only the needed social interaction among agencies, but also the sharing of their skills to the mutual benefit of all.

Crisis Intervention services today are offered through a variety of professional, paraprofessional and lay agencies throughout the country. Specialized community-funded agencies, such as rape crisis and suicide prevention centers, staffed with mental health professionals, paraprofessionals and nonprofessional volunteers exist in larger cities. General service crisis centers and hotlines for emergency intervention and referral seem to be more prevalent. They are manned by lay persons, who may or may not have had formalized training, or by paraprofessionals, although they may have professionals on staff. The quality of service offered often varies widely, as do the facilities used to provide such services. Where public funding is not available, or when such agencies cannot qualify for funds, money is often obtained from private donors. As a result some agencies may be able to rent better space, buy higher-quality equipment, entice more highly-trained staff or consultants and afford greater training for all personnel. The better funded agencies seem to last longer than those less fortunate.

Both volunteer and paid-staff agencies often experienced high burnout rates; continual motivation of volunteers was often seen as a major personnel problem for such agencies. In addition, while crisis agencies of various descriptions sprung up regularly in this country, they disappeared from existence almost as regularly. By the time *Hotline: Crisis Intervention Directory* was published, many of the agencies in operation during the research phase of the book no longer existed. Change of individual and group priorities, inadequate funds, decline of interest, lack of personnel, absence of leadership, withdrawal of public grants and the like all seemed to contribute to the demise of crisis intervention agencies.

The agencies that survived funding problems and worked out staffing contingencies provided an invaluable refuge for those who experienced crises resulting from highly stressful, sudden and unexpected emotional and psychological trauma. Telephone hotlines supplied information, crisis intervention and referral to additional or ongoing assistance. Rape crisis centers and spouse and child abuse centers offered individual and advocacy services to those in need. Many agencies also afforded ongoing counseling and residential and other specialized services for those who initially sought help because of a personal crisis. A concern of some centers was the families of those who are experiencing a crisis, including the survivors of suicide victims, the families of those undergoing an alcohol crisis and the children and spouses who have been physically or emotionally abused by the primary crisis victim.

Crisis Intervention services have also become increasingly available from trained police officers in the field. Domestic disputes, suicides, rape and critical incident stress are being more sensitively handled than ever before because of greater emphasis on emergency intervention training for all officers. A slow change in the attitudes of police officers toward the effects of crime on the public has also taken place. When crimes such as robbery, burglary, assault, rape and murder are viewed as potential crisis situations for victims, police officers can demonstrate a greater degree of sensitivity to either avoid or manage such crisis while still maintaining a high degree of job efficiency (see Figure 22.1. Crime-Crisis Continuum). The younger officers in the police academies seem to be more receptive to such training than ever before. Although they may not always receive it, because of archaic departmental or state certification policies, police officers seem to be asking for more training in interpersonal skills than they are now receiving. It has even been suggested by this author that police training curricula need to be revised based on actual time spent each day utilizing particular skills in the field. Such a revision in training standards would result in a much deeper indoctrination in Crisis Management and Critical Incident Stress Management techniques for all police personnel.

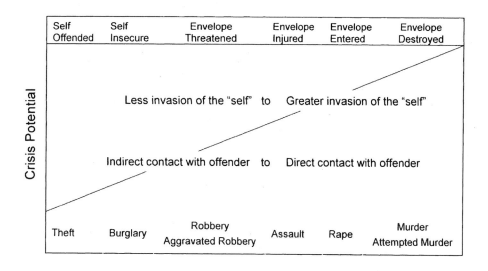

Seriousness of Crime

Figure 22.1. The Crime-Crisis Continuum (James L. Greenstone).

Crisis Intervention training has been available in this country in many forms and has been presented in various ways. Pockets of training and trainers from various disciplines continue to appear and disappear from coast to coast. As the public becomes more familiar with the term "crisis," books with titles that capitalize on the growing attention to this area continue to proliferate. Crisis Intervention has come to mean everything from psychotherapy to emergency first aid to critical incident stress management. The inconsistency of meaning, and consequently of training, has created much confusion for those who need to find appropriate skill-building assistance to perform their specific Crisis Management functions. In an attempt not only to standardize the definitions of Crisis Intervention, but also to establish a separate distinct discipline, two national training academies were formed in the 1970s; the American Academy of Crisis Interveners (AACI) in 1976 and the Southwestern Academy of Crisis (SWACI) in 1978.

Both academies were dedicated to the professionalization of crisis interveners and the specialty of Crisis Intervention. The Southwestern Academy developed training standards, set up regularly scheduled training sessions and introduced a certification program for interveners. The two academies jointly published *Emotional First Aid: A Journal of Crisis Intervention*, which was the only journal in the field of crisis management and was abstracted by the American Psychological Association. In addition, the *Crisis Intervener's Newsletter* was available four times a year to all members' of both academies and their affiliates. Other national, state and local groups as well as international agencies were invited to join ranks with the SWACI and the AACI in further standardization of the discipline. Many inquiries were made to the academies and several state-level groups formed in various areas. While the major academies were closely related to each other by brand of training and perspective, each was a separately incorporated group that encouraged others who were interested to organize in similar fashion. Both the Southwestern Academy and the American Academy were available to assist in the formation of new groups. The American Board of Examiners in Crisis Intervention certified the first group of graduates from the two academies in late 1980.

This national movement resulted in the establishment of a sense of identity for those who work in the field of Crisis Intervention regardless of the level of other professional or paraprofessional training. Crisis Interveners had developed their own professional academies, heritage and future.

It became increasingly clear to this author that psychotherapeutic experience does not in itself supply adequate Crisis Intervention expertise. In order to fully understand crises and intervention into such situations, specific definitions, procedures and training are essential. In short, Crisis Management must be recognized as a professional discipline with a tradition, a definite place in today's professional and paraprofessional community and a future within the overall health care system (Leviton, 1979). It must be understood as a set of tools, abilities and skills that can be used independently as situations dictate or in conjunction with any current psychotherapeutic or counseling system. It must have its own professionals, organizations, training academies, certifications, journals and recognition to allow its development as a significant and viable scientific entity. Individuals and groups who claim to offer crisis training exist at various places around the country. Goals differ and so does the quality of training. There has been no national standard until recently, and as a result those who need the training the most often get the least of it. What is offered may be incomplete as to range and variety of crises studied and inconsistent with training given elsewhere.

Nevertheless, the Crisis Intervention Movement has progressed on many fronts. Despite the monetary limitations imposed by the current economic situation, which may doom many agencies working in the field, those agencies that continue to provide services can look to several areas for support. Those in the field of Crisis Management had their own professional organizations that they could call upon for assistance. Never before had there been such a global interest in this particular field as a distinct discipline. The Crisis Intervener Certification Program and the American Board of Examiners in Crisis Intervention was established to ensure the highest quality of training and of services to those who utilize crisis workers. The designation of Certified Crisis Intervener served not only to acknowledge accomplishment, but also to assure those charged with staffing responsibilities that whether professional, paraprofessional or nonprofessional volunteer, individuals with such training, regardless of other background, can meet the vital challenge of delivering Crisis Management services.

Overall, Crisis Intervention services proliferated in the United States during the 1980s and 1990s and nonprofessional crisis workers were increasingly utilized to meet the growing needs of even the smallest communities. The senior citizen found a role as a much-needed crisis staff person who could provide experience of life and perhaps spend more time on the job than a younger person with other commitments. More and more people who might have felt that they are not equipped to handle the problems of others were pressed into service and found that they are more than adequately qualified for the task. Professionals in all helping fields were asked to shoulder a greater burden of providing crisis agencies with their expertise as a backup to the crisis intervener.

Crisis Intervention

Crisis Intervention is the immediate attempt to deal with immediate problems. The major emphasis is on the re-establishing of pre-crisis functioning and assisting the individual to achieve high levels of functioning as appropriate. While effective and immediate Crisis Intervention often reduces the need for additional treatment of psychotherapy if additional help is needed, the intervener must be ready to make proper and meaningful referrals. Follow-up of these referrals is equally important to be sure that the victim of crisis has received the aid that he needs as quickly as possible. While in any human condition, the history of the condition is important, the emphasis of the Crisis Intervener and Crisis Intervention as described is the immediate crisis and the management thereof. In many forms of psychotherapy or counseling, the role of the therapist is nondirective or indirect. The role of the Crisis Intervener, however, may be directive and active in an attempt to assist the victim as quickly as possible. In addition, whereas psychotherapeutic intervention may occur over a relatively lengthy period of time, Crisis Intervention occurs within a much more limited time span. This time is often measured in minutes and seconds; any additional time becomes a luxury. This rapid assistance in helping the victim to regain his pre-crisis efficiency may take the form of both emotional and physical support as needed and judged to be beneficial.

The intervener in crisis situations has two major objectives: (a) to reduce emotional trauma, and (b) to utilize the crisis situation to help those who are suffering, not only to manage present difficulties but also to attempt to master future problems by the use of more effective and more adaptive coping mechanisms.

Maladaptive Behavior

Recognition of Maladaptive Behavior

Our effectiveness as interveners is strengthened through our recognition of those individuals who can and do experience crisis. The person who is prone to crisis can be characterized by several indicators. These include:

1. An alienation from lasting and meaningful personal relationships.
2. An inability to utilize life support systems such as family, friends, and social groups.
3. A difficulty in learning from life experience so that the individual continues to make the same mistakes.
4. A history of previously experienced crises which have not been effectively resolved.
5. Feelings of low self-esteem and/or a history of emotional disorders.
6. Provocative, impulsive behavior resulting from unresolved inner conflicts.
7. Poor marital relationships.
8. Excessive use of drugs including alcohol abuse.
9. Marginal income.
10. Lack of regular, fulfilling work.
11. Unusual or frequent physical injuries.
12. Frequent encounters with law enforcement authorities.
13. Frequent changes in address.

Events Which May Precipitate a Crisis

There are a number of events which may precipitate a crisis in the life of an individual. These include:

1. An accident in the home.
2. An automobile accident with or without physical injury.
3. Being arrested, appearing in court, or even anticipating a court appearance.
4. Changes in job situation and income.
5. Changes in school status involving either promotion or demotion.

6. The death of a significant person in one's life.
7. Divorce or separation.
8. A delinquency episode.
9. Entry into school.
10. Out-of-wedlock pregnancy.
11. Physical illness or acute episodes of mental disorder.
12. Natural disaster.
13. Man-made disasters and terrorism.

Individuals who seem most crisis prone are those who are sensitive to relatively minor stress. Of course, the likelihood of crisis in increased when many stresses occur simultaneously or in rapid succession. While a particular stressful situation may not induce crisis, a combination of several such stressful events may push the individual to the crisis point.

In considering the above, it now becomes important to our overall effectiveness as an intervener to recognize when a crisis is occurring. People will indicate crises in different ways. Some may cry out and be very obvious about their crisis. Others may withdraw and become depressed. It is helpful to obtain information from the victim's family and friends concerning pre-crisis behavior. Disruptions in previous behavior are also important to assess, as well as the modes used by the individual to support his ineffective functioning.

A person in crisis may evidence any of the following mental states as characterized by their verbal responses:

1. *Bewilderment*: "I've never felt this way before."
2. *Danger*: "I'm so nervous and frightened."
3. *Confusion*: "I can't think clearly."
4. *Impasse*: "I feel stuck. Nothing I do seems to help."
5. *Desperation*: "I've just got to do something."
6. *Apathy*: "Nothing I do seems to help, so why bother anymore?"
7. *Helplessness*: "I can't take care of myself."
8. *Urgency*: "I need help now!"
9. *Discomfort*: "I feel miserable. I'm restless and unsettled."

In order to better understand crisis development, it may be helpful to refer to Appendix 1, Form 5. The Cube is a pictorial, three-dimensional representation of how a crisis develops and the effects of both proper and improper intervention. Specific crises may vary somewhat from this chart.

Crisis, in general, will usually follow the patterns outlined. Stress and minor crises are inherent in daily living and people develop problem-solving techniques to function effectively. However, when stress and tension begin to build in our lives because of the occurrence of unusual, sudden, and unexpected events, we may find that our usually effective coping mechanisms do not provide the expected relief.

Stress continues to mount and the crisis intensifies. The victim will then resort to various types of trial-and-error problem solving in an attempt to develop new ways of subduing the problem. This usually does not work either, and panic sets in. The behavior of the victim becomes increasingly maladaptive. Maladaptive behavior is distinguished from mentally-ill behavior by the fact that without the crisis, the maladaptive behavior would not exist. The maladaptive response is directly connected to the crisis. This is not to infer that persons who are in crisis may not also have a mental illness. In fact, they may. Mental illness, however, is not a requirement for the development of a crisis. Anyone may experience crisis and yet not be mentally ill.

Maladaptive behavior may take the form of aggressive, hostile actions, or may be manifested by complete withdrawal from the world. The crisis victim is not in total control of his life and feels the panic resulting from this realization.

Effective intervention into the life of the crisis victim must begin as soon after the crisis is experienced as is possible. The more immediate the intervention, the less is the likelihood that emotional damage needing subsequent psychotherapy will occur. The victim may require guidance in developing new resources or help in strengthening old ones.

At the point at which effective intervention is accomplished, the crisis victim can be helped to rely once again on his own resources and abilities. A crisis is self-limiting. It will cease even if intervention does not occur. However, we must consider the potential personal and/or emotional destruction that could result if the crisis were allowed to run its course.

Intervention Procedure

Effective intervention into crisis situations requires that the intervener ask two sets of questions. The first area of concern is the intervener's emotional and physical preparedness to intervene in the particular situation at hand. The questions include:

1. Is this an intervention that I can physically and emotionally handle?
2. Will personal, unresolved biases or prejudices interfere with my ability to be effective? The most blatant example of bias often exists in child abuse cases, where the intervener may not be willing to acknowledge the crisis being experienced by the abuser and may focus only on the crisis of the child. This attitude can potentiate crisis for the intervener and increase the stress level of those already in crisis.
3. Is my physical safety in jeopardy if I intervene in this situation? Do I need additional support personnel before I enter the case?
4. If I am working on an intervener team, is the line of communication between my partner and me fail-safe?
5. Have our individual roles been clearly defined and agreed-upon in order to avoid confusion and conflict?

If the intervener experiences ambiguity in his answers to these questions and is unwilling to resolve the problems immediately, the intervener runs the risk of sabotaging his effectiveness. His lack of clarity could exacerbate the suffering of the victim and cause a personal crisis. If, however, the intervener is clear about his goal, reasonably certain of safety, in agreement with a team partner on procedure, and prepared to intervene regardless of the situation, then the intervener should proceed with the intervention.

Effective crisis intervention consists of five components: immediacy, control, assessment, disposition, and referral and follow-up (see Figure 22.2).

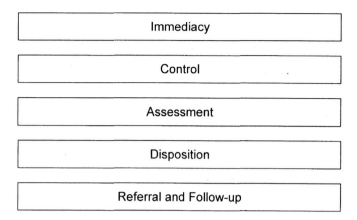

Figure 22.2. Intervention Procedures.

General Guidelines for Effective Intervention into Crisis Situations

1. Attempt to limit the personal disorganization that the victim is experiencing by calming and relieving as much of the anxiety and stress as possible.
2. If possible, remove the victim from the crisis situation and provide a place to relax and to self-compose.
3. Explain the situation to the victim and what is being done about the problems.
4. Remain confident and be firm and reasonable at all times.
5. Do not agree or disagree with the victim. The way that the world is perceived at this time in life is real for the victim.
6. Encourage family members to be with the victim if appropriate. Some family members may be disruptive or in crisis themselves. The intervener must assess the helpfulness or nonhelpfulness of all significant others before bringing them into contact with the victim.
7. Encourage the victim to relax and to tell what is currently troubling.
8. Help the victim to see the crisis as temporary rather than chronic. Recovery is usually quicker when the problems are viewed in this way rather than as an unsolvable situation which may never be fully resolved.
9. Allow the victim to speak freely and to ventilate feelings.
10. In a multiple victim situation (such as a domestic violence inci-

dent or a family dispute), allow each person to speak without interruption by the other parties. Establish this ground rule immediately and insist that it be followed.

11. Avoid unnecessary interruptions while the crisis victim is talking.

12. Try to build a sense of structure to which the victim can relate as you talk. In crisis, the sufferer may see things as chaotic and out of his control. The more the victim understands and the more quickly a sense of structure can be secured, the quicker the victim will recover and be able to function effectively.

13. Avoid arguing with the victim. There are many ways of viewing a situation. The role of the intervener is to help direct the problem solving.

14. Whenever possible, obtain information from others who are aware of the victim's situation and who can supply facts that may be helpful to the intervention.

15. If the victim is currently involved in psychotherapy, contact the therapist and apprise the situation. The therapist may be able to supply additional facts. At this time, check to see if the victim is taking any type of medication which may have adverse effects.

Creativity, judgment, response to one's intuition in a given situation, and adaptation of procedures to one's own profession all become part of a responsible, skillful crisis intervention.

Critical Incident Stress Management

In an effort to reduce the number of psychological casualties among emergency service workers, a relatively new form of Crisis Intervention was developed (Mitchell, 1983). This procedure was designed to assist these workers and one form is known as a Critical Incident Stress Debriefing. The main goal of this Crisis Intervention procedure, and of the overall Critical Incident Stress Management program, is to support those who are involved in emergency operations under condition of extreme stress. A "debriefing" under this procedure is designed to alleviate the acute stress responses which appear at the scene and immediately afterwards. Doctor Mitchell suggested that it will also inhibit, or eliminate delayed stress reactions.

Critical incidents occur whenever those who work in emergency service and other civilian situations encounter situations which engender strong stress reactions which could interfere with the worker's ability to function either on the job or afterwards. At least one type of incident which may cause unusually strong, and potentially devastating, stress are natural or man-made disasters. Almost any emergency which is highly charged, regardless of the source of the unusual stress, could be considered a critical incident. The main focus of the Critical Incident Stress Debriefing is the emergency service worker and not the primary victim of the crisis at hand. Mitchell (1983) points out that critical incidents produce a characteristic set of responses both psychological and physiological. Such reactions have been noted since the American Civil War. Even Freud found remarkable the quality and intensity of stress reactions of soldiers in World War I. He found that those who had been exposed to unusual traumatic events experienced severe reactions not unlike those which we observe today in post critical incidents. It is important to note that the symptoms which may be seen under such circumstances are normal. In fact, it could be said that they are the normal and expected reactions to abnormal and unexpected situations. It should be noted that, while the reactions to abnormal situations may be normal, the potential for severe emotional injury to the sufferer is high. If the stress is denied or not effectively dealt with, those who experience it could experience both long and short-term psychological and physical debilitation.

Debriefings are divided into at least three types according to Doctor Mitchell who is credited with the expansion, if not development, of this subset of Crisis Intervention. These include:

1. Initial Defusing.
2. Formal Critical Incident Stress Debriefing.
3. Follow-up Critical Incident Stress Debriefing.

The on-scene defusing is the briefest form of CISM. At this point, it is important to check on the well-being of personnel involved, provide encouragement and to take note of those who may need additional assistance. Such assistance may include a break or a change in duties which are being performed. Assistance on or near the scene by someone who is willing to listen and to respond supportively, had been found to be prophylactic for long-term stress reactions.

Within eight hours of the critical incident, a defusing may also prove extremely effective. A mental health professional, a team leader or even the workers themselves can provide this assistance. The spontaneous positive talking of the emergency workers with each other can be extremely helpful. Feelings and reactions become the main focus, and support and understanding is the rule. One format for defusings could be a team meeting within a few hours after the incident has subsided.

The formal Critical Incident Stress Debriefing usually occurs from 24–72 hours after the critical incident and is led by a mental health professional. This formal Crisis Intervention may not be effective prior to this time because emergency workers may be too worked up to appropriately participate.

The process consists of three basic phases:

1. The first phase of the process consists of initial ventilation of feelings by the emergency service personnel and assessment by the facilitator of the intensity of stress response.
2. The second phase of the process consists of a more detailed discussion of the signs and symptoms of the stress response, and provides for education, support and reassurance.
3. The final closure of a Critical Incident Stress Debriefing occurs when information is provided and, if necessary, a plan of further action is developed or a referral is made by the mental health professional.

In most cases, the Critical Incident Stress Debriefing will follow the following format:

1. *Introductory Phase.* The peer leader introduces himself, describes the rules for the debriefing, and emphasizes the need for confidentiality. Participants are to be assured that the open discussion of their feelings will not be used against them in any way. Often, members need to be reminded that this is not to be a discussion of the tactical or operational aspects of the incident. The peer leader then introduces the facilitator.
2. *Fact Phase.* The facilitator asks the participants to describe facts about themselves and their activities during the incident, as well as facts about the incident itself. Members should be encouraged to describe what activities they performed during the incident and what they heard, saw, smelled, and did as they worked at the scene.

3. *Thought Phase.* The facilitator asks the members of the group to discuss their first thought during the incident. Personal thoughts often get hidden behind the facts and bringing them out into the open affirms that one's own thoughts are important and not to be forgotten and buried beneath the facts of the situation.

4. *Feeling Phase.* When enough information has been provided to make the incident vividly clear, the facilitator encourages a sharing of feelings by all participants. The facilitator emphasizes that all feelings, positive or negative, important or unimportant, should be expressed and listened to. Members are encouraged to share with others the feelings they had at the scene and are having now, and whether they have ever had these feelings before.

5. *Unfinished Business Phase.* The facilitator opens the discussion to include past critical incidents which may have resurfaced due to the present situation.

6. *Reactions Phase.* The facilitator asks members of the group to describe any reactions they have experienced since the incident. The facilitator focuses on the behavioral, psychological and physical reactions.

7. *Teaching Phase.* Members are reminded that the symptoms they have experienced are normal responses to extraordinary circumstances and the facilitator explains the rationale for the stress response. Coping techniques are discussed at this time (What has worked before?)

8. *Re-entry Phase.* This phase seeks to wrap up the debriefing, answer outstanding questions, and establish a plan of further action. Summary comments are offered by the facilitator and thepeer leader, advising members on how to seek further help if they need it.

Follow-up Critical Incident Stress Debriefing can be done several weeks post-incident or post-formal CISD. If any portion of this process borders on "therapy," this portion does. The educational nature of CISD may need to be extended if the problems dealt within the formal CISD continue to create major difficulties for a worker. Individual or group follow-ups may be effective. More than one session may be necessary and a formal referral may be in order.

Psychotherapeutic vs. Psychoeducational

When we speak of Crisis Intervention, we are referring to the timely process of entering into the life of an individual, because of unusual stress which renders the person's usual coping mechanisms ineffective, in order to defuse the destructive effects of the unusual stress experienced, in order to return the individual in crisis to his or her level of pre-crisis functioning (Greenstone, 1979). Greenstone (1983) and Corsini (1983) both discussed the necessity for psychotherapists to know and understand Crisis Intervention procedures. The importance here is that Crisis Intervention is not a form of psychotherapy and therefore is an added skill that therapists need to know in order to handle such emergencies. Historically, psychotherapy training has not included Crisis Intervention training, probably because it was not considered a therapeutic skill.

Greenstone (1982) compared three methods of assisting individuals at risk. These included psychoanalysis, short-term counseling and Crisis Intervention. Crisis Intervention should not be construed as short term counseling or psychotherapy. It is not intended that the Crisis Intervener be or becomes a psychologist, counselor or psychiatrist. In fact, the paraprofessional may actually be the better intervener. This was discovered early on in the Crisis Intervention movement by therapists themselves in the 1970s. "Litman's Law," referred to earlier developed from the work of the Los Angeles Suicide's Prevention Center, and indicated from their experiences that the nonprofessional or the paraprofessional may really be in a better position to help victims manage their crisis.

The emphasis of Crisis Intervention is the immediate management, not resolution, of the crisis being experienced. In many forms of psychotherapy or counseling, the role of the therapist may be nondirective or indirect at best. The role of the Crisis Intervener may be a quite active and directive attempt to assist the victim as quickly as possible. In addition, whereas psychotherapeutic intervention may occur over a relatively lengthy period of time, Crisis Intervention is time-specific and time-limited. For the Crisis Intervener, time is often measured in minutes or seconds rather than in weekly sessions. The intervener in a crisis situation has a dual objective. These include the objective of reducing trauma wherever possible, and utilizing the crisis situation to help those affected, not only to manage present problems, but also to become strengthened in mastering future difficulties by use of more effective and adaptive coping mechanisms (Parad, 1965). This additional mastery is not the direct result of Crisis Intervention, but the side-effect of skillful education and assistance in returning a person in crisis to pre-crisis levels of functioning. Crisis Intervention is always the attempt to provide immediate management to an immediate problem rather than long term solution to ongoing problems (Greenstone, 1982, 1983). Critical Incident Stress Debriefing provides this assistance to emergency service personnel as well as to others affected in the form of support and education (Mitchell, 1983).

Summary

Such necessity came directly from the author's perception that significant confusion may exist about the professional areas known as Critical Incident Stress Management and Crisis Intervention. Those attempting to work in these fields, as well as those who are newcomers to either, may well benefit from the clarification attempted here:

1. Is Crisis Intervention a form of psychotherapy? "Crisis" and Crisis Intervention have been used to describe many activities ranging from economic travails to counseling. In our context, Crisis Intervention is not psychotherapy. It is a related approach which approximates in the emotional sense, "first aid" in the physical sense. It is Emotional First Aid administered prior to the advent of psychotherapeutic assistance. In many cases, properly administered Emotional First Aid can reduce the need for intensive psychotherapeutic intervention later. Crisis Intervention is a "front line" procedure. Psychotherapy may be equivalent to rear echelon care. The relationship between the two is crucial. If proper "first aid" is done on the front line, rear echelon care if needed will be enhanced significantly.

2. Is the Critical Incident Stress Debriefing a form of Crisis Intervention? Because the focus of the Critical Incident Stress Debriefing is the unusual stress experienced by emergency service workers and civilians and the effects, both short and long-term, of this stress on them, it seems that CISD is a logical extension of the discipline of Crisis Intervention. Critical Incident Stress Debriefing may be seen as the inward turning of Crisis Man-

agement skills toward those who are responding to the crises of others. Rather than a completely separate focus, as some would see it, CISD deals with the crises of crisis workers. It attempts to prevent crisis on the job through defusings; and subsequent to the job, by debriefing. Crisis Intervention theory offers assistance to interveners preparing to enter into the crisis of another. Such preparation is called "Intervener Survival" training.

3. Is Critical Incident Stress Debriefing a psychotherapeutic or psychoeducational process? Crisis Intervention is not psychotherapeutic in scope. Therefore, if we accept that Critical Incident Stress Management is an extension of Crisis Intervention, we must also accept that CISM is not a psychotherapeutic process. Describing Critical Incident Stress Management as a process which seeks to educate, that emergency service workers may experience normal emotional reactions to abnormal man-made and natural occurrences, places such a procedure in the educational arena.

4. What is the role of the Intervener in either Crisis Intervention or Critical Incident Stress Debriefing? The role of the properly trained and supervised intervener is to administer emotional first aid to those experiencing crisis in their life. The intervener may also direct or refer those who may need more than Crisis Intervention provides, to sources of psychotherapeutic assistance. Specifically, within the purview of CISD, the intervener assists the mental health professional in performing those functions designed both to educate and to stem the development of crises in the lives of the emergency service workers as well as others who are being debriefed. As a support to the mental health professional, the intervener adds credibility to the professional's involvement, and to the process. If a crisis develops, the crisis intervener can be available to take immediate steps to interrupt the course of the exhibited maladaptive behavior.

5. Do mental health professionals do Crisis Intervention? Clearly, yes! Psychotherapeutic and Counseling training does not always train the therapist in the skills of Crisis Intervention. Few patients seen by a therapist come to the therapy office in crisis. Definitions should help clarify this point. However, patients may go into crisis once they are in the therapy session. Doctor Raymond Corsini, Editor of *Innovative psychotherapies*

(1981), points out that while Crisis Intervention is not therapy, it is a procedure that should be studied by all therapists. The ability to "change hats" and to administer effective Crisis Intervention may be the difference between being able to continue a therapy session or having to abort it. Therapists do psychotherapy. They also do psychoeducation. Additionally, their skills should include Crisis Intervention. Special training is needed to accomplish this much as special training is required to do Critical Incident Stress Management.

6. Are mental health professionals required for Critical Incident Stress Debriefing purposes? Again, clearly yes! The reasons are several. Just as the crisis intervener adds credibility to the professional, the use of a mental health professional adds credibility to the process of the CISD. Rightly or wrongly, it seems to work that way. Additionally, the mental health professionals, by their actions, assume the responsibility for what occurs in the debriefing session. Such responsibility, not to mention malpractice insurance coverage, may be beyond the scope of the crisis intervener. Additionally, properly trained mental health professionals will have the depth of background to make important distinctions in the reactions of those being defused, as well as to maintain the psychoeducational/psychotherapeutic distinctions necessary for a successful debriefing.

7. Are mental health professionals required for Crisis Intervention procedures to be utilized? The history of the Crisis Intervention Movement in this country and abroad, has demonstrated that the mental health professional, with this traditional training, may not be the best Crisis Intervener. It is espoused by some that the more critical the crisis, the better equipped are the Crisis Intervener, nonmental health professional, to handle them. Interestingly, this discovery was made by mental health professionals. Mental health professionals can provide vital back-up to the intervener during times when the intervener's training is insufficient to handle a severe mental problem. In no way should the above indicate that Crisis Intervention trained therapists could not be extremely effective interveners.

8. Are both Crisis Intervention and Critical Incident Stress Debriefing designed each for separate or similar groups? If so, when? If not, why not? Crisis Intervention is an attempt by

emergency service personnel, peer counselors, crisis interveners, etc., to assist those who may be experiencing a crisis in their life in order to reduce the destructive effects of that crisis if allowed to go unchecked. CISD, in many ways, is designed to prevent and to reduce crisis in the lives of those who care for the crises of others. Crisis Intervention includes Critical Incident Stress Debriefing; and Critical Incident Stress Debriefing is Crisis Intervention.

9. Should mental health professionals desist from their primary role while acting in the role of a debriefer? The role of the debriefer is that of psychoeducator rather than psychotherapist. Given this, it is sometimes assumed that the therapist should somehow not react to the psychotherapeutic needs that may arise in the debriefing. Some mental health professionals may elect this stand. Perhaps the most important point is, not the cessation of a psychotherapeutic role but the understanding of the professional responsibility levied when such a line is crossed. As a professional, they must do what is needed. Additionally, they should always understand the duties that such actions may cause the therapist to assume.

10. What is the relationship of Crisis Intervention to psychotherapeutic thought, Crisis Counseling, short-term counseling theory, group theory, and to the procedures advocated in Critical Incident Stress Debriefing and Defusing? Crisis Intervention procedures are based on current and accepted psychotherapeutic thought. In fact, Crisis Intervention does not seem to be theory-bound. Regardless of psychotherapeutic theoretical background, Emotional First Aid seems adaptable and usable. Crisis Intervention is the immediate intrusion into a person's life at the time of crisis in their life. Crisis Counseling is the subsequent longer involvement which may be necessary once the initial intervention has been done or the crisis has subsided. Psychotherapy, group counseling, short-term counseling, and the like, may be utilized as a result of additional problems resulting from, or not resolved or managed by the initial intervention. The "Crisis Cube," Appendix 1, Form 5, may be helpful in understanding these relationships.

It is apparent that there are many additional questions to be raised and to be answered. Perhaps others will do so as our discipline continues to grow. Hopefully, what is presented here will allow those who labor in this vineyard to better understand themselves, their work and their roots.

APPENDICES

Appendix 1

UTILIZE THESE HANDY FORMS IN THE FIELD

Intervener Forms

FORM 1. INITIAL MISSION SHEET

UNIT			
Statement of mission			

Activities to accomplish mission
1
2.
3.
4.
Resources to accomplish mission
1.
2.
3.
4.

Incident Commander	Name	Contact Phone	Email address
Administration	Name	Contact Phone	Email address
Operations	Name	Contact Phone	Email address
Logistics			
Planning			

Status	Total Personnel	
	MD's/DO's	
	PA's	
	RN's	
	Med Tech's	
	Mental Health	
	Others	
	Shift organization	

Personnel Breakdown				
	MD's/DO's	Name	Contact Phone	Email Address

FORM 1–*Continued*

	PA's	Name	Contact Phone	Email Address
	RN'	Name	Contact Phone	Email Address
	Med Tech's	Name	Contact Phone	Email Address
	Mental Health	Name	Contact Phone	Email Address
	Others	Name	Contact Phone	Email Address
Other information about what your force is doing				

FORM 2. INCIDENT COMMAND FOR MENTAL HEALTH

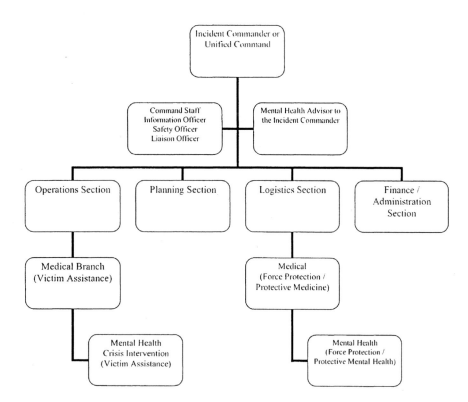

FORM 3. MEDICATIONS FORM

MEDICATIONS							
NAME			TIME		DATE		
MEDICATIONS HELD			MEDICATIONS RETURNED				
MEDICATIONS AND TIMES	SAT	SUN	MON	TUE	WED	THU	FRI
OTC MEDS							

FORM 4. VOLUNTEER MILEAGE LOG

Page # ___ of ___   Mileage Log 20   Name of Volunteer:

Starting Mileage		Ending Mileage	Total:	
Date	RT Miles	Destination	Activity	Notes
Page Total		Total Balance Brought Forward =		

FORM 5. THE CRISIS CUBE

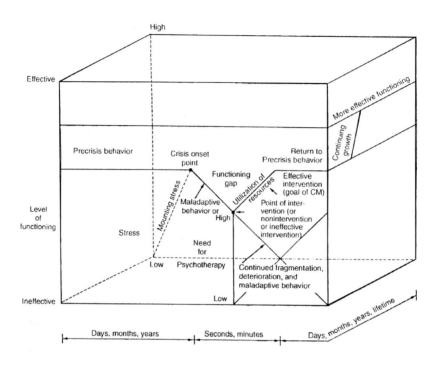

Source: From James L. Greenstone and Sharon C. Leviton, *The Elements of Crisis Intervention* (2nd Ed.) (Belmont, CA: Wadsworth Publishing, 2001). Reproduced by permission.

FORM 6. AFTER ACTION ISSUE REPORT

Date:

Submitted by:
Phone:
e-mail:
Unit:
Position:

Issue: (Provide a specific, detailed statement or two describing the issue.)

Discussion: (Provide a discussion about the issue – background, details of what occurred, etc.)

Recommendation: (Provide your recommended solution and who you recommend should address the issue, if possible. (Recommendation may be that someone or a working group tackle the problem.)

FORM 7. MENTAL STATUS EXAMINATION

For use by: Mental Health Personnel and Crisis Interveners / Responders

Name of subject: Date form completed: by:

Attitude and General Behavior

Physical	WNL*	disheveled	untidy	unkempt
Cooperation	WNL*	fair	poor	
General Manner	WNL*	mistrustful	suspicious	antagonistic
	Negativistic		defiant	preoccupied

Activity   Motor retarda-   hyperactivity   stereotype   compulsion
tion persevera-   mannerisms   echopraxia   echolalia   tics
tion

Stream of talk and mental activity

Accessibility   indifferent   self-absorbed   inaccessible
Productivity   voluble   circumstantial   flight of ideas   underpro-
retarded   mute   ductive
Thought   illogical   irrelevant   incoherent   verbigera-
progression   Blocking   Neologisms   tion

Emotional Reactions

Quality of   WNL*   elation   exhilaration   mild depression
affect   fear   euphoria   exaltation   moderate depression
anxiety   apprehension   emotional   severe depression
instability
Appropriateness   incongruity with thought content
of affect   ambivalence   emotional deterioration

Content of thoughts

Thinking   phobias   obsessive ideas
disorders   ideas of reference   psychosomatic complaints
persecutory trend   grandiose ideas
depressive delusions   nihilistic delusions
hypochondriac ideas   ideas of unreality
deprivation of thought   delusions of influence
autistic thinking
Perceptive   auditory hallucinations   visual hallucinations
disorders   olfactory hallucinations   tactile hallucinations
reflex hallucinations   hypnagogic hallucinations
psychomotor hallucinations   illusions

Sensorium and General Knowledge

Disorders of consciousness   confusion   clouding   dream state
                               delirium   stupor
Disorders of apperception   mild   severe
Disorders of orientation   time   place   person
Disorders of personal identification and memory
                               general amnesia   circumscribed amnesia
                               confabulation   retrospective falsifica-
                               hyperamnesia   tion
Disorders of retention and immediate recall   mild   severe
Disorders of counting and calculation   mild   severe
Disorders of reading   mild   severe
Disorders of writing   mild   severe
Disorders of school and general knowledge   mild   severe
Disorders in attention, concentration, and thinking capacity   mild   severe
Disorders in intelligence   inconsistent with education   mild   severe
Disorders in judgment   mild   severe
Disorders in insight   mild   severe

<u>Suicidality:</u>   mild   moderate   severe   immediate

Summary of mental status examination

☐   Mental status examination essentially negative
☐   Disturbance in attitude and general behavior
☐   Disturbance in stream of mental activity
☐   Disturbance in emotional reaction
☐   Disturbance in mental trend – content of thought
☐   Disturbance in sensorium, mental grasp and capacity

*Within normal limits.

FORM 8. FIELD DIAGNOSTIC WORKSHEET

Date:

Name of incident:

Name of Victim Profiled:
Profiler:

⊗Diagnosis/Profile:

Below, list the specific characteristics observed in the victim or sufferer, or related to the victim, that ultimately justifies the above diagnosis:

1.

2.

3.

4.

5.

6.

7.

8.

9.

10.

Proposed Strategies and Goals based on the primary diagnosis:

1.
2.
3.
4.
5.

Notes:

FORM 9. CHECKLIST FOR CRISIS INTERVENTION

Do	*Notes*
Have a good opening statement.	
Be Empathetic.	
Be credible.	
Have good voice control.	
Good stress tolerance.	
Gather information as needed	
Establish a psychological profile.	
Listen actively.	
Pause to listen.	
Encourage ventilation.	
Use self-disclosure carefully.	
Be flexible.	
Nurture the recovery potential.	
Ask open-ended questions.	
Be reassuring.	
Make the victim feel responsible for themselves.	
Help the victim to accept responsibility.	
Talk in terms of WE meaning the intervener and the victim.	
Talk on the level of the victim.	
Use reflective responses.	
Acknowledge the victim's feelings.	
Use reassuring phrases.	
Give positive approval.	
Keep the victim in a decision-making mode to the extent possible.	
Do Not	*Notes*
Interrupt the victim.	
Ask superfluous questions.	
Be argumentative.	
Make decisions for the victim if not needed.	
Make promises that you cannot keep.	
Use trigger or "bullet" words.	
Irritate the victim.	
Volunteer information.	
Talk too much.	
Get mad or irritated.	
Make assumptions.	
Get angry with the victim or circumstances.	
Be authoritarian.	
Be tough except if planned.	
Be too soft unless planned.	
Be defensive.	

FORM 10. STANDARD WORDS AND PHRASES

Standard Words and Phrases for the Intervener

When you may not know what to say next, this is the place to look. Below are listed several words and phrases that have little or no emotional load associated with them. They are non-judgmental, encourage talking and deal with feelings. Used properly when you do not know where to go next, they will give you time to think and will demonstrate your ongoing interest in the victim/sufferer and the victim's problems and current circumstances. Use them individually and judiciously for best results. At times, all of us are at a loss for words. These "pat" words and phrases have been tested repeatedly, and will help you get going again.

"First, I'd like to get to know you better."

"Could you tell me about it?"

"I would like to hear what you have to say..."

"Could you share that with me?"

"I guess that's pretty important to you."

"Tell me about it."

"That's interesting."

"I see."

"Is that so?"

"Oh."

"Uh huh."

Note: You may find that a well-placed grunt will do wonders for your communications skills.

FORM 11. BASIC FORMAL INCIDENT COMMAND STRUCTURE

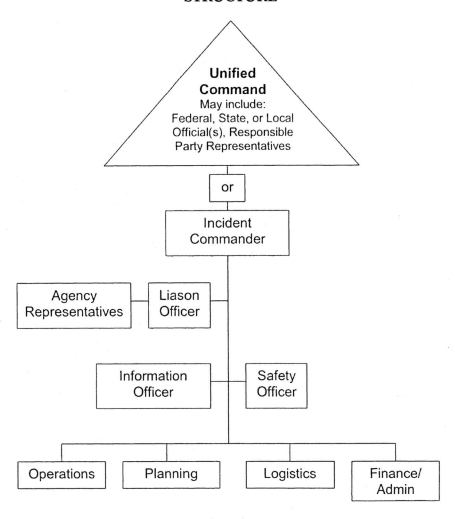

FORM 12. INCIDENT COMMAND SYSTEM 206: MEDICAL RESOURCES

	1. Incident Name	2. Date Prepared	3. Time Prepared	4. Operational Period

MEDICAL AID STATIONS	LOCATION	PARAMEDICS

NAME	ADDRESS	PHONE	PARAMEDICS

NAME	LOCATION	PARAMEDICS

NAME	ADDRESS	TRAVEL TIME AIR	TRAVEL TIME GRND	PHONE	HELIPAD	BURN CENTER

	9. Prepared By: (Medical Unit Leader)	10. Reviewed By: (Safety Officer)

FORM 13. INCIDENT COMMAND SYSTEM 201: INCIDENT BRIEFING

INCIDENT BRIEFING	1. Incident Name	2. Date Prepared	3. Time Prepared

4. MAP SKETCH
(Could include maps showing the total Area of Operation, the Incident site, overflight results, trajectories, impacted shorelines, or other graphics depicting situation and response status.)

Form ICS 201	Page of	5. Prepared By: (Name and Position)

FORM 14. INCIDENT COMMAND SYSTEM 204:
ASSIGNMENT LIST

1. Branch	2. Division/Group	
3. Incident Name	4. Operational Period (Date/Tim)	
5. Operations Personnel		

6. Resources Assigned This Period						
Strike Team /Task Force/ Resource Identifier	Leader	Phone	# of Pers.	Trans Needed	Drop Off Point/Time	Pick Up Point/Time

7. Assignments

8. Special Instructions/Safety Message

Function		Freq.	System	Chan.	Function		Freq.	System	Chan.
Command	Local				Support	Local			
	Repeat					Repeat			
Div./Group/Unit Tactical					Ground-To-Air				

Prepared By:	11. Approved By: (Planning Section Chief)	Date/Time Approved

ICS 204

FORM 15. INCIDENT COMMAND SYSTEM 213:
MESSAGE FORM

	POSITION	
FROM	POSITION	
SUBJECT	DATE	

MESSAGE:

DATE	TIME	SIGNATURE/POSITION
ICS 213		

FORM 16. INCIDENT COMMAND SYSTEM 214: UNIT LOG

	1. Incident Name	2. Date Prepared	3. Time Prepared
4. Unit Name/Designators	5. Unit Leader (Name and Position)	6. Operational Period (Date/Time)	

7. Personnel Roster Assigned

NAME	ICS POSITION	HOME BASE

8. ACTIVITY LOG (CONTNUE ON REVERSE)

TIME	MAJOR EVENTS

	9. Prepared By:

FORM 17. INCIDENT COMMAND SYSTEM 221:
DEMOBILIZATION CHECKOUT

DEMOBILIZATION CHECKOUT		
1. INCIDENT NAME/NUMBER	2. DATE/TIME	3. DEMOB NO.
4. UNIT/PERSONNEL RELEASED		
5. TRANSPORTATION TYPE/NO.		
6. ACTUAL RELEASE DATE/TIME	7. MANIFEST YES NO NUMER _____	
8. DESTINATION _____	9. AREA/AGENCY/REGION NOTIFIED NAME _____ NAME _____	
10. UNIT LEADER RESPONSIBLE FOR COLLECTING PERFORMANCE RATING		

11. UNIT/PERSONNEL You and your resources have been released subject to signoff from the following:
(Demob. Unit Leader Check Appropriate Box)

<u>LOGISTICS SECTION</u>

☐ SUPPLY UNIT _____

☐ COMMUNICATION UNIT _____

☐ FACILITIES UNIT _____

☐ GROUND SUPPORT UNIT LEADER _____

<u>PLANNING SECTIONS</u>

☐ DOCUMENTATION UNIT _____

<u>FINANCE/ADMINISTRATION SECTION</u>

☐ TIME UNIT _____

<u>OTHER</u>

☐ _____   _____

☐ _____   _____

12. REMARKS

_____

_____

ICS 221

FORM 18. INCIDENT COMMAND SYSTEM 202: RESPONSE OBJECTIVES

RESPONSE OBJECTIVES	1. Incident Name	2. Date Prepared	3. Time Prepared

4. Operational Period (Date/Time):

5. Overall Incident Objective(s):

6. Objectives for specified Operational Period:

7. Safety Message for specified Operational Period:

8. Weather: See Attached Weather Sheet

9. Tides/Currents. See Attached Tide/Current Data

10. Sunrise: Sunset:

11. Attachments (Yes if attached, No if not attached)

___ Organization List (ICS 203)   ___ Medical Plan (ICS 206)   ___ Resources at Risk Summary (ICS0)S-232)

___ Assignment List (ICS 204)   ___ Incident Map(s)   ___ _____

___ Communication Plan (ICS 205)   ___ Traffic Plan   ___ _____

ICS 202	12. Prepared By: (Planning Section Chief)

FORM 19. TEAM INTERVENTIONS

Single intervener intervention

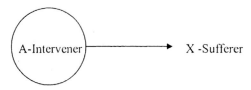

Single team intervention

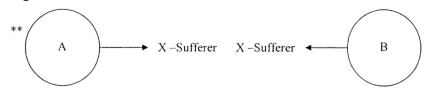

Multiple team intervention

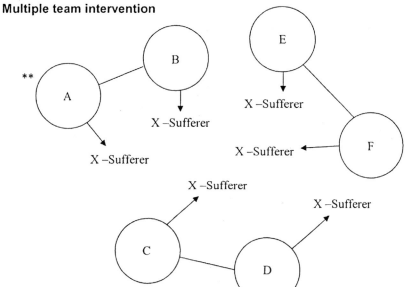

O = Interveners
X = Sufferers/Victims
———————— = Team Relationship
** = Lead/Control Intervener

Originated by Dr. Sharon C. Leviton. Reprinted and adapted with permission.

FORM 20. THE DISASTER–CRISIS CONTINUUM

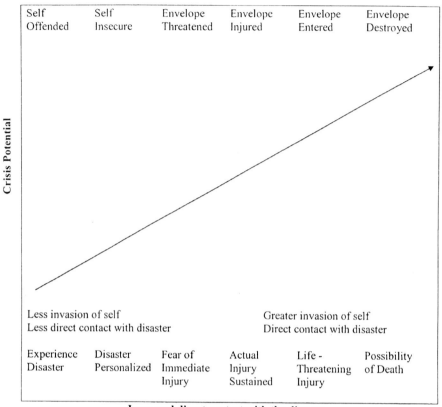

Increased direct contact with the disaster.

FORM 21. PACKING LIST

Personalize this list as needed. Make it your own. Adapt to your specific situations. Divide into short term pack and long term pack, as needed.

- Hat
- Rain gear
- Uniform if required
- Water
- Bandanna
- Personal identification
- Unit identification
- Money
- Credit cards
- Passport if needed for particular deployment.
- Emergency phone numbers
- Extra glasses
- Eye protection
- Ear protection
- Leather work gloves
- Flashlight and batteries
- Knife
- Personal first aid kit
- Medical equipment as needed for your specific deployment or specialty function.
- Paper and pens
- Disposable gloves
- Personal battery powered radio.
- Creature comforts as possible and practical.
- Extra clothing or uniforms.
- Extra undergarments
- Shoes or boots depending on possible assignment.
- Extra footwear
- Swimwear
- Socks

- Sweater depending on season
- Jacket
- Gloves
- Food
- Snacks/power bars
- Mess kit
- Knife, spoon and fork
- Canteen or bottled water
- Water purification tablet
- Razor/blades
- Shave cream
- Chargers as needed
- Toothbrush
- Toothpaste
- Toilet paper
- Soap
- Shampoo
- Hand lotion
- Deodorant
- Comb / brush
- Handiwipes
- Personal medications
- Sunglasses
- Foot care products
- Sleeping bag
- Foam pad
- Ground cloth
- Pillow
- Extra batteries
- Matches or disposable lighter
- Face/Dust mask
- Goggles or safety glasses
- Sewing kit
- Duct tape
- Towels
- Wash cloth
- Hand mirror

- Parachute cord or nylon cord
- Large trash bags
- Nail clippers
- Trail mix
- Shoe shine kit
- Copies of professional licenses
- Lip balm
- Dental floss
- Feminine hygiene products as appropriate
- Tylenol or Aspirin
- Contact lenses with case and cleaner
- Athletic shoes
- Sleepwear
- Sunscreen
- Shower shoes
- Hangers
- Clock
- Lock, combination or key
- Zip lock plastic bags
- Insect repellant
- Books
- Clipboard
- Cell phone and charger
- Handkerchief
- No personal weapons
- No expensive jewelry or watches
- No large amounts of cash
- No unauthorized guests

Appendix 2

STUDY THESE HELPFUL WEBSITES

General Health Information

http://www.healthweb.org
http://www.healthfinder.gov
Mayo Clinic. . . . . http://www.mayoclinic.com
National Institute of Health. Health Info Page. . . http://www.health.nih.gov
National Library of Medicine . . . . http://www.nlm.nih.gov
New York Online Access to Health . . . . http://www.noah-health.org

Advanced Search

Combined Health Information Database . . . . http://chid.nih.gov
Video Option . . . .
. . . . http://www.med.stanford.edu/healthlibrary/resources/videos.html

Finding Doctors and Hospitals

http://www.familydoctor.org
American Medical Association . . . . http://www.ama-assn.org
Medline Plus. . . . . http://www.medlineplus.gov
Quality Check® . . . . http://www.qualitycheck.org

Diseases and Conditions

Agency for Healthcare Research and Quality. . . . . http://www.ahrq.gov
American Heart Association. . . . . http://www.americanheart.org
CDC Health Topics. . . . . http://www.cdc.gov/ncidod/diseases
National Cancer Institute. . . . . http://www.cancer.gov

Specific Audiences

Administration on Aging . . . . http://www.aoa.gov
Kids Health. . . . . http://www.kidshealth.org
Men's Health (American Academy of Family Physicians) . . . .
. . . . http://www.familydoctor.org/men.xml
National Institute on Aging . . . . http://www.nia.nih.gov
National Women's Health Information Center. . . . http://www.4women.gov

Miscellaneous Special Interest

AIDS Knowledge . . . . http://www.HIVinsite.com
American Board of Examiners in Crisis Intervention. . . . .
. . . . http://www.emotionalfirstaid.com
American Psychiatric Association. . . . . http://www.psych.org/
American Psychological Association . . . . http://www.apa.org/
American Red Cross . . . . http://www.redcross.org/
Baptist Men. . . . . . . http://www.bgct.org/TexasBaptists/Page.aspx?&pid=198
Center for Disease Control. . . . . http://www.cdc.gov
Consumer Health Information. . . . . http://www.medlineplus.gov
Family Medicine. . . . . http://www.familydoctor.org
Federal Emergency Management Agency. . . . . http://www.fema.gov/
Health. . . . . http://www.healthfinder.com
International Critical Incident Stress Foundation . . . . . http://www.icisf.org/
Law. . . . . http://www.dshs.state.tx.us/comprep/ogc/default.shtm
Medical Reserve Corps. . . . . http://www.medicalreservecorps.gov/
Salvation Army. . . . . . . http://www.salvationarmyusa.org/usn/www_usn.nsf
Storms. . . . . http://www.nhc.noaa.gov/
Texas State Guard Medical Brigade (MRC) . . . .
. . . . http://www.texasmedicalrangers.com
United Way . . . . http://national.unitedway.org/
Water Purification . . http://www.thefarm.org/charities/i4at/surv/bleach.htm

BIBLIOGRAPHY

Ackerman, N. W. (1958). *The psychodynamics of family life: Diagnosis and treatment of family relationships.* New York: Basic Books.

Ackerman, N. W. (1970). Family psychotherapy and Psychoanalysis: Implications of difference. In N.W. Ackerman (Ed.), *Family process.* New York: Basic Books, Inc.

After Action Report (September, 2005). Texas State Guard Medical Brigade, San Antonio, Texas.

Aguilera, D. C., Messick, J. M., & Farrell, M. S. (1970). *Crisis intervention: Theory and methodology.* St. Louis: C.V. Mosby Co.

Allen, N. (1971). History and background of suicidology. In C. L. Hatton, S. M. Valente, & A. Rink (Eds.), *Suicide: Assessment and intervention.* New York: Appleton-Century-Crofts.

Altrocchi, J., & Batton, L. (1968). *Suicide prevention in an under-populated area.* Paper read at the American Association of Suicidology, Chicago, March.

Altrocchi, J., & Gutman, V. (1968). *Suicide prevention in an under-populated area.* Paper read at the Southeastern Psychological Association, Roanoke, Virginia, April.

American Association of Marriage and Family Counselors (1981). *Distress signals in marriage and family relations.* New York: Author.

American Psychiatric Association (1994). *Diagnostic and statistical manual of mental disorders* (4th ed.). Author, Washington.

American Psychiatric Association (2001). *Guidelines for teen suicide and intervention.* Washington, D.C.

Arieti, S. (1963, October). Psychopathic personality: Some views on its psychopathology and psychodynamics. *Comprehensive Psychiatry, 7–14.*

Baard, M. (1975). *The function of the police in crisis intervention and conflict management: A training Guide.* Washington, D.C.: Government Printing Office.

Bard, M., & Ellison K. (1974). Crisis intervention and investigation of forcible rape. *The Police Chief, 41*(5), 68–73.

Bard, M., & Zacker, J. (1976). *The police and interpersonal conflict: Third party intervention approaches.* Washington, D.C.: Police Foundation.

Barton, D. (1976). The dying patient. In H.S. Abram (Ed.), *Basic psychiatry for the primary care physician.* Boston: Houghton Mifflin.

Berggreen, S. (1971). A study of the mental health of the near relatives of 20 multi-handicapped children. *Acta Paed. Scandanavia, 9,* 16–23.

Bernstein, E., & Rommel, B. (1975). Rape exploding the myths. *Today's Health,*

35(10), 36–39.

Biggs, J. R. (1987, May). Defusing hostage situations. *The Police Chief.*

Bloom, B. C. (1963). Definitional aspects of the crisis concept. *Journal of consulting Psychology, 27,* 498–502.

Bolz, F. (1979). *Hostage cop.* New York: Rawson, Wade Publishers.

Briefing Reports (2005, September). Personal Communications.

Brown, M. (1972). Family therapy and family group therapy, In H. I. Kaplan, & B. J. Sodock (Eds.), *Group treatment of mental illness.* New York: E. P. Dutton.

Brownmiller, S. (1975). *Against own will: Men, women, and rape.* New York: Simon & Schuster.

Burgess, A., & Holmstrom, K. (1974). *Rape: Victims and crisis.* Washington, D.C.: Robert J. Brady Co.

Burnes, J. L., & Dixon, M. C. (1974). Telephone crisis intervention and crisis volunteers. *American Journal of Community Psychology, 2,* 120–125.

Caplan, G. (1960). Patterns of parental response to the crisis of premature births. Psychiatry, *23,* 365–374.

Caplan, G. (1961). *An approach to community mental health.* New York: Grune & Stratton.

Caplan, G. (1963). Emotional crises. *The Encyclopedia of mental health, 3,* 521–532.

Caplan, G. (1964). Symptoms of preventative psychiatry. New York: Basic Books.

Capozzoli, J., & Zubenko, W. N. (2002). *Children and disasters: A practical guide to healing and recovery Missouri-Kansas.* Oxford, UK: Oxford University Press.

Collins, H. A. (1965). Introversion and depression in mothers of cerebral palsied children. *Missouri Medicine, 62,* 847–850.

Cooper, H. H. A. (1997, Spring). Negotiating with terrorists. *The International Journal of Police Negotiations and Crisis Management,* 1–8.

Corsini, R. (1981). *Innovative psychotherapies.* New York: John Wiley Interscience.

Cullen Inspection Report, United States Surgeon General's Office, Personal Communications, September, 2005.

Davis, R. C. (1987, September). Three prudent considerations for hostage negotiators. *Law and Order,* 10–15.

Dolan, J. T., & Fuselier, G. D. (1987, April). A guide for first responders to hostage situations. *FBI Law Enforcement Bulletin,* 10–15.

Dublin, I. J. (1969). Suicide. In E. S. Schneidman (Ed.), *In the nature of suicide.* San Francisco: Jossey-Bass.

Edwards, C. H. (1970). *The identification, training, and utilization of paraprofessional key personnel in the delivery of crisis intervention services in nonmetropolitan areas.* Paper read at the Mid-south Conference on Crisis Intervention and Suicide Prevention, Athens, Georgia, January.

Ehlers, W. H. (1966). *Mothers of retarded children: How they feel, where they find help.* Springfield, IL: Charles C Thomas.

Engel, G. L. (1961). Is grief a disease? A challenge for medical research. *Psychosomatic Medicine, 23,* 18-22.

Erickson, E. (1953). Growth and crisis of the healthy personality. In C. Kluckhohn, H. A. Murray, & D. M. Schneider (Eds.), *Personality in nature, society, and culture.*

New York: Alfred A. Knop, Inc.

Evarts, W. R., Greenstone, J. L., Kirkpatrick, G., & Leviton, S. C. (1984). *Winning through accommodation: The mediator's handbook.* Dubuque: Kendall/Hunt.

Ewalt, P. L. (1967). *Mental health volunteers.* Springfield, IL; Charles C Thomas.

Farber, B. (1959). Effects of a severely retarded child on family integration. *Society for Research in Child Development Monographs, 24,* 36-38.

Farber, B. (1963). Some effects of a retarded child on the mother. In M. B. Sussman (Ed.), *Sourcebook in marriage and the family.* Boston: Houghton Mifflin Co.

Farberow, N. W. (1967). Crisis, disaster, and suicide: Theory and therapy. In E. S. Schneidman (Ed.), *Essays in self-destruction.* New York: Science House.

Figley, C. R. (2002). *Treating compassion fatigue.* Belmont, CA: Routledge – Taylor Francis.

Forer, B. (1963). The therapeutic value of crisis. *Psychological Reports, 13,* 275–281.

Fowler, R. (2005, September). Daily Briefings, Personal Communications.

Fowler, R. (2005, September). Multiple Quotations, Personal Communications.

Fowler, W. R. (1997, Spring). Dealing with defenestrators: Immediate intervention. *The International Journal of Police Negotiations and Crisis Management,* 1–10.

Fowler, W. R., & Greenstone, J. L. (1983). Hostage negotiations. In R. Corsini (Ed.), *Encyclopedia of Psychology.* New York: John Wiley and Sons.

Fowler, W. R., & Greenstone, J. L. (1987). *Crisis intervention compendium.* Littleton, MA: Copley Publishing Group.

Fowler, W. R., & Greenstone, J. L. (1987). Hostage negotiations for police. In R. Corsini (Ed.), *Concise Encyclopedia of Psychology.* New York: John Wiley Interscience.

Fowler, W. R., & Greenstone, J. L. (1989). *Crisis intervention compendium.* Littleton, MA: Copley Publishing Group.

Fowler, W. R., & Greenstone, J. L. (1996). Hostage negotiations for police. In R. Corsini (Ed.), *Concise encyclopedia of psychology,* Second Edition.

Fox, S., & Scherl, D. (1972). Crisis intervention with victims of rape. *Social Work, 25,* 37.

Fuselier, G. W. (1981, June/July). A practical overview of hostage negotiations. *FBI Law Enforcement Bulletin,* 2–5.

Fuselier, G. W. (1986). What every negotiator would like his chief to know. *FBI Law Enforcement Bulletin, 1.*

Garmire, B. L., Rubin, J., & Wilson, J.Q. (1972). *The police and the community.* Baltimore: Johns Hopkins University Press.

Gil, D. G. (1970). *Violence against children: Physical abuse in the United States.* Cambridge: Harvard University Press.

Glaser, B. G., & Strauss, A. L. (1965). *Awareness of dying.* Chicago: Aldine Publishing Company.

Greenstone, J. L. (1966). *A study of small group development.* Thesis: North Texas State University.

Greenstone, J. L. (1968). *Ministers and attorneys marital inventory.* Dallas: Self published.

Greenstone, J. L. (1969, June). *Tuning in with our children.* The Single Parent.

Greenstone, J. L. (1970). *The meaning of psychology: A human subject.* Dubuque: Kendall Hunt.

Greenstone, J. L. (1971, November). *The crisis of discipline.* The Single Parent.

Greenstone, J. L. (1981, October). *Crisis intervention: Stress and the police officer.* Paper presented to the Society for Police and Criminal Psychology, Baton Rouge, LA.

Greenstone, J. L. (1981, December 21). Job related stress: Is it killing you? *National Law Journal,* Law Office Management Section.

Greenstone, J. L. (1986, Winter). The laws of terrorism. *Emotional First Aid: A Journal of Crisis Intervention.*

Greenstone, J. L. (1992, Vol.1). The art of negotiating: Tactics and negotiating techniques–the way of the past and the way of the future. *Command: Journal of The Texas Tactical Police Officers Association.*

Greenstone, J. L. (1992). The key to success for hostage negotiations teams: Training, training and more training. *The Police Forum.*

Greenstone, J. L. (1992). The negotiator's equipment: Tools of the trade; mark of the professional. *Law Enforcement Product News.* 1–3.

Greenstone, J. L. (1993). *Critical Incident Stress Debriefing and Crisis Management.* Austin, Texas: Texas Department of Health.

Greenstone, J. L. (1993). Violence in the courtroom: Culpability, personal responsibility, sensitivity and justice - The courtroom risk analysis checklist. *National Social Science Perspectives Journal,* 4(1), 15–36.

Greenstone, J. L. (1993, Summer). Crisis intervention skills training for police negotiators in the 21st century. *Command.*

Greenstone, J. L. (1993, October). Violence in the courtroom, part one. *Texas Police Journal.* 17–19.

Greenstone, J. L. (1993, November). Violence in the courtroom, part two. *Texas Police Journal.* 15–18.

Greenstone, J. L. (1993, November/December). Dr. Greenstone's 150 laws of hostage and crisis negotiations. *Police and Security News.* 36–38.

Greenstone, J. L. (1994–1996). Editor-in-Chief, *The Journal of Crisis Negotiations.* Dallas: The Texas Association of Hostage Negotiators.

Greenstone, J. L. (1995). Hostage negotiations team training for small police departments. In M. I. Kurke, & E. M. Scrivner (Eds.), *Police Psychology Into the 21st Century.* Hillsdale. New Jersey: Lawrence Erlbaum Associates.

Greenstone, J. L. (1995). Tactics and negotiating techniques (TNT): The way of the past and the way of the future. In M. I. Kurke, & E. M. Scrivner (Eds.), *Police Psychology Into the 21st Century.* Hillsdale, New Jersey: Lawrence Erlbaum Associates.

Greenstone, J. L. (1995, August). Crisis intervention skills training for negotiators. *The Police Chief.*

Greenstone, J. L. (1995, Fall). Police crisis negotiations with AIDS patients and HTLV III/HIV positive persons. *The Journal of Crisis Negotiations.*

Greenstone, J. L. (1996-1999). Editor-in-Chief, *The International Journal of Police Negotiations and Crisis Management.* San Marcos, Texas: The Society for Police and Criminal Psychology.

Greenstone, J. L. (1998, January). Domestic violence. *Signal 50*, Fort Worth Police Officers Association.

Greenstone, J. L. (1998, February). Domestic violence II: signals of violence and murder. *Signal 50*, Fort Worth Police Officers Association.

Greenstone, J. L. (1998, April–December). The role of tactical emergency medical support in hostage and crisis negotiations. *Prehospital and Disaster Medicine.*

Greenstone, J. L. (1999). *Elements of Police Psychology.* Unpublished Manuscript.

Greenstone, J. L. (2000, March/April). Peer support in a municipal police department. *The Forensic Examiner.*

Greenstone, J. L. (2001). *Terrorism and Our Response to It: The New Normalcy.* Booklets prepared for: Fort Worth Police Department; City of Fort Worth; Civil Air Patrol, U.S.A.F.

Greenstone, J. L. (2001, March). Fit to serve: Failure to address stress can cause emotional problems. *Civil Air Patrol News*, 10.

Greenstone, J. L. (2001, September). Fit to serve: Teen suicide. *Civil Air Patrol News*, 5–6.

Greenstone, J. L. (2001, Fall). Case study: Why did it work? *Journal of Police Crisis Negotiations*, 127–130.

Greenstone, J. L. (2001, Fall). New initiatives: The role of tactical emergency medical support in hostage and crisis negotiations. *Journal of Police Crisis Negotiations*, 29–33.

Greenstone, J. L. (2001, November). Fit to serve: Holiday stress – Some steps to help you avoid a crisis at Christmas. *Civil Air Patrol News*, 10.

Greenstone, J. L. (2001, November). Terrorism and our response to it: The new normalcy. *Signal 50*, Fort Worth Police Officers Association, 34–35.

Greenstone, J. L. (2002, Winter). The role of tactical emergency medical support in hostage and crisis negotiations. *The Tactical Edge, 20*(1), 33–35.

Greenstone, J. L. (2002, February). Fit to serve: Terrorism and our response: Getting on with our life and our mission. *Civil Air Patrol News*, 10 & 19.

Greenstone, J. L. (2002, June). Fit to serve: The drugs of abuse: Knowledge can reduce the demand; Ignorance can hurt us and impede our mission. *Civil Air Patrol News*, 6.

Greenstone, J. L. (2003, Spring). Case study: How to be a mental health consultant. *Journal of Police Crisis Negotiations, 3*(1), 121-130.

Greenstone, J. L. (2003, Spring). Crisis and hostage negotiations: Six steps to the training and performance of police negotiators. *Journal of Police Crisis Negotiations, 3*(1), 51–58.

Greenstone, J. L. (2003, Fall). Case study: Hostage and crisis negotiation unit crisis situation debriefing sheet – "The ten minute debriefing." *Journal of Police Crisis Negotiations*, 79–80.

Greenstone, J. L. (2003, Fall). Teen suicide: Negotiating with the youthful actor. *Journal of Police Crisis Negotiations*, 61–64.

Greenstone, J. L. (2003, Fall). Terrorism and how we prepare ourselves psychologically to survive it: The new normalcy. *Journal of Police Crisis Negotiations, 3*(2), 91–94.

Greenstone, J. L. (2004, Winter). Crisis management for mediators: The unrecognized elements. *ACResolution,* 24–27.

Greenstone, J. L. (2004, Summer). Crisis negotiation: Why did it work? Crisis Negotiation Section, *Association for Conflict Resolution Newsletter.* Retrieved August 14, 2004 from ACR HN Website.

Greenstone, J. L. (2004, Fall). Communicating effectively for successful hostage negotiations and crisis intervention. *Journal of Police Crisis Negotiation,* 43–52.

Greenstone, J. L. (2004, Fall). Up close and personal: Red flag indicators for negotiators/ interveners. *Journal of Police Crisis Negotiation,* 71–73.

Greenstone, J. L. (2004, November). Fit to serve: Health services: Greater evidence of programs, policies in months ahead. *Civil Air Patrol News,* 13.

Greenstone, J. L. (2005). *The Elements of Police Hostage and Crisis Negotiations: Critical Incidents and How to Respond to Them.* Binghamton, New York: The Haworth Press, Inc.

Greenstone, J. L. (2005, March). Fit to serve: The tsunami effect: Crisis abroad, crisis at home. *Civil Air Patrol News,* 3–5.

Greenstone, J. L. (2005, May). Fit to serve: The tragedy of teenage suicide especially when it is one of our own. *Civil Air Patrol News,* 7–8.

Greenstone, J. L. (2006, Winter). *Medical support.* Foreword for Winter 2006 Monograph Series. Maryland: State Defense Forces Publication Center, 3–5.

Greenstone, J. L. (2006, Winter). *The Texas Medical Rangers in the military response of the uniformed medical reserve corps to Hurricane Katrina and Hurricane Rita 2005: The new and tested role of the medical reserve corps in the United States.* Monograph, State Defense Forces Publication Center.

Greenstone, J. L. (2006, February). Negotiations success factors: How they work. *The Negotiator Magazine.* http://www.negotiatormagazine.com

Greenstone, J. L. (2006, Spring). The military emergency management specialist qualification (MEMS) and the medical units of the state defense forces: It just makes sense. *State Defense Force Journal,* 2(1), 27–28. http://www.sdfpc.org/sdfjvol2.pdf

Greenstone, J. L. (2006, May). The most serious errors made by negotiators: Twenty-five to consider. *The Negotiator Magazine.* http://www.negotiatormagazine.com

Greenstone, J. L. (2006, October). MEMS and the medical units of the state defense forces. *The MEMS Academy Report,* 12.

Greenstone, J. L., Dunn, J. M., & Leviton, S. C. (1994). Promotion of mental health for police: The departmental peer counselling programme. In D. R. Trent, & C. A. Reed (Eds.), *Promotion of Mental Health, 4,* 319–340. Aldershot, Hants, England: Avebury, Ashgate Publishing Limited.

Greenstone, J. L., Kosson, D. S., & Gacono, C. B. (2000). Psychopathy and hostage negotiations: Some preliminary thoughts and findings. In Carl B. Gacono (Ed.) *The clinical and forensic assessment of psychopathy: A practitioner's guide.* Hillsdale, New Jersey: Lawrence Erlbaum Associates, 385–404.

Greenstone, J. L., & Krakover, B. (2007). Medical implications during hostage negotiation. In R. Schwartz, J. McManus, & R. E. Swienton (Eds.), *Tactical and operational emergency medical services command and support.* Philadelphia, PA: Lippincott,

Williams & Wilkins. Manuscript in preparation.

Greenstone, J. L., & Leviton, S.C. (1979). *The Crisis Intervener's Handbook, Volume 1.* Dallas: Crisis Management Workshops.

Greenstone, J. L., & Leviton, S. C. (1979). *Crisis management and intervener survival.* Tulsa: Affective House.

Greenstone, J. L., & Leviton, S. C. (1979). *Stress reduction: Personal energy management.* Tulsa: Affective House.

Greenstone, J. L., & Leviton, S. C. (1980). *The crisis interveners handbook, Volume II.* Dallas: Rothschild Publishing House.

Greenstone, J. L., & Leviton, S. C. (1980, January). Crisis management: A basic concern. *Crisis Interveners Newsletter.*

Greenstone, J. L., & Leviton, S. C. (1980–1987). *Crisis intervention in mediation.* Training presentation to Mediator Training Courses, Dispute Mediation Service of Dallas, Texas.

Greenstone, J. L., & Leviton, S. C. (1981). Crisis management and intervener survival. In R. Corsini (Ed.), *Innovative Psychotherapies.* New York: John Wiley Interscience.

Greenstone, J. L., & Leviton, S. C. (1981). *Hotline: Crisis intervention directory.* New York: Facts on File.

Greenstone, J. L., & Leviton, S. C. (1981). *Training the Trainer.* Tulsa: Affective House.

Greenstone, J. L., & Leviton, S. C. (1982). *Crisis Intervention: Handbook for Interveners.* Dubuque: Kendall-Hunt.

Greenstone, J. L., & Leviton, S. C. (1983) Crisis intervention. In R. Corsini (Ed.), *Encyclopedia of psychology.* New York: John Wiley and Sons.

Greenstone, J. L., & Leviton, S. C. (1983). Executive survival. In R. Corsini (Ed.), *Encyclopedia of psychology.* New York: John Wiley and Sons.

Greenstone, J. L., & Leviton, S. C. (1986, Summer). Referrals: a key to successful crisis intervention. *Emotional First Aid: A Journal of Crisis Intervention.*

Greenstone, J. L., & Leviton, S. C. (1986, Fall). Intervention procedures. *Emotional First Aid: A Journal of Crisis Intervention.*

Greenstone, J. L., & Leviton, S. C. (1986, December). *Mediation: The police officer's alternative to litigation.* Psychological Services for Law Enforcement. Washington, D.C.: U.S. Department of Justice, Federal Bureau of Investigation, U.S. Government Printing Office.

Greenstone, J. L., & Leviton, S. C. (1987). Crisis intervention. In R. Corsini (Ed.), *Concise encyclopedia of psychology.* New York: John Wiley Interscience.

Greenstone, J. L., & Leviton, S. C. (1987). Executive survival. In R. Corsini (Ed.), *Concise encyclopedia of psychology.* New York: John Wiley Interscience.

Greenstone, J. L., & Leviton, S. C. (September, 1987). Crisis management for mediators in high stress, high risk, potentially violent situations. *Mediation Quarterly.*

Greenstone, J. L., & Leviton, S. C. (1991). *Parents, Kids and War.* Brochure of Information to Assist Parents and Children in Handling War and Its Consequences. Dallas and New York: National Broadcasting Company and Columbia Broadcasting System.

Greenstone, J.L., & Leviton, S.C. (1991). *War, and how to respond to it.* Dallas: Leviton

& Greenstone.

Greenstone, J. L., & Leviton, S. C. (1993). *Elements of crisis intervention.* Pacific Grove, CA: Brooks/Cole.

Greenstone, J. L., & Leviton, S. C. (2001). *Parents, Kids, War and Our Mission,* A brochure to be used by Civil Air Patrol personnel, counselors, critical incident team members, parents and cadets in an attempt to minimize the psychological trauma resulting from terrorism and war. Fort Worth, Texas: Leviton & Greenstone.

Greenstone, J. L., & Leviton, S. C. (2001, 2d). *Parents, kids and war.* Information to Assist Parents and Children in Handling War and Its Consequences, Booklet, Second Edition. Fort Worth, Texas: Leviton & Greenstone.

Greenstone, J. L., & Leviton, S. C. (2002). *Elements of Crisis Intervention,* Second Edition. Pacific Grove, CA: Brooks/Cole.

Greenstone, J. L., & Leviton, S. C. (2005, Polish Translation). *Interwencja Kryzysowa.* Gdansk: Gdanskie Wydawnictwo Psychologiczne.

Greenstone, J. L., & McManus, J. (2007). Psychological effects and management of law enforcement and medical providers in the tactical environment. In R. Schwartz, J. McManus, & R. E. Swienton (Eds.), *Tactical and Operational Emergency Medical Services Command and Support.* Philadelphia, PA: Lippincott, Williams & Wilkins. Manuscript in preparation.

Greenstone, J. L., & Mole, D. (2007). Hostage survival. In R. Schwartz, J. McManus, & R. E. Swienton (Eds.), *Tactical and Operational Emergency Medical Services Command and Support.* Philadelphia, PA: Lippincott, Williams & Wilkins. Manuscript in preparation.

Griffin, S. (1971, September). Rape – the all-American crime. *Ramparts.* 27–37.

Grosser, C., Henry, W.E., & Kelly, J. G. (1969). *Non-professionals in the human services.* San Francisco: Jossey-Bass.

Grossman, D. (1995). *The psychological cost of learning to kill in war and society.* New York: Little, Brown and Company.

Groth, A. N. (1979). *Men who rape.* New York: Plenum Press.

Guerney, B. G. (Ed.) (1969). *Psychotherapeutic agents: New roles for non-professionals, parents, and teachers.* New York: Holt, Rinehart, & Winston.

Haley, J. (1972). Family therapy. In C. J. Sager, & W. J. Singer (Eds.), *Progress in group and family therapy.* New York: Brunner/Mazel Publishers.

Halpern, J., & Tramontin, M. (2006). *Disaster mental health: Theory and practice.* Belmont, CA: Wadsworth Publishing Company.

Hare, R. D. (1995, September). Psychopaths: New trends and research. *The Harvard Mental Health Newsletter,* 1–5.

Hatton, C. L., Valente, S. M., & Rink, A. (1977). Suicide: Assessment and intervention. New York: Appleton-Century-Crofts.

Heilig, S. M. (1970). Training in suicide prevention. *Bulletin of Suicidology,* 6, 41-44.

Heilig, S. M., Farbernow, N. L., Litman, R. E. & Schneidman, E. S. (1968). The role of the non-professional volunteer in a suicide prevention center. *Community Mental Health Journal,* 4, 287–95.

Hendricks, J., & Greenstone, J. L. (1982, March). *Crisis intervention in criminal justice.*

Paper presented at the meeting of the Academy of Criminal Justice Sciences, Louisville, KY.

Heppner, P. P., & Heppner, M. (1977). Rape: Counseling the traumatized victim. *The Personal and Guidance Journal, 15*(10), 45–47.

Hillmann, M. (1988, February). Tactical intelligence operations and support during a major barricade/hostage event. *The Police Chief,* 20–26.

Holt, K. S. (1958). The home care of the severely retarded. *Pediatrics, 22,* 744–755.

Hurricane Rita (September, 2005). Washington, D.C.: National Hurricane Center, the National Oceanic and Atmospheric Administration, and the National Weather Center. http://www.nhc.noaa.gov/

Hutt, M. L., & Gibby, R. G. (1976). *The retarded child: Development, education, and treatment.* Boston: Allyn & Bacon, Inc.

Jackson, D. D. (1966). The marital guide pro quo. In G. Zuk, & I. Boszormenzi-Nagy (Eds.), *Family therapy for disturbed families.* California: Science and Behavior Books.

Jackson, D. D. (1970). The study of the family. In N. W. Ackerman (Ed.), *Family process.* New York: Basic Books, Inc.

Jackson, G. (1999). *Disaster mental health: Crisis counseling programs for the rural community.* Washington: U.S. Department of Health and Human Services.

Justice, B., & Justice, R. (1976). *The abusing family.* New York: Human Sciences Press.

Kelly, G. A. (1961). Suicide: the personal construct point of view. In N. L. Fabernow, & E. S. Schneidman (Eds.), *The cry for help.* New York: McGraw-Hill Book Co.

Kempe, C. H. Helfer, R.E. (1972). *Helping the battered child and his family.* Philadelphia: J. B. Lippincott.

Kirk, S. A. (1972). *Educating exceptional children.* Boston: Houghton Mifflin Co.

Klein, D., & Lindemann, E. (1961). Preventative intervention in individual and family crisis situations. In G. Caplan (Ed.), *Prevention of mental disorders in children.* New York: Basic Books.

Kosson, D. S., Steuerwald, B. L., Forth, A. E., & Kirkhart, K. J. (1997). A new method for assessing the interpersonal behavior of psychopaths: Preliminary validation studies. *Psychological Assessment, 9,* 89–101.

Kubler-Ross, E. (1969). *On death and dying.* London: Macmillan.

Lanceley, F. J. (March, 1981). The antisocial personality as a hostage taker. *Journal of Police Science and Administration,* 30–40.

Langsley, D. G., & Kaplen, D. M. (1970). *The treatment of families in crisis.* New York: John Wiley & sons.

Lebovici, S. (1970). The psychoanalytic theory of the family. In E.J. Anthony, & C. Koupernik (Eds.), *The child in his family.* New York: John Wiley & Sons.

Lester, D., & Brockopp, G. (1973). *Crisis intervention and counseling by telephone.* Springfield, IL: Charles C Thomas.

Leviton, S. C., & Greenstone, J. L. (1980). Intervener survival: Dealing with the givens. *Emotional First Aid: A Journal of Crisis Intervention, 2,* 15–20.

Leviton, S. C., & Greenstone, J. L. (1980, Winter/Spring). Intervener survival: Dealing with the givens. *Emotional First Aid: Journal of Crisis Intervention.*

Leviton, S. C., & Greenstone, J. L. (1983). Conflict mediation. In R. Corsini (Ed.),

Encyclopedia of Psychology. New York: John Wiley and Sons.

Leviton, S. C., & Greenstone, J. L. (1983). Intervener survival. In R. Corsini (Ed.), *Encyclopedia of Psychology*. New York: John Wiley and Sons.

Leviton, S. C., & Greenstone, J. L. (1984). Mediation in potential crisis situations. *Emotional First Aid: A Journal of Crisis Intervention, 1*, 150–155.

Leviton, S. C., & Greenstone, J. L. (1984). Team intervention. *Emotional First Aid: A Journal of Crisis Intervention, 1*, 20–25.

Leviton, S. C., & Greenstone, J. L. (1984, Winter). Mediation in potential crisis situations. *Emotional First Aid: A Journal of Crisis Intervention*.

Leviton, S. C., & Greenstone, J. L. (1984, Spring). Team intervention. *Emotional First Aid: A Journal of Crisis Intervention*.

Leviton, S. C., & Greenstone, J. L. (1987). Conflict mediation. In R. Corsini (Ed.), *Concise Encyclopedia of Psychology*. New York: John Wiley Interscience.

Leviton, S. C., & Greenstone, J. L. (1987). Intervener survival. In R. Corsini (Ed.), *Concise Encyclopedia of Psychology*. New York: John Wiley Interscience.

Leviton, S. C., & Greenstone, J. L. (1997). *Elements of Mediation*. Pacific Grove, CA: Brooks/Cole.

Leviton, S. C., & Greenstone, J. L. (2002, Fall). The hostage and crisis negotiator's training laboratory. *Journal of Police Crisis Negotiations*, 21–33.

Lopez-Ibor, J. J., Christodoulou, M. M., & Sartorius, N. (2004). *Disasters and mental health*. New York: John Wiley and Sons.

McMains, M. J., & Mullins, W. C. (1996). *Crisis negotiations: Managing critical incidents and hostage situations in law enforcement and corrections*. Cincinnati: Anderson Publishing Company.

McMains, M. J., & Lanceley, F. J. (1995, Fall). The use of crisis intervention principles by police negotiators. *The Journal of Crisis Negotiations*, 25–28.

Mitchell, J. T., & Resnik, H. L. P. (1981). *Emergency response to crisis*. Bowie, MD: Robert J. Brady Company.

Mordock, J. B., Ellis, M. H., & Greenstone, J. L. (1969, October). The effects of group and individual psychotherapy on sociometric choices of disturbed adolescents. *International Journal of Group Psychotherapy*.

Myers, D., & Wee, D. F. (2005). *Disaster mental health services: A primer for practitioners*. New York: Brunner – Routledge.

Norris, F. H., Galea, S., Friedman, M. J., & Watson, P. J. (2006). *Methods for disaster mental health research*. New York: Guilford Press.

Pastel, R. H. (2005, June). *Psychological Impact of an all hazards incident*. PowerPoint presentation at the Homeland Security Medical Executive Course, Austin, Texas.

Pederson, P. A. (1988). *A handbook for developing multicultural awareness*. New York: American Association for Counseling and Development.

Podeanu-Czehofsky, I. (1975). Some aspects of family life cerebral palsied children. *Rehabilitation Literature, 3*, 308–311.

Polansky, N. A., Hally, C., & Polansky, N.T. (1975). *Profile of neglect: A survey of the state of knowledge of child neglect*. Washington, D.C.: U.S. Department of Health, Education & Welfare.

Rapoport, L. (1972). The state of crisis: Some theoretical considerations. *Social Service Review, 36*, 211–217.

Resnik, H. L. P. (1964). A community anti-suicidal organization. *Current Psychiatric Therapies,* 55–56.

Resnik, H. L. P. (1968). A community anti-suicide organization: The friends of Dade County, Florida. In H.L.P. Resnik (Ed.), *Suicidal behaviors: Diagnosis and management.* Boston: Little, Brown.

Reiff, R., & Reissman, F. (1965). The indigenous nonprofessional. *Community Mental Health Journal,* Monograph I.

Reuch, J. (1961). *Therapeutic communication.* New York: W.W. Norton & Co., Inc.

Ritchie, E. C., Watson, P. J., & Friedman, M. J. (2006). *Interventions following mass violence and disasters: Strategies for mental health practice.* New York: The Guilford Press.

Rosenbluh, E. S. (1974). *Techniques of crisis intervention: Emergency mental health first aid.* Louisville: Rosenbluh & Associates.

Rosenbluh, E. S. (1976). Crisis techniques for everyone. *Innovations, 3*, 38.

Rosenbluh, E. S. (1986). *Crisis counseling: Emotional first aid.* Dubuque: Kendall/Hunt.

Schonell, F. J., & Roarke, M. A. (1960). A second survey of the effects of a subnormal child on the family unit. *American Journal of Mental Deficiency, 64*, 862–868.

Schneidman, E. S. (1979). An overview: Personality, motivation, and behavior theories. In L. D. Hankoff, & B. Einsidler (Eds.), *Suicide: Theory and clinical aspects.* Littleton, Mass.: PSG Publishing Co.

Schneidman, E. S. (1974). *Deaths of man.* Baltimore Penguin Books.

Sewell, James D. (1983, April). Police Stress. *FBI Law Enforcement Bulletin,* 10–12.

Sherif, M., & Sherif, C. *Social psychology.* New York: Harper & Row, 169.

Slaikeu, K. A. (1984). *Crisis intervention: A handbook for practice and research.* Boston: Allyn and Bacon.

Sobey, F. (1970). *The non-professional revolution in mental health.* New York: Columbia University Press.

Soskis, D. A., & Van Zandt, C. R. (1986, Autumn). Hostage negotiations: Law enforcement's most effective non-lethal weapon. Department of Justice, *FBI Management Quarterly,* 15–21.

Sowder, B. J., & Lystad, M. (1986). *Disasters and mental health: Contemporary perspectives and innovations in services to disaster victims.* Chicago: American Psychiatric Association Press.

Strentz, T. (1979, April). Law enforcement policy and ego defenses of the hostage. *FBI Law Enforcement Bulletin,* 10–13.

Strentz, T. (1983, March). The inadequate personality as a hostage taker. *Journal of Police Science and Administration,* 30–35.

Thacker-Zocklein, P. (1975). *Rape.* Paper presented to National Institute on Training in Crisis Intervention, Louisville, Kentucky.

Uniform Crime Reports for the United States. (1968). Clarence M. Kelly, Director, Federal Bureau of Investigation, Department of Justice. Washington, D.C.: Government Printing Office.

Ursano, R. J., Fullerton, C. S., & Norwood, A. E. (2003). *Terrorism and disaster: Indivi-*

dual and community mental health interventions. Cambridge: Cambridge University Press.

U.S.A. Today (2006, August 9). USA Today Snapshots, Gallup Poll. *Jittery World.* 1.

Varah, C. (1965). *he Samaritans.* New York: Macmillan.

Walters, D. R. (1975). *Physical and sexual abuse of children: Causes and treatment.* Bloomington: Indiana University Press.

Weaver, J.D. (1995). *Disasters: Mental health interventions.* Sarasota, FL: Professional Resource Press.

Weiss, J. (1981). Crisis and the Child. In J. L. Greenstone, & S. C. Leviton (Eds.), *The crisis intervener's handbook,* 2. Dallas: Rothschild Publishing House.

Weiss, R., & Payson, H. (1967). Gross stress reaction. In *Comprehensive textbook of psychiatry.* Boston, Houghton Mifflin.

Wesselius, C. L. (1983, Vol. 1, No. 2). The anatomy of a hostage situation. *Behavioral Sciences and the Law,* 10–15.

Whitaker, J. F. (1976). *Personal marriage contract.* Dallas: O.K. Street, Inc.

Wolfensberger, N. (1967). *Counseling parents of the retarded.* Chicago: Aldine Publishing Co.

Zalbra, S. R. (1976). The abused child: A typology for classification and treatment. *Social Work, 12,* 70–79.

LEGAL REFERENCES

73 N. Dak. L. Rev. 109, 113 (1997).

Arizona Revised Statute for Privileged Communications, § 32-2085 (1965). (Privileged Communications)

Berkovitz by Berkovitz v. U.S., 108 S.Ct. 1954.

Berkovitz v. United States, 486 U.S. 531 (1988).

Buwa v. Smith, 84-1905 NMB (1986). (Duty to Warn)

Canterbury v. Spense, 464 F. 2d. 772 (D.C. Cir. 1972), cert. den. 93 S.Ct. 560 (1972). (Informed Consent)

Cutter v. Brownbridge, Cal. Ct. App., 1st Dist. 330 (1986). (Privileged Communications)

Hales v. Pittman, 118 Ariz. 305, 576 P. 2d. 493 (1978). (Informed Consent)

Howlett v. Rose, 496 U.S. 356 (1990).

Jones v. United States, 249 F2d 864(7th Cir. 1957).

Lidie v. California, 478 F2d 552 (9th Cir. 1973).

Liebeck v. McDonald's Restaurants, 1995 WL 360309 (D.N.M.1994).

Louisiana Public Service Commission v. F.C.C., 476 U.S. 355 (1986).

Mafrige v. U.S., 893 F.Supp.691, (S.D.Tex.1995).

McDonald v. Clinger, 446 N.Y.S. 2d. 801 (1982). (Confidentiality)

McIntosb v. Milano, 403 A. 2d. 500 (N.J.S.Ct. 1979). (Duty to Warn) New Jersey Revised Statutes, New Jersey Marriage Counseling Act, Annotated § 45: 8B–29 (1969). (Exceptions to Confidentiality)

New York v. F.E.RC., 122 S.Ct.1012 (2002).

People v. District Court, City and County of Denver, 719 P. 2d. 722 (Colo. 1986). (Privileged Communications)

Rest. (2nd) of Torts' 324A. *Dorking Genetics v. U.S.*, 76 F.3d 1261 (2nd Cir. 1996).

Rodriguez v. Jackson, 118 Ariz. 13, 574 P. 2d. 481 (App. 1978). (Informed Consent)

Rodriguez v. U.S., 968 F.2d 1430 (1st Cir.1992).

Santillo v. Chambersburg Engineering Co., 603 F. Supp. 211 (E.D.Pa. 1985).

Sard v. Hardy, 291 Md. 432, 379 A. 2d. 1014 (1977). (Informed Consent)

Section 458.305(3), Florida Statutes (1999).

Tarasoff v. Regents of California, 131 Cal. Rptr. 14, 551 P. 2d. 334 (1976). (Duty to Warn)

Torres v. United States, 979 F. Supp. 1054, 1056 (DV.I 1997).

U.S. v. DeVane, 306 F.2d 182 (5th Cir. 1992).

U.S. v. S.A. Empresa de ViacaoAerea Rio Grandense (Varig Airlines), 467 U.S. 797 (1984).

U.S. v. Gaubert, 499 U.S. 315 (1991).

U.S.C.A. Const. Art. 6, cl. 2.

United States v. Faneca, 322 F.2d 872.

United States v. Testan, 424 U.S. 392 (1976).

West's RCWA4.24.300. *Maynard v. Ferno-Washington, Inc.*, 22 F.Supp.2d 1171 (1998).

Whitree v. State of New York, 56 Misc. 2d. 693, 290 N.Y.S. 2s. 486 (1968). (Record Keeping)

NAME INDEX

SUBJECT INDEX

DISASTER PSYCHOLOGY–ELEMENTS BY SPECIFIC AUDIENCE INDEX

DISASTER PSYCHOLOGY–ELEMENTS BY SPECIFIC ACTIVITY DESIRED INDEX

ABOUT THE AUTHOR

JAMES L. GREENSTONE, ED.D., J.D., DABECI has been in practice for forty years in Dallas and Fort Worth, Texas. He served as the Police Psychologist and Director of Psychological Services for the Fort Worth Police Department. His work in Crisis Intervention and disaster response began in the mid-1960s, and continues to this day. He has written widely in this as well as other areas.

He serves on a Department of Health and Human Services Disaster Medical Assistance Team as a Supervisory Mental Health Specialist, is a member of the Texas State Guard Medical Brigade (MRC), is a Certified Crisis Intervener, Certified Traumatologist, an Emergency Medical Technician, and a Master Peace Officer. Doctor Greenstone has earned the Master Military Emergency Management Specialist Qualification, and teaches in the Basic and Advanced Disaster Life Support program sponsored by the National Disaster Life Support Foundation.

While with the Fort Worth Police Department he supervised the department's Peer Support Team; was the Coordinator of the Critical Incident Stress Management program and a member of the department's Hostage and Crisis Negotiation Team.

Formerly, he was an Adjunct Professor of Law at the Texas Wesleyan University School of Law and was Lead Hostage and Crisis Negotiations Instructor at the North Central Texas Council of Governments Regional Police Academy. He is a licensed professional counselor, licensed marriage and family therapist, and a dispute mediator and arbitrator. He holds earned degrees in Clinical Psychology, Education, Criminal Justice and Law. He interned at the Devereux Foundation in Devon, Pennsylvania.

He is the Editor-in-Chief of the *Journal of Police Crisis Negotiations*, an international journal published by Haworth Press, Inc. Doctor Greenstone also edited the *Journal of Crisis Negotiations* and *The International Journal of Police Negotiations and Crisis Management*. These journals were the predecessors of the current publication. Previously, he was the Editor-in-Chief of *Emotional First Aid: A Journal of Crisis Intervention*.

Doctor Greenstone is a Diplomate in Crisis Intervention from the American Board of Examiners in Crisis Intervention; a Diplomate in Police Psychology from the Society for Police and Criminal Psychology; a Diplomate of the American Board of Forensic Examiners; a Diplomate in Traumatic Stress from the American Academy of Experts in Traumatic Stress, and a Fellow of the College of The American College of Forensic Examiners. He is a Practitioner Member of the Academy of Family Mediators/Association for Conflict Resolution.

Doctor Greenstone is a member of the Graduate Faculty of Walden University and of the Harold Abel School of Psychology at Capella University.

Doctor Greenstone was an Associate Professor of Psychology and Criminal Justice at Tarrant County College, Adjunct Faculty at the University of North Florida, Institute for Police Technology and Management, and has been a member of the Adjunct Faculty in the Psychology Departments of Brookhaven College, El Centro College, Northlake College and Northlake College Police Academy, Tarrant County Junior College, an Adjunct Professor of Psychology at Columbia College and Northwood Institute, an Associate Professor in Crisis Management at Texas Women's University Graduate School of Nursing, Adjunct Faculty in the Graduate School of Southeastern University, a member of the Continuing Education Faculty of Richland College and the Human Resource Center in the Graduate School of Social Work at the University of Texas at Arlington, and has presented numerous workshops and training seminars in Crisis Intervention, Stress Management and Dispute Mediation to professionals, paraprofessionals, executives and lay volunteers throughout the country.

Doctor Greenstone served as Director of the National Training Conference for Crisis Intervention, and as Director of the National Institute for Training in Crisis Intervention. He has been invited to present to such groups as the International Association of Chiefs of Police National Training Symposium, the Third, Fourth, Fifth and Sixth International Congress on Family Therapy, the Academy of Criminal Justice Sciences, the National Conference on Peace and Conflict Resolution, the Second Annual Conference on Problem Solving Through Mediation, the Federal Bureau of Investigation Academy, the National Conference of the Academy of Family Mediators, the American Academy of Matrimonial Lawyers, and was one of seven national experts in Crisis Intervention invited to present at the Brigham Young University Conference on Crisis Intervention. He was invited to, and participated in The Advanced Study Institute on Psychopathy: Theory, Research and Implications for Society, sponsored by the North Atlantic Treaty Organization.